MASTERING THE DYNAMICS OF INNOVATION

Mastering the Dynamics of Innovation

James M. Utterback

HARVARD BUSINESS SCHOOL PRESS   Boston, Massachusetts

Published by the Harvard Business School Press in hardcover, 1994; in
paperback, 1996

Printed in the United States of America
   06 07 08 09   15 14 13 12 10 11   (pbk

Library of Congress Cataloging-in-Publication Data

Utterback, James M., 1941–
     Mastering the dynamics of innovation / James M. Utterback.
         p.   cm.
     Includes bibliographical references and index.
     ISBN 0-87584-342-5 (acid-free paper) (hc)
     ISBN 0-87584-740-4 (pbk)
     1. Organizational change—Management.   2. Industrial management.
     3. Technological innovations—Management.   4. Strategic planning.
     I. Title.
     HD58.8.U87   1994
     658.4'06—dc20   93-38429
                                                                CIP

The paper used in this publication meets the requirements of the American
National Standard for Permanence of Paper for Printed Library Materials
Z39.49—1984.

Contents

Preface

Innovation in industry is a process that involves an enormous amount of uncertainty, human creativity, and chance. It takes place in small and large ways, and in some times and some places more than in others. Over the years, scholars have observed patterns of successful industrial innovation, but the identification of patterns does not suggest that successful innovation is entirely predictable. These patterns do, however, indicate that relationships exist between product and process changes, the state of evolution of an industry, and the competitive climate faced by individual firms. Understanding these relationships is crucial, both to the scholar, who seeks keys to the general behavior of firms and their abilities to innovate, and to the practicing manager, whose mission is to plan and act.

This book attempts to develop a practical model of the dynamics of industrial innovation—a model with explanatory power for the scholar, and action ideas for the manager. Clearly, this model will not be generalizable to all settings, industries, cultures, and times. Like all attempts to explain behavior, it is a creature of its sources, which in this case are the American industrial experience of the past 150 years, with a smattering of evidence from Europe and Japan. It also draws primarily on products for which cost and product performance are the commanding factors, rather than those for which fashion, novelty, or advertising are important competitive variables. Within these limits, however, it should be readily apparent to the reader that innovation is conditioned by a firm's competitive environment, technology, organization, and conscious strategic choices. Every attempt has been made to clarify the implications of the model for the practicing manager.

ORIGINS AND ACKNOWLEDGMENTS

Like all books, this one was much longer in the making than in the writing, and is the outcome of many influences. Years ago, Professor Donald Marquis and I discussed an outline for a wide-ranging review of work on innovation and the management of technology. Although our work was cut short by Don Marquis' untimely death, we pursued differences between types of innovations, products, and processes, and differences in patterns of innovation among different industrial sectors. We concluded that firms persisted in particular types of innovation, and that there were striking differences between firms and between technologies and sectors. At the time, little was known and less could be stated to explain these differences.

Further research on innovation was required to develop an operational model to account for interfirm and interindustry differences. I began to develop such a model by looking at differences in product innovation among firms and industries and attempting to relate those differences to firms' explicit competitive strategies for growth and competition. I expected to find that firms which focused on customer perception of product performance would emphasize product innovation, while those focusing on cost and quality would emphasize process innovation.

This endeavor was largely fruitless until 1974, when I had the good fortune to meet Professor William Abernathy, who was beginning his work on the dynamics of innovation in the production process and its relationship to product innovation. We immediately saw that together we had the elements of understanding a complex set of relationships linking a firm's products and process technologies to its competitive environment and organizational structure. We continued to develop this dynamic theory of innovation, which was reported in his book, *The Productivity Dilemma*.

I was also influenced and encouraged by another Harvard colleague, Richard S. Rosenbloom. He stressed the importance of understanding differences between groups of competing firms in the process of innovation. Professor Rosenbloom arranged for me to teach his seminar at the Harvard Business School for two years as visiting associate professor. Lacking that opportunity and his generous and continuous encouragement, I doubt if this project would have been started, much less completed in its current guise. Most important, the position at Harvard gave Bill Abernathy and me the chance to work together while our ideas were in their formative stages.

When I left Harvard for a full-time position at MIT, I was fortunate to receive half-time research support for two years from the National Science Foundation to start gathering the industry cases that form the basis of this work.[1] Dr. Alden Bean, who was then head of the NSF's Policy Research and Analysis Division, Dr. William Hetzner, and later Dr. David Roessner, who served as project monitors, provided many ideas and much helpful criticism as well as personal encouragement to me. In 1983 the project was interrupted by a long period of administrative service to MIT when I was given assignments to head a laboratory of the School of Engineering, a major research project, and then the Industrial Liaison Program. I have been fortunate that, on my return to full-time teaching and research in 1989, the new Leaders for Manufacturing Program at MIT awarded me a term chair that afforded the chance to pick up the research and writing tasks that finally resulted in this work. I also appreciate help granted by MIT's new International Center for Research in the Management of Technology for support needed by Dr. Suárez for the completion of Chapter 2.

Most important, over my years at MIT three close colleagues, the late Professor J. Herbert Hollomon, Professor Edward Roberts, and Professor Tom Allen have provided constant encouragement and help, without which I certainly would not have persisted in the work.

Dr. Linsu Kim worked extensively with me in the early stages of the project that led to this book. He classified a number of discontinuous innovations in the framework of hypotheses now seen in Chapter 9, and also wrote a paper, not included here, on the evolution of technology in the civil aircraft industry. Teresa Costanza Nolet, under my guidance, analyzed first the flat glass industry, starting with Scoville's seminal work, and later the rayon industry, working mainly from primary sources. Dr. Fernando Suárez helped develop Chapter 2 by expanding my original observations on the automobile, calculator, and transistor industries to the other industries covered. Doctors Andre Ghirardi, Paul Horwitz, and Jinjoo Lee, each working under my direction, provided analyses of the evolution of products and processes in the electrical equipment, machine tool, and synthetic rubber industries, respectively. These cases were helpful in developing the ideas set out here, but again were not included owing to the need for brevity. Prof. James R. Bright first introduced me to the early MIT studies of innovations and provided many helpful comments.

Later, I was fortunate to encounter a book by Professor Burton Klein, entitled *Dynamic Economics*. Klein was pursuing answers to the same questions but from a much different perspective. Looking at aggregates of firms competing in an industry, he reached conclusions that were remarkably consistent with those that Bill Abernathy and I were reaching. He provided a number of helpful comments with respect to the need to understand the implications of our work for the renewal of large, established corporations.

Al Lehnerd, currently with Steelcase, provided the details of the Black & Decker experience with modular portable power tool designs from his time there as leader of the project as well as much helpful commentary on the model developed in the introduction and Chapter 4. John Rydz generously checked his notes and records from his years at RCA to provide details on the cases of televisions and television picture tubes as given in Chapter 2. He also provided many helpful comments on the topic of innovation as a basis for corporate renewal. Dr. George White gave a vivid firsthand account of his experiences at Xerox and a valuable critique of the concept of a dominant design in Chapter 2. Dr. Jacob Goldman, who as vice president of research, development, and engineering at Xerox founded its Palo Alto Research Center, provided valuable commentary on that experience as well as valuable ideas related to many of the themes in this book.

Dr. Henry Montrey wrote his masters thesis, on the case of oriented strand board replacing plywood, at MIT under my guidance. Similarly Allan Afuah analyzed the case of the massively parallel supercomputer challenging von Neumann designs, while Hidetaka Kai described and analyzed the personal computer industry. I thank each of them for the use of ideas and materials from their research.

Dr. Dennis Oliver introduced me to the Pilkington Corporation and to Sir Alastair Pilkington. He not only arranged a tour of the then most modern float glass plant in Europe, but also generously shared his own knowledge of its development as well as comments on Chapter 5.

Professor Clayton Christensen was extremely helpful in allowing me to use and re-analyze material from his doctoral dissertation on the rigid disk drive industry, and thoughtful in providing comments not only on that case but also on the entire manuscript. Professor Robert Stobaugh kindly gave permission to use ideas and data from his ground-breaking book on innovation in the petrochemical industry in Chapter 6 and offered me much personal support and encouragement. Professor JoAnne Yates helped with materials and comments on Chapter 1. Professor Michael Rappa generously helped me with the design of the manuscript sent out for reviewers' comments and, in particular, drawing many of the figures.

Professor Michael Tushman has been familiar with this work from its beginning, first as a student in the doctoral seminar that I taught with Bill Abernathy at the Harvard Business School in 1975. Later, when my intention was to publish the work as part of the series edited by Tushman and Professor Andrew Van de Ven, he provided extensive comments on the original manuscript. Tushman and his associate Philip Anderson have built on my ideas, integrating them with the broader theory available in the social sciences, and, more recently, extending Nolet's and my analyses of innovation in the glass and rayon industries to the cases of glass containers, cement, and minicomputers. I have in turn benefited from their insights. Van de Ven also provided an extensive review of the current manuscript as did Professor Donald Frey, each from a different perspective, for which I am most grateful.

During the past two years Professors Richard Rosenbloom and Richard Nelson provided welcome opportunities for me to present the work at their Sloan Foundation Seminars at Harvard University and Columbia, respectively, as well as written reviews and helpful personal comments which have greatly improved the work. Professor Bengt Arne Vedin gave me an amazingly detailed critique of the manuscript, in particular of Chapter 8, based on his extensive knowledge of the photographic industry, which helped me add many ideas as well as correct some errors and inconsistencies.

Professor Chris Freeman of the Science Policy Research Unit at Sussex University has been a constant source of inspiration and support for my work since its beginning, as have Professors Keith Pavitt, Roy Rothwell, and Will Walker. Professor Will Mitchell gave me valuable suggestions during a seminar at the University of

Michigan, as did Professor Steven Klepper of Carnegie-Mellon. Klepper also sent me an extensive and helpful technical review. While I have tried to take all of their comments into account, I have not been able to do so in all cases, and any errors in the final text are my own.

When I agreed to publish this work through the Harvard Business School Press I had the great good fortune to have Richard Luecke as its editor. In many respects Luecke should be credited as co-author, as he constantly argued for brevity and clarity. He gathered additional research materials for all of the cases and checked facts and data for me. We debated and rewrote each of the chapters for clarity and consistency. His hand is particularly evident in Chapters 1, 3, 5, 7, and 8. Finally, Carol Franco, as acquisitions editor for the Harvard Business School Press, helped me believe from the beginning that there really was a book, a story worth telling in my work. She kept the final goal in view even when reviewers' comments were occasionally discouraging and during the long periods when I was caught up in administrative assignments. I thank all of these friends, especially Dick and Carol, for their unstinting help and encouragement.

This book is dedicated to the memory of William J. Abernathy. To the very end of his life Abernathy's concern was with his family and colleagues, and with scholarship having the potential to make industry more productive and innovative. Typically Bill helped the rest of us see things in new ways, to widen our vision. He was able to bring disparate, sometimes contradictory, facts together to reveal fresh insights and relationships. His many original ideas set the stage for research that has led us to a deeper and more powerful structure for thinking about and managing industrial innovation. No one book could possibly build on all of Bill's many important contributions, but I am deeply grateful for the help he gave me in starting this project. I hope that in it I have managed to capture some of his creative insights as well as my own and to make them fresh and clear for others.

Note

1. National Science Foundation, Division of Policy Research and Analysis grant No. PRA 76-82054 to the Center for Policy Alternatives at the Massachusetts Institute of Technology.

Introduction

A walk around the MIT neighborhood in Cambridge, Massachusetts today reveals a neighborhood stunningly different from the one I first encountered as a graduate student 25 years ago. In 1970, the area was truly derelict, a clutter of boarded-up buildings, all relics of New England's heyday as the center of American manufacturing. Today, many of those buildings house new companies that have crawled like hermit crabs into the abandoned shells of the industrial past. The American Twine building is now home to a laser printer company. An old piano factory has become an incubator for new software companies. Just across the street is the headquarters of Lotus Corporation, an icon of the software industry. The Biltrite factory that made shoe soles and heels has been razed to make room for one of several new biotechnology companies in town. Names like Biogen, Genzyme, and Repligen are seen on buildings here and there, while a gleaming new MIT biology laboratory is being completed where the Carr division of TRW once stamped out metal fasteners for the auto industry.

Today, a few pounds of glass fiber can carry the telephone calls that once required a ton of copper cable made by the Simplex Wire and Cable Company, whose buildings have been replaced by a technology park. In this same neighborhood, during the 1940s, MIT researchers and engineers of the newly formed Raytheon Company created miniature vacuum tubes for proximity fuses, a technology that decidedly influenced the outcome of World War II. Modern researchers in the same building explore ways to develop the ocean's resources, while the staff of MIT's Industrial Liaison Program, which I led for five years, work to transfer current research findings to productive commercial uses.

The new and growing companies around this part of Cambridge and places like it testify to the notion that technological change, broadly considered, contributes as strongly to economic growth and wealth creation as do the traditional factors of production: labor and capital. Such was the conclusion of Robert Solow, whose office is nearby.[1] Though Solow's findings earned him the Nobel Prize in economics, few industrial leaders have heard of him, and one suspects that even fewer would act on his findings. Instead, today's corporate managers and directors seem more obsessed than ever with producing short-term results, with reducing staffs, with closing plants and streamlining current businesses. Research and engineering are viewed more as costs than as investments in the future. Few scientists or engineers are found in boardrooms or in the top ranks of corporations.

As the industrial giants of our time struggle to reinvigorate themselves through downsizing, reengineering, joint ventures, and other prescriptions, the importance of technological innovation has not been adequately addressed. Innovation is at once the creator and destroyer of industries and corporations. Over the years, new technologies have made industrial giants out of many upstart firms, invigorated older ones that were receptive to change, and swept away those that were not. Today, when competitiveness hinges on the ability to develop or adapt new technologies in products, services, and processes, understanding the dynamics of industrial innovation and change is essential for survival and success. The purpose of this work is to clarify the importance of technological change in the course of enterprise, both as a creative force in the growth of corporations, and as a destructive force making those same corporations vulnerable to competitors.

Traditionally, the growth and survival of firms have been studied indirectly through the economics of business cycles. Only recently have they been the focus of more direct study by researchers in strategy and population ecology applied to organizations. Strategy researchers point to linkages between survival, financial strength, and the timing of firms' entry into the marketplace. Advocates of population ecology argue that the survivability of organizations is affected by the population density of firms at the time of their founding and by the size and growth of the markets they address. This book examines the role of technological evolution and innovation in shaping the destinies of industries and firms. It sees these explanations as complementary, each strengthening the other. Its goal is to address a number of important problems that puzzle managers and researchers, and to provide a framework for thinking about the important issues of technology, innovation, and industrial change. Issues addressed in this book include the following:

- The role of innovation in industrial competition
- The sources of industry-shattering innovations
- The relationship between product and process innovation in the cycle of industry development and competition, with special attention to the differences between assembled products (such as automobiles and typewriters) and nonassembled or homogeneous products (such as rayon and glass)
- The behavior of established firms when a radical innovation invades a stable industry
- The habits of mind and strategy that so often prevent today's dominant firms from bridging from the product technologies of the present to those of the future
- How firms can successfully renew their competitiveness as one generation of technology succeeds another

Large firms impress us as durable and persistent features of the economic landscape for obvious reasons; they have greater resources and the forward momentum of established products and customers to carry them through times of distress and mismanagement. But in the longer term, survival concerns even the largest enterprises. Examine a list of the largest U.S. firms over any appreciable time span, and you will see a surprising degree of movement: many of what were once the biggest, best financed, and most professionally managed have slid from the top ranks. Others have dropped off the lists entirely. Still others, previously small or nonexistent, have risen to displace them. Many of the newcomers were formed around semiconductors, software, supercomputers, and biotechnology—technologies that few would have imagined a generation ago. And many long-term survivors, such companies as Motorola and Hewlett-Packard, have so altered their products and underlying technologies that they would be unrecognizable to the time traveler from even 30 years ago.

The broader concerns of firm competitiveness and survival were not as compelling when national markets were largely self-contained. That is all changed today. Loss of market share and industrial competence by one domestic producer more than likely represents a gain by some foreign producer, resulting in a transfer of economic benefits across borders, with devastating effects on employment, its suppliers, and the economic vitality of entire cities and regions. Equally, firms must seek opportunities for expansion in international markets. This means that products must be originally designed with the idea of global appeal and cost-value leadership in mind. This new fact of life has heightened interest by scholars, managers, government, and the public in the forces that lead to the competitiveness and survival of firms, industries, and nations.

My purpose here is to view technology neither as a given nor in isolation, but in terms of its necessary place within and linkages to other aspects of the firm. Here, competitiveness is viewed as a systemic issue, rather than as a consequence of weakness or strength of one component or another. I plan to look at a number of products and industries as they have developed over time, moving from the particular to the general, to see whether we can begin to understand the process of innovation and its importance to business in a larger and dynamic context.

A LONG-TERM PERSPECTIVE AS A
BASIS FOR UNDERSTANDING

The process of innovation in industry is fascinating in its complexity, particularly when described in concert with the inventors, entrepreneurs, and industry builders who are its catalysts. Both are here described in a number of extended cases—short histories, really—of industries in the midst of innovation and change. I hope that these cases will render the essential ideas about innovation, competition, and corporate survival in more tangible form. The industries treated in the cases are viewed over very long periods, making it possible to identify patterns of change that would be missed by standing too close to the subject.

The first of our extended cases begins in 1874, two years before the centennial of the United States. Other cases have even earlier origins. Far from being curious and unfamiliar, the study of events of over 100 years ago casts new light on today's developments and provides foundations for understanding the present in cases as diverse as the personal computer, refrigeration, and electronic imaging. Science and enterprise in late nineteenth-century Europe and America were in many ways as dynamic as they are in our own time. In his book *Head To Head,* Lester Thurow reaches the same conclusion, noting that leadership, investment, and creativity in production and product development must be aligned as they were in the last century if American firms are to build and sustain competitive success.[2]

The purpose for presenting the extended cases and related scholarship is to explain how innovations enter and transform industries, to examine why managers so often respond in ways that ensure their ultimate failure, and to suggest strategies for mastering innovation as a force for corporate renewal.

A MODEL OF PRODUCT AND PROCESS INNOVATION

From 1975 to 1978, William Abernathy and I published several articles that laid out a model of the dynamics of innovation in industry.[3] This model, shown here as Figure I-1, hypothesizes that the rate of major innovation for both products and processes fol-

FIGURE I–1. **The Dynamics of Innovation**

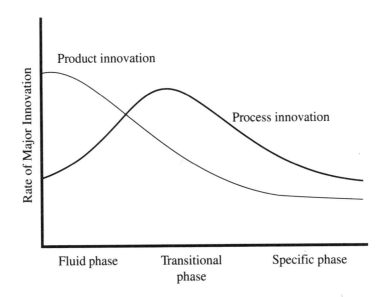

lows a general pattern over time, and that product and process innovation share an important relationship.

As the figure indicates, the rate of product innovation in an industry or product class is highest during its formative years. This is a period called the "fluid phase," during which a great deal of experimentation with product design and operational characteristics takes place among competitors. A good example of the fluid phase is found in the early years of the automobile industry, when a bewildering variety of machines—including electric and steam-driven cars—emerged from the workshops of dozens of manufacturers. Each hoped to capture the allegiance of the public with a novel new design and driver amenities; the great product variety of this period makes design innovation in the modern auto age seem sterile by comparison. During this fluid period of high product innovation, much less attention is given to the processes by which products are made, so the rate of process innovation is significantly less rapid.

The period of fluidity, according to the model, typically gives way to a "transitional phase" in which the rate of major *product* innovation slows down and the rate of major *process* innovations speeds up. At this point, product variety begins to give way to standard designs that have either proven themselves in the marketplace as the best form for satisfying user needs, or designs that have been dictated by accepted standards, by legal or regulatory constraints. As the form of the product rapidly becomes settled, the pace of innovation in the way it is produced quickens. Again the auto industry provides an example, as the imaginative designs of the early auto age gave way to a set of fairly standard designs in which the form and features of the automobile achieved a measure of uniformity. By this time auto companies had developed a set of technologies and the driving public had developed a set of expectations that together essentially defined the modern automobile. At the same time, great progress was being made in the ability of firms to manufacture automobiles at lower cost.

Some industries enter what Abernathy and I described as a "specific phase," in which the rate of major innovation dwindles for both product and process. These industries become extremely focused on cost, volume, and capacity; product and process innovation appears in small, incremental steps.

Naturally, not all industries or products pass through these tidy phases, but over the years the model has proven valuable in explaining the pace of innovation as a factor of industrial competition over periods of time. The Abernathy-Utterback model has found a place in the growing literature on this important subject and on the subject of corporate strategy as well. This book will revisit the subject of industrial innovation from the vantage point of more than a decade of scholarship and with broader evidence. We now understand much better, for example, the importance of technological "discontinuities" in reshuffling the deck of competition and industrial leadership. A key observation drawn from a 100-year perspective is the extent to which industries experience waves of innovation interspersed with periods of stability and consolidation. When a wave of radical innovation sweeps across an industry, by definition it renders one or more existing technologies obsolete, and the firms with products and internal capabilities bound up by those existing technologies must either get aboard the new one or expect to be swept away or relegated to some new role in the industry. In later chapters I will show how so many established firms fail to switch to new technologies and why that switch is so difficult.

Finally, this book forms a connection between the study of technological innovation and more recent understandings of organizational learning and the core competencies that make it possible for established firms to bridge the discontinuities caused by technological change. To avoid the grim reaper that has carried off so many proud and prosperous firms over the past century, modern managers must develop and nourish organizational capabilities that will carry them successfully from one generation of product and process technology to the next. This may be the ultimate managerial challenge.

SYNOPSIS

Chapter 1 is the first of five extended cases. It traces the development of the typewriter, a commonplace device today but a marvelously useful innovation in the late nineteenth century. This chapter describes the development of the typewriter from existing technologies and mechanical systems of the 1870s, the rise of a number of alternative designs, and the eventual appearance of a dominant design of the machine and keyboard layout. The course of industry development is analyzed through several waves of innovation—namely, the age of electric typewriters, and the early period of computer-based word processors—both of which have dramatically changed the industry.

Many of the themes to be explored later in detail surface in Chapter 1. For example, established firms must occasionally attempt to renew and diversify their core businesses rather than simply improve and expand their well-established products. A drive for renewal is often stimulated by external pressures. In this case—and as we will see later, in many other cases—the first appearance of a new product led to many imitations by both established firms and new entrants. Each new entry and product offering may be thought of as an experiment that results in feedback or data from the marketplace, leading to rapid progress in the development of the new product. At first an innovation such as the typewriter may be almost entirely a combination of design elements tried out in earlier uses or prototypes. As the market grows, greater emphasis will usually be given to development of components tailored especially for the product itself. Ultimately these may be synthesized into a model that includes most features and meets most user requirements, a model we have termed a "dominant design."

Chapter 2 develops an important concept raised in the story of the typewriter industry, the creation of a dominant design. This concept is underpinned by a rich body of academic literature and managerial experience. William Abernathy and I introduced the concept of a dominant product design and suggested that its occurrence may alter the character of innovation in a firm and an industry.[4] A dominant design usually takes the form of a new product synthesized from individual technological innovations introduced independently in prior product variants. A dominant design has the effect of enforcing or encouraging standardization so that production or other complementary economies can be sought. Then effective competition begins to take place on the basis of cost and scale as well as of product performance.

Dominant design milestones can be identified in many product lines. The sealed refrigeration unit for home refrigerators and freezers is one example; another is the advent of the Douglas DC-3, which effectively established the commercial aircraft industry. The standard diesel locomotive used by the railroad industry is a third example. Many others are examined throughout the book.[5] The many features implicit in a dominant design often result in a drastically reduced number of performance requirements to be met by a product. Once such a design is accepted it can have a profound impact both on the direction and rate of further technical advance and on the structure of competition.

Chapter 3 studies the development of the incandescent electric light and the early lighting industry from the perspective of product innovation. It continues our exploration of the relationships between innovation and its impact on competitive success. Here we observe that successive waves of change occur within an industry. Incandescent lighting through carbon filament electric lamps displaced gas lighting and was itself later displaced by metal filament lamps. These in turn were challenged by fluorescent lighting, which is challenged today by various new designs for highly efficient lamps. Later cases will show how waves of innovation are a recurring pattern as new technology enters an industry.

It is essential that we understand the linkages of product technologies with manufacturing process, corporate organization and strategy, and the structure and dynamics of an industry. Lacking balance and integration among all essential factors means that by investing heavily in one area, a firm could allow its competitors to exploit the new product or process technology first. Focusing on manufacturing (or on product development, or on finance) alone is wholly insufficient. Product design for manufacture, change in organization, and appropriate strategy are also prerequisites for competitive strength. By the same token, potential for product innovation and competitiveness depends increasingly on ability to innovate in manufacturing processes. Chapter 4 revisits the dynamics of the innovation model (see Figure I-1), describing it and supporting scholarship in detail. The implications for firms in each of its several stages are discussed.

A great number of the examples of innovation examined here and in other works involve assembled products such as typewriters and television sets, automobiles and electric lamps. Nonassembled products such as chemicals and materials have received relatively less attention, but understanding them from the perspective of innovation is required for our purposes. Chapter 5 considers developments within the plate glass manufacturing industry, which has undergone a dramatic reduction of process steps and an equally dramatic increase in efficiencies over the past century as a result of innovation.

This study of the glass industry leads naturally into Chapter 6, which examines the innovation differences and similarities between assembled and nonassembled products. The work of John Enos and Robert Stobaugh on the petrochemical industry, J.A. Allen's study of polyethylene, Daniel Hollander's evaluation of DuPont rayon operations, and others are used to enrich our understanding of process industries and the roles of breakthrough and incremental innovation.

In assembled products, a dominant design incorporating many of the performance requirements needed in the product may be reached after a long period of experimentation in both manufacture and use of the product. This idea appears to hold as well for non-assembled products. However, because nonassembled products contain fewer diverse materials than do assembled products, there is a more concentrated focus of technological effort and experimentation in the production process, which goes through similar periods of variation and experimentation, resulting in what might be called an enabling technology. This enabling technology incorporates many of the elements needed in a continuous production process and allows the focus of technological effort to shift to process improvement rather than process innovation and design.

For assembled products, process innovation usually takes the form of automation, which appears first as islands of automation and progresses through their linkage via materials transfer and other mechanisms. This phenomenon occurs much more dramatically in the production of nonassembled products. Here, process innovations often eliminate entire manual and automated steps of production, ultimately converging on a continuous process of production. This phenomenon in nonassembled product lines appears to be linked not to product change but to major equipment innovations, often those that combine in one step operations previously done in two or three separate steps. Since the separate steps may have been done in separate productive units, their combination in a new process requires a new organizational form.

Chapter 7 describes the invasion of a stable business by a radical innovation. What are the likely sources of such an invasion? What are usual consequences? And how should established firms respond? Here we consider another extended case, that of the natural ice industry which, after years of growth and the enrichment of many in New England, was fatally undermined by the innovation of mechanically made ice. The difficulties faced by firms whose fortunes are based on technology under attack is here examined. The pattern of response to attack is too often contrary to long-term survival. The period of technological turbulence caused by the invading innovation is a challenge that calls for a bold response by established firms. More often than not, however, the boldness comes from upstart firms with no standing in the industry in change.

Chapter 8 continues the earlier discussion of the power of innovation in the creation of an industry and a growing market. Here the focus is on the evolution of an industry—photography—in which innovation in both product and process technology were key factors in eventual success. George Eastman grew up in the age of glass plate photography but revolutionized the industry with his successful development of photosensitive rolls of celluloid film. This innovation fundamentally altered the picture-taking business, changing the construction of cameras and the way pictures were developed and creating a huge world market for amateur photography. It also opened the way for a rewarding collaboration with Thomas Edison in the development of cinematography. The chapter reinforces and enlivens many lessons for the practicing manager with respect to innovation and industrial change: waves of technological innovation, the linkage of product and process innovation, and the importance of "systems" in creating a market.

Chapter 9 draws together some of the lessons of earlier chapters and academic research to consider the relationship between the behaviors and strategies of firms with respect to technological innovation and long-term survival. Central to this discussion are the technological discontinuities created by innovations and their impacts on the competencies that sustain established firms. Some of these discontinuities are shown to be compatible with a firm's existing capabilities, while others fly in the face of existing strengths, requiring new skills and methods that established firms are either incapable or unwilling to master. A broader analysis of the cases is provided to determine the source of discontinuities in product and process industries. In brief, established, dominant firms are more attracted to incremental innovations than to radical innovations.

Finally, Chapter 10 addresses the perennial management issue of how corporations can renew their technology, products, and processes as a basis for continued competitive vitality. The struggle for survival in industry is unceasing and is characterized by a continuing series of challenges—usually at points of technological discontinuity or "generations" of technology. Only a small percentage of firms succeed in meeting any one of these tests. And those that survive one test must be prepared to face a succession of others. Here managers are advised to increase the quality and robustness of the product architectures that are the foundation of their product families and to extend their core competencies across the discontinuities that periodically appear.

Findings in fields as diverse as the history of technology, corporate strategy, and the dynamics of innovation have reached a common and disturbing conclusion. An unhappy by-product of success in one generation of technology is a narrowing of focus and vulnerability to competitors championing the next technological generation. If these findings are correct, then we are in the midst of a period of great peril for established but highly focused firms that may be swept away by the opening of many new fields of commercial endeavor for which they are ill equipped. Even if we do not accept such a dramatic thesis, there are many reasons for pessimism about the future of today's dominant competitors. Commodity products are being challenged by more highly engineered and tailored designs on every front. Long-accepted products and operations are increasingly open to safety and environmental concerns.

Failure to innovate is a prime source of business failure. During periods of revolutionary change, nearly all established competitors fail. But during periods of evolutionary change, most growing firms also fail to master change. In either case firms seem to fail by learning the lessons of survival in the short term too well. Must failure be the norm, or will understanding the dynamics of product and process change help managers find ways to create success instead? Failing firms are remarkably creative in defending their entrenched technologies, which often reach unimagined heights of elegance in design and technical performance only when their demise is clearly predictable.

A BROADER PERSPECTIVE

The method pursued to create this book has been to study a number of industries producing diverse products from their birth to their demise and possibly their rebirth or re-creation in an entirely new guise. The emphasis of the underlying research has been to examine primarily the details of product and process change with attention to organizational, economic, and market factors as well whenever practical. Though events in countries other than the United States are covered in several parts of the book, the emphasis has been primarily on the origins and development of industries here. Similarly, my viewpoint has been that of the "productive unit" engaged in competition in a particular market segment rather than that of a multidivisional corporation engaged in myriad markets. Thus I have looked at entry into and exit from particular market segments, which often—but certainly not always—corresponds with the birth or death of a firm as a whole. This approach, working from details to generalities, from technology to all other factors, and from local to global events, has obvious biases and limitations. The study itself started with a relatively narrow focus in time and variables and grew in scope as I realized how unsatisfactory a limited coverage would be. Through the work, I have come to appreciate just how interconnected a system the process of innovation is and how intimately it is tied to the firm and influences its fortunes. It is this understanding that the cases and analyses in *Mastering the Dynamics of Innovation* are meant to convey.

Yet the approach taken in the study is not exactly the approach I would repeat, given what has been learned from this work and others in recent years. What are the unique characteristics of the few firms that survive the "winds of creative destruction"? Would the conclusions change if the study examined a sample of more diversified corporations? Would the conclusions change if the work had a broader international and global texture? Fortunately, two outstanding recent studies take a broader view and resonate with this more narrowly focused work.

Business historian Alfred Chandler in 1990 completed a monumental work, *Scale and Scope: Dynamics of Industrial Capitalism*. In it he examines the world's 200 largest manufacturing enterprises, firms accounting for some two-thirds of world industrial output from the 1880s through the 1930s.[6] Chandler contends that

> whether we look at chemicals and electrical equipment in the
> 1880s and 1890s, motor vehicles in the 1920s, or computers today,
> the same pattern recurs. The dominant companies are those whose
> founders and senior executives understood . . . the logic of mana-
> gerial enterprise, that is, the dynamic logic of growth and competi-
> tion that drives modern industrial capitalism.[7]

My work has a focus rather different from Chandler's, starting with the welter of companies that rush into an industry at its beginnings. However, I find that only a few survive, those that adopt a so-called dominant design at a fortuitous time and then shift their attention to process integration and large-scale production. My conclusion seems in harmony with Chandler's major findings. He cautions that scale is not always an unalloyed good, particularly when a firm loses its bearings and drifts from the technological underpinnings and intimate understanding of related businesses that lead to its major success. I emphasize the dangers inherent in large scale, which often leads to overemphasis on tending the current well-established business, a lack of entrepreneurial dynamism, and vulnerability to innovative competitors.

In his most recent and most comprehensive work, *The Competitive Advantage of Nations,* Michael Porter has studied the national attributes that foster competitive advantage in particular industries. His massive research addresses more than 100 industries in 10 countries in a sample designed to cover as wide a range of differences as possible. Porter postulates that sustained productivity growth, in his view the most pertinent measure of national competitiveness, requires that a nation continually upgrade its economy.[8] This occurs when firms raise product quality, improve features and functions, improve product technology and performance, or improve production processes. Moreover,

> a nation's firms must also develop the capabilities required to compete in more and more sophisticated industry segments, where productivity is generally higher. At the same time an upgrading economy is one which has the capability of competing successfully in entirely new and sophisticated industries.[9]

In essence Porter seeks to determine how valuable skills and technology are created by firms in a region. The evidence leads him to conclude that the process of creating comparative advantage is more stable than one might imagine and that the creation of advantage remains nationally and even regionally based, despite widening international competition and the increasing presence of multinational firms in the world economy. Porter concludes in part that "innovations shift competitive advantage when rivals either fail to perceive a new way of competing or are unwilling or unable to respond," and that "possibilities for new ways of competing usually grow out of some discontinuity or change in industry structure," often created by new technologies or by new demands that bring existing technologies to market in new combinations and forms.[10] Porter finds that "often innovators are 'outsiders' . . . to the existing industry," and that "where innovators are large firms, they were often new entrants to the industry from an established position in another industry." Finally, "a firm's ability to sustain its success is most likely a result of constant innovation to adapt to changing circumstances."[11] Despite a much different sample and approach, these conclusions are remarkably similar to those drawn in the following chapters.

This book argues that innovation is a central determinant of longer-run success and failure for manufacturing firms. Moreover, most industry-shattering innovations do not spring from the established competitors in an industry but from new firms or from established firms entering a new arena. This is true even though such radical innovations often are seen to be based on the synthesis of well-known technical information or components, occur step by step, and exist in embryonic form for many years before they become commercially significant. One reason for the lethargy of well-established competitors in a product market in the face of potentially disruptive innovation is that they face increasing constraints from the growing web of relationships binding product and process change together. At the start of production of a new product, general-purpose equipment, available components, and highly skilled people may suffice to enter the market. As both product and market increase in sophistication more specialization is generally required in equipment, components, and skills. Thus change in one element, the product, requires changes throughout the whole system of materials, equipment, methods, and suppliers. This may make changing much more onerous and costly for the established firm than for the new entrant. Porter makes the further point that newcomers are outside the system of social constraints and may be less aware or less concerned about the disruptive nature of the changes that they promote to the existing web of mutual obligations and understood limits.

A pattern emphasized in the cases in this study is the degree to which powerful competitors not only resist innovative threats, but actually resist all efforts to understand them, preferring to further entrench their positions in the older products. This results in a surge of productivity and performance that may take the old technology to unheard-of heights. But in most cases this is a sign of impending death.[12]

How is it that a large and powerful firm can respond with great creativity in its defense while rarely exhibiting the creativity required to embrace the new and abandon the old? After sifting the evidence we believe this is primarily the result of the habits of mind, commitments and strategy, or patterns of behavior of the organization's elite. Perhaps it is only human to defend the known and resist the unknown, a point that has been made by students of fields as diverse as history, psychology, and the philosophy of science. Change does not come easily to human societies, and there is no reason to expect the societies we call firms to behave differently. What is often astonishing is the degree to which the same societies, the same collections of people who behave so defensively toward radical change in its first appearance, can pull together and perform remarkable feats of courage and creativity when mortally threatened. This finding leads us to the conclusion that to sustain its success and renew its products, the firm must focus not on the products but on the people involved! James Brian Quinn puts this well in "The Intelligent Enterprise" when he looks at the renewal of the firm as a whole based on its portfolio of human resources. Quinn claims, and I agree, that "looking beyond mere product lines to a strategy built around core intellectual or service competencies provides both a rigorously maintainable strategic focus and long-term flexibility."[13] This is the most important point on which Chandler, Porter, Quinn, and the present work converge, and it is the subject of the concluding chapter.

Notes

1. Robert M. Solow, "Growth Theory and After," *American Economic Review,* vol. 78, no. 3 (June 1988), pp. 307–317.
2. Lester Thurow, *Head to Head: The Coming Economic Battle among Japan, Europe and America* (New York: William Morrow, 1992).
3. William J. Abernathy and James M. Utterback, "Patterns of Industrial Innovation," *Technology Review,* vol. 80, no. 7 (June/July 1978), pp. 40–47.
4. James M. Utterback and William J. Abernathy, "A Dynamic Model of Product and Process Innovation," *Omega,* vol. 3, no. 6 (1975), pp. 639–656.
5. Abernathy and Utterback, "Patterns of Industrial Innovation."
6. Alfred D. Chandler, Jr., *Scale and Scope: Dynamics of Industrial Capitalism* (Cambridge, Mass.: Harvard University Press, 1990) and its extension in Alfred D. Chandler, Jr., "The Enduring Logic of Industrial Success," *Harvard Business Review,* vol. 90, no. 2 (March–April 1990), pp. 130–140.
7. Chandler, "The Enduring Logic of Industrial Success," p. 131. This logic begins with an understanding of the cost advantages that large scale and broad scope provide in technologically advanced and capital-intensive industries. It

continues with large investments in coordinated global investments in manufacturing, marketing, and distribution. Chandler shows that those companies that first made such investments, those he describes as "first movers" quickly dominated their industries and continued to do so for decades. He concludes that "geographic expansion was usually based on economies of scale, while moves into related product markets more often rested on economies of scope. In both cases, however, organizational capabilities . . . provided the dynamic for continuing growth" (p. 133).

8. Michael E. Porter, *The Competitive Advantage of Nations* (New York: The Free Press, 1990), p. 6.

9. Ibid., p. 7.

10. Ibid., pp. 45–47. Innovation is defined broadly by Porter to include both improvements in a technology and better methods and ways of doing things. In his terms it can be manifested in product changes, process changes, new approaches to marketing, new forms of distribution, and new conceptions of scope (p. 45).

11. Ibid., p. 65.

12. Only rarely does the struggle of old ways against impending death drive the new from the market. Ironically, one of the defenses of the old against the new involves its adoption and incorporation, but in a defensive rather than an offensive posture. Examples include the steaming sailing ship, super sterilization of still refrigerated milk, film cameras stuffed with electronics to improve amateur picture-taking quality, and serial supercomputers with limited added-in parallel-processing capabilities.

13. James Brian Quinn, "The Intelligent Enterprise: A New Paradigm," *Academy of Management Executive,* vol. 6, no. 1 (1992), p. 50.

CHAPTER 1

The Dynamics of Innovation in Industry

There is an idea that will revolutionize business.
Henry Benedict to Philo Remington on the Sholes typewriter

I N THE SUMMER OF 1874, Mr. Samuel Clemens (Mark Twain) had come from Hartford to Boston to deliver a series of readings. He and a friend, humorist "Petroleum" V. Nasby, were out for a walk one afternoon when they spied a new contraption called a "type writing machine" in a store window. Clemens was a great fan of American ingenuity in any form and had a weakness for the gadgets and inventions that sprang from the minds and workshops of his countrymen. In today's parlance, Clemens was a "lead user," invariably the first in his circle to have the latest technical gizmo.

Entering the store, Clemens asked to see how the device worked. The sales clerk was happy to oblige and offered that it could write 57 words per minute. He had a young lady demonstrate the machine, and her performance so astonished Clemens and Nasby that they asked her to do it again, this time while they timed her work on their pocket watches. Clemens was impressed, and he bought the machine on the spot.

Back in Hartford, he pecked out a letter to his brother Orion:

TRYING TO GET THE HANG OF THIS NEW FANGLED
MACHINE . . . [it] COSTS 125 DOLLARS. THE MACHINE
HAS SEVERAL VIRTUES. I BELIEVE IT WILL PRINT

1

FASTER THAN I CAN WRITE . . . IT PILES AN AWFUL
STACK OF WORDS ON A PAGE.[1]

MR. CLEMENS'S NEW MACHINE

The machine Clemens purchased was a Remington No. 1, the
first ever offered to the general public. The large, cumbersome
device came mounted on its own platform, enclosed in a japanned
black metal case, with a keyboard and a roll of paper on top. It
could print only uppercase letters and had no tabs. Still, many
today would recognize this first commercial typewriter for what it
was.

The Remington machine was actually a synthesis of many
existing technologies and mechanical elements in widespread use
at the time. Clockwork suggested the idea of the *escapement*—i.e.,
moving the carriage one letter at a time. The keys and their con-
necting arms were adaptations of the telegraph key. A sewing
machine pedal returned the carriage, and the piano suggested a
model for the free-swinging arms and hammers that struck the letter to the paper.[2] It was noisy, in the words of its inventor going
"thump, thump at every letter" and "back with a crash sufficient
to wake the dead."

This chapter considers the case of the typewriter as an assembled product innovation. Here we will see how an innovation often
draws from existing technologies and models for its application but
uses these elements creatively in combination with new ones to
form a uniquely different product. We will see how the characteristics of the innovation are molded by forces of competition, invention, and customer use until they crystallize into a product with a
certain standardized form, set of features, and technical capability.
Most important, we will extend the case of the manual typewriter
to its successor forms—the electric typewriter, the dedicated
word processor, and the personal computer—each of which
appeared as a new wave of technological innovation washing
through the industry with tremendous effects on the nature of competition.

The Remington No. 1 typewriter purchased by Samuel Clemens was based on the invention of a former Milwaukee newspaper editor named Christopher Latham Sholes. Like most other
inventions, Sholes's was part of a stream of inventions. As early

as 1714, an English engineer named Henry Miller had obtained a patent for a "writing engine," of which all descriptions are now lost. In the United States, William Burt of Mt. Vernon, Michigan patented a crude "typographer," which apparently interested almost no one. The government official who gave Burt his patent document wrote it out in longhand, of course, attesting to the need for some kind of mechanical writing device, but Burt's contraption did not fit the bill. A good writer with a pen could not do more than 30 words per minute—the official speed record in 1853. This, and the fact that telegraphers and shorthand stenographers of the time could now take down information at speeds of up to 130 words per minute, created the imperative for an effective fast writing machine. Dozens of prototypes appeared and received patents between the time of Burt and the Sholes inventions, but none were put into commercial use.[3]

Sholes had first developed a machine using narrow wooden keys that connected to the type hammers by means of wires. An ink-saturated ribbon passed beneath. He made improvements using telegraph-like keys that dispensed with the wires of the older model, and he received patents in July 1868.[4] Sensing the need for a partner with the money and the moxie to take his invention into successful commercial development, Sholes in 1869 took on as partner a burly, swaggering, salesman character named James Dunsmore. Dunsmore did not have two nickels to rub together, but he had plenty of grit and saw in the typing machine a chance to make a fortune. First, however, he wanted Sholes to improve the crude device, and he imposed on the inventor for a succession of some 50 models—each reflecting some minor improvement—before he had the machine he wanted. At that point, Dunsmore began approaching manufacturers.

After an unsuccessful attempt to sell exclusive manufacturing rights to Western Union Company for a reported $50,000, Dunsmore and an associate approached Mr. Philo Remington, president of the Remington Company. With the boom times of the Civil War behind it, Remington had been trying to diversify into other areas, and by then had gone into farm machinery, sewing machines, horse-drawn fire engines, and cotton gins—generally with disastrous results.[5] The idea of the typewriter appealed to Philo Remington and his associates; their plant in Ilion, New York was underutilized, and they wanted to expand their line of consumer products. In 1873, Remington agreed to be exclusive manufacturer of the Sholes typewriter and dedicated two top mechanics to the problem of perfecting the machine for production in a section of its Ilion plant.[6]

THE NEW MACHINE MEETS THE PUBLIC

By July 1874, the first production models, including the one purchased by Samuel Clemens, were in stores across the country. They had some unusual operating characteristics. The keys of the No. 1 struck the paper *inside* the machine, making it impossible for the operator to see his or her work until the first four rows were typed, at which time the paper began emerging from the machine. And, of course, no one knew how to type.

The fact that it had only uppercase letters did not endear the No. 1 to users or readers, which is made clear in many letters of the time. The uppercase script led some early readers to believe that the letters sent to them were in fact printed handbills—that is, junk mail—which they tossed out without reading. Still others, like this Texas banker, took offense at the first typewritten correspondence:

> I realize, Mr. John, that I do not possess the education which you have. However, until your last letter I have always been able to read the writing. I do not think it necessary to have your letters to me taken to a printer and set up like a handbill. I will be able to read your writing and am deeply chagrined to think you thought such a course necessary.[7]

Even Clemens, who was committed to making a go of the new writing machine, grew frustrated with it. "I DONT KNOW WHETHER I AM OGING TO MAKE THIS TYPE-WRITING MACHINE GO OR NTO," he wrote to his Cambridge literary friend, W.D. Howells, after a short time with the new machine. Six months later he shipped the beast to Howells, preceding it with a note that warned, "You just wait a couple of weeks & if you don't see the Type-Writer come tilting along toward Cambridge with the raging hell of an unsatisfied appetite in its eye, I lose my guess." The typewriter did arrive, and Howells kept it, returning at least two witty letters to Clemens in payment, both at the expense of the Remington device: "I have begun several letters to My d ar lemans, as it prefers to spell your respected name . . . It's fascinating, in the meantime, and wastes my time like an old friend."

After a few years with the typewriter, Howells could tell Clemens that "The wretch who sold you that typewriter has not yet come to a cruel death."[8]

How the Typewriter Keyboard Got that Way

The development of the QWERTY, or Universal, keyboard is subject to some debate. Both Sholes and Dunsmore had experience as printers. Thus, according to one explanation, they were familiar with the type case, the sectioned box in which the printer's pieces of type were arranged. Because letters such as A, E, and I were used more often than others, the type case was arranged not alphabetically, but in a way that made picking out the most frequently used letters more convenient. The typewriter inventors supposedly used this principle as they experimented with various keyboard layouts. One problem they encountered was the jamming together of type bars as an operator's speed increased. Sholes and Dunsmore found that they could minimize this problem by altering the arrangement of the keys so that letters frequently struck in close succession would converge from opposite sides of the machine.

Historian Bruce Bliven disputes the type case story. According to Bliven's sources, Sholes originally laid out the keyboard alphabetically (the FGH and JKL sequences are surviving relics). As Sholes struggled through many model changes, he reportedly made modifications to keep the keys from jamming up. According to Bliven, the machine offered to Remington for manufacture in 1873 bore this keyboard arrangement:[1]

2 3 4 5 6 7 8 9 - ,

Q W E . T Y I U O P

Z D F G H J K L M

A X & C V B N ? ; R

Whichever story was accurate, the inventors were aware that keyboard standardization would be important to successful adoption of the new machine. Typing a letter to his stepson on a new keyboard arrangement that he and Sholes had just concocted, Dunsmore complained, "I had to unlearn as well as learn" the new arrangement. This concern has made the modern QWERTY keyboard, named after the order of the top left-hand row of letters, a standard (except in France), despite subsequent attempts to improve typing efficiency through keyboard redesign.[2] Paul David, who has considered the effect of the keyboard arrangement on competing alternatives offers these comments:

> Under competitive conditions, and in the absence of public policy interventions, the existence of significant increasing returns to scale, or analogous positive feedback mechanisms such as "learning by doing," and by "using," can give the result that one particular formulation of a network technology—VCRs, or QWERTY-formatted keyboard—will be able to drive out other variants and so emerge as the de facto standard for the industry. By no means need the commercial victor in this kind of systems rivalry be more efficient than the available alternatives.[3]

Paul David and others have pointed to the persistence of the QWERTY keyboard as an example of how high "switching costs" from one design standard to another make it possible for less efficient artifacts—like the original Sholes key layout—to persist, even though more efficient alternatives exist. They point out that technological changes in typing (with respect both to the change from type bars to type balls and daisy wheels on modern typewriters and to the digital underpinnings of computer-based typing) have virtually eliminated the problem of jamming keys. The Dvorak keyboard, introduced by August Dvorak in 1936 as a more ergonomically efficient system that balanced the frequently used letters between the two hands and loaded the strong fingers more heavily, is often pointed to as *the* better system that high switching costs have effectively kept off the market. The fact that so many individuals and business establishments have an investment in QWERTY skills and equipment, the reasoning goes, has prevented adoption of the Dvorak keyboard. This same switch-cost issue is important in other fields where product innovations are rapid.[4]

The latest salvo in the continuing argument about QWERTY versus Dvorak keyboards and the power of design standards comes from S.J. Liebowitz and Stephen E. Margolis, who challenge the entire notion of the superiority of the Dvorak design. According to these scholars, the assumption of the Dvorak superiority has never been established by scientific tests. To Liebowitz and Margolis, the persistence of the QWERTY design is not an indication of market failure due to an entrenched product standard, but an indication that the Dvorak design failed to prove its superior value in an open marketplace.[5] They point to the high variety of typewriter designs in the early days of the industry, the many typing contests that pitted the performance of one design against another, and the economic incentives for modern corporations to invest in switching to improve typing systems as an indication of the inherent fitness of the QWERTY design and an explanation for its persistence over time.

Notes

1. Bruce Bliven, *The Wonderful Writing Machine* (New York: Random House, 1954), p. 143.
2. Richard Nelson Current, *The Typewriter: And the Men Who Made It* (Champaign, Ill.: University of Illinois Press, 1954), pp. 55–58.
3. Paul A. David, "Heroes, Herds and Hysteresis in Technological History," *Industrial and Corporate Change,* vol. 1, no. 1 (1992), p. 139.
4. See Paul A. David, "Clio and the Economics of QWERTY," *American Economic Review,* 75 (May 1985), pp. 332–337; and "Understanding the Economics of QWERTY: The Necessity of History," in W.N. Parker, ed., *Economic History and the Modern Economist* (New York: Basil Blackwell, 1986).
5. S.J. Liebowitz and Stephen E. Margolis, "The Fable of the Keys," *The Journal of Law & Economics,* vol. XXXIII (1) (April 1990), pp. 1–25.

Sales of the No. 1 were slow. Impeded by its high price and poor performance, Remington managed to sell only 400 during the first six months. But the company made improvements in both the product and its manufacturing process, and by 1877 it had sold 4,000 machines. In 1878, the company introduced a new machine, the No. 2, with the now-familiar double typeface and shift keys, making lowercase writing possible. This machine did much better, selling 100,000 units during its lifetime.[9] Remington catalogs described the wonders of its new machine in glowing terms—"A Machine To Supersede the Pen," they proclaimed. And "Persons traveling by sea can write with it when pen writing is impossible."[10]

The typewriter was on its way, and over the course of the next 30 years it would create a totally new industry with many competitors offering a variety of innovative products. Old methods of writing in newsrooms, offices, and homes gave way to typewriting. It was helped along by the expansion of business enterprise in general and the growing requirements for written documents, reports, and records. Even the rudimentary Remington No. 1 could produce up to 75 words per minute in the hands of an expert typist.[11] The literary community caught the spirit; Samuel Clemens delivered the first typewritten manuscript—*Life on the Mississippi*—to his publisher, and others followed suit.

THE NEW PERSON IN THE OFFICE

The typewriter was soon a ubiquitous fixture of the workplace. As early as 1887 it would be said that "its monotonous click can be heard in almost every well-regulated business establishment in the country."[12] It would make broad ripples of change in the social environment of the office, creating, as JoAnne Yates has documented, "a whole new class of clerical workers"—largely female—to handle the production of written documents.[13] U.S. Bureau of the Census figures on occupations, begun in 1890 and cited by Yates, tell the story of the expanded role of typewriting in the American economy (Table 1-1).

A major consequence of this development was the opening of the office workplace to women. Women had shared the work of men on America's farms for hundreds of years, and their daughters

TABLE 1–1.   **Typists and Stenographers in the United States**

1890	33,000
1900	134,000*
1910	387,000
1920	786,000

*Starting in 1900, this occupational category included secretaries.

left those farms for work in the textile mills of New England in the mid-nineteenth century. But the office had always been a male bastion of managers who ruled and male clerks who were ruled over, hoping to be managers one day. The demand for typists changed that situation permanently; men still ruled the bastion, but women were now let in. Typewriters did for the office what automated equipment did for the mill—it separated thinking from doing. Now the manager could do all the thinking, and the typist could manually transcribe those thoughts into documents. By 1890, 64 percent of all typists were women; by 1920, the percentage had risen to 92.[14]

The aptitude of women for the new occupation of typist was hotly debated, even in the presuffrage era of the 1880s and 1890s. "Women," it was claimed in their favor, "are superior to men, their greater quickness of perception and motion giving them obvious advantages," while men were decried as "more frequently absent because of their vices."[15]

Natural abilities aside, pay levels probably had much more to do with the recruitment of women for the boom in typing jobs. Then, as now, women were usually paid less for the same work—perhaps by 25 percent in those times. But at $15 per week in 1886, the typist's pay was far better than what could be had in the factory or the retail shop, and the working environment was said to be much better.

NEW COMPETITORS AND INNOVATIONS

The commercial possibilities of the typewriter were not lost on potential competitors, and before long a number had entered the field with machines of many designs. The first of these was the Yost Caligraph, a cheap version of the Sholes machines offered by the former sales agent of Remington. Dunsmore had a financial interest in this operation as well. In 1881, the Caligraph No. 2 came onto the market with upper- and lowercase functions; but unlike the Remington, the Caligraph did not use a shift key—it had two entirely separate keyboards. In 1885, the Crandell, the Hammond, and the Hall machines appeared—each based on a uniquely different design for striking type to paper.[16]

By 1886, *Scientific American* estimated that 50,000 typewriters of all makes had been produced; and by 1888, Remington Standard Typewriting Company[17] was turning out some 1,500 machines each month. Its Ilion plant had adopted mass-production techniques to reach this level. Specialized departments performed the die-casting, tempering, forging, annealing, plating, and assembly operations. Specialized equipment was developed and brought on line, and skilled workers assembled each machine individually.

Remington knew that it had the best-made and most functional machine and was aggressive in letting the public know about it. In 1888, the company's sales agency put up a "$1,000 Challenge" to Caligraph and the handful of other competitors, proposing a public contest with impartial referees to determine which machine was the fastest. Caligraph did not shrink from this challenge, but sent its typing champion with the double-keyboard machine to take on Remington in a highly publicized event in Cincinnati in July 1888. Caligraph was soundly thrashed.

If Remington's public victory confirmed its position as top dog in the typewriting world, it did nothing to stop a torrent of new competitors from entering the field, particularly as Sholes's patents began to expire. Between 1885 and 1890, the number of firms doubled to ten. A community of some 20 supplier firms grew up in their shadow, and collectively, in 1890, they employed some 1,800 people and produced $3.6 million in finished goods sales.[18] But the real threat to Remington's dominance was a yet-unhatched innovation by Franz X. Wagner. Wagner had designed the Caligraph machine for Yost, and now he and his brother had a new design with an important new feature: visible type. The Wagner design had the type arms swing out and strike the paper front and center, where the operator could observe any mistake and correct it immediately. John T. Underwood and his father, who were in the ribbon and carbon business, saw the virtue of this innovation. They bought the design from Wagner and put the new machine into production in 1895.

The Underwood No. 1 was an immediate success, and was followed in short order by several models that refined its basic design, the most important of which was the Model 5 (1899). The Model 5 had the look and feel of the modern manual typewriter that anyone today who has ever used such a device (a vanishing breed) would quickly recognize and feel comfortable with; it had visible type, a light touch, a tab function, quiet operation, and a design that made corrections easy. Its placement of the type bars— like its predecessor models—represented a successful departure from the design of competing machines. So successful was this machine that Underwood immediately shifted production to a larger factory in Hartford to meet the skyrocketing demand. With its market leadership decimated by the new challenger, Remington rushed out its Monarch model in 1901; L.C. Smith & Brothers—another big producer—followed with its No. 8 (1908). From photographs, it is clear that these competitors were look-alikes of the design pioneered by Underwood.[19] Imitation, however, did nothing to shore up their sales, and by 1920 Underwood had a lock on the business, selling as many machines as all of its rivals combined.[20]

The Royal Company (1904), was perhaps the last of the new entrants to gain any real standing, but this did not prevent other startups from joining the fray. Some 89 manufacturers had tried their luck in the American market by 1909, but almost all were marginal operations, and many came and went quickly. Underwood, Remington, Royal, and L.C. Smith & Brothers (later merged with Corona) were to dominate the American market until the next chapter was opened. With everyone settled on the design and features of the typewriter, the pace of product innovation slowed dramatically, and the big producers concentrated on manufacturing and costs.

THE ELECTRIC AGE

In 1933, one of the fringe players in the industry—Electrostatic Typewriters, Inc.—was purchased by International Business Machines (IBM). Both Remington and Underwood had passed up the opportunity to buy it; both had disappointing experiences with electrics as early as 1925. Electric-powered typewriters had been around since 1906 but had never made a dent in the market—home or office. The 1930s were not good years for the industry anyway. The Great Depression decimated economic growth, and with it expenditures for office equipment. Of the four leaders, only Royal had a positive growth rate, and its was anemic. Firms were leaving the business at a high rate.

IBM was not in the typewriter business, but it did make record-accounting and tabulating machines and thought it might acquire some useful keypunch technology from the Electrostatic acquisition.[21] There is little information about the early IBM electric machines, except that the War Department gave the company a great many orders during the war, while requiring its principal competitors to forego typewriter production altogether in favor of military production. This gave IBM years of design and manufacturing experience that put it well down the learning curve. In the postwar economic boom, demand for the IBM electrics was poised to intensify.[22]

Electrics did not represent a radical innovation so much as a mixing of two well-understood technologies to provide better performance: more uniform print, better-quality copies, and less physical stress on the typist over long periods. But the business market was not yet convinced. Perhaps secretaries found these early electrics too crude and too noisy; perhaps they did not find their virtues overwhelming. For whatever reason, electrics were slow to catch on; but once they did, they rapidly displaced manual office typewriters (Figure 1-1).

In terms of total machine sales, both office and nonoffice, a similar picture prevailed. In 1950, electrics had only 10 percent of the total office/nonoffice market, but by 1965 they were capturing 50 percent of all sales. By 1970, only 24 percent of total machine sales went to manuals, mostly for the home market.

FIGURE 1–1.   **Electrics as a Percentage of Office Typewriter Sales, 1948–1967**

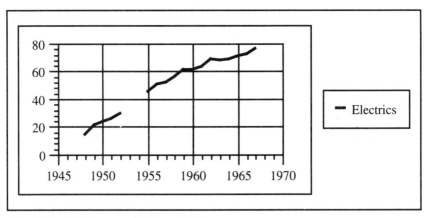

Note: No data for years 1954 and 1955.

Source: Based on data in George Nichols Engler, *The Typewriter Industry: The Impact of a Significant Technological Innovation*, Ph.D. diss. (Los Angeles: University of California at Los Angeles, 1970), pp. 276–277.

By 1967, IBM controlled 60 percent of the electric market and 74 percent of the high-end, full-featured electric market. SCM, Royal, and Olivetti-Underwood each had about 10 percent. Remington was barely on the map. The stage was now set for an invasion of the office market by another wave of innovation, this time something so radical that Sholes, Dunsmore, Wagner, and other pioneers of the typewriter business would have had trouble understanding it, but which Mr. Samuel Clemens would surely want to get his hands on.

THE SMARTER MACHINES

At the time that the business community was excitedly buying Underwood's Model 5, there were about 5 million office workers in America—about 20 percent of the working population. Today, more than 55 million are white-collar workers—clerical and professional—and they represent about half of all employed people in the United States.[23] By all accounts they are not the most productive workers, and no one has been able to measure any appreciable rate of productivity increase over many years. Thus, with half of the working population in a state of productive lethargy, and some four-fifths of office costs going for labor, any technologies that suggested improvements in white-collar productivity were welcomed.

The office-machines industry was ripe for radical change, but when change first appeared it was as an adaptation of a new technology to an old form. The IBM Magnetic Tape Selectric, introduced in 1964, combined electric typewriter technology with digital computing technology to make text editing possible for the first time. By the early 1970s, stand-alone "word processors" with CRTs for true text editing began to appear and replace standard office typewriters.[24] A group of new companies, some from unrelated industries, read the tea leaves and determined that what the "office of the future" needed was an integrated system of dedicated word processors—that is, smart typewriters with CRTs, microprocessor systems, and text-processing software—that would improve productivity. Wang, Xerox, Exxon, ITT, AT&T, Olivetti, IBM, and others (as many as 55 by one count[25]) developed elaborate and expensive systems that intended to do for text processing what Henry Ford had done for auto assembly. Exxon alone, in its bid to diversify from the oil business, spent an estimated $2 billion on its office equipment division, developing such fanciful products as Vydec word processors, Qwip fax machines, and Qyx electronic typewriters. All signs pointed to big success, and by 1975, some 200,000 word-processing devices had been installed. By 1986, over 4 million word processors had been sold in the United States alone.

But the electronic office proved not to be the factory of the future. The millions spent on word processors could not be shown to generate any productivity improvements, except in law offices and other establishments where boilerplate documents were heavily used. Secretaries dreaded the prospect of being corralled into word-processing "centers" like so many assembly-line drudges; managers sensed they would be lost without their secretaries; and companies that organized word-processing pools faced heavy reorganizing efforts and costs. Office workers wanted something else, and when they found it, the word-processor firms took big losses. Wang went belly up. Exxon retreated to the oil patch after selling its product line to Lanier for pennies on the dollar. ITT and AT&T pulled back. The "something else" that office workers wanted was the personal computer.

THE NEXT WAVE OF INNOVATION

Like the innovation of the typewriter a century earlier, the personal computer was destined to draw from many existing technologies of the time, came in a variety of designs offered by many competing firms, and ultimately crystallized around a fairly uniform set of product features and specifications. And, like the Sholes/Remington typewriter, it was an innovation destined to both create a major industry and affect the way people did their work. Further, the personal computer represented a wave of technological innovation that swept through the same market occupied by the typewriter and the dedicated word processor. These pattern similarities support the earlier contention that the study of older innovations is not just a form of academic recreation, but a way to enrich our understanding of developments taking place today.

Development of the PC Industry

The first device that deserved the name "personal computer" was the Altair 8800, designed by a small electronic kit maker in Albuquerque (MITS), and offered to the public for $395. How this machine was invented and the early history of the personal computer industry are engagingly told in *Fire In the Valley*[26] and other books. The Altair 8800 was an instant hit among electronic gadgeteers and the new breed of digital enthusiasts; by 1977, there were at least 30 firms making personal computers, including Apple, Commodore, Tandy (Radio Shack), and Heathkit.[27] That year, the Apple II was introduced—a 16K RAM machine that sold for $1,195 without a monitor. Its skyrocketing sales were encouraged by the development of the spreadsheet and word-processing software that would eventually create a business market for it and other machines. By 1981, an estimated half-million personal computers had found their ways to the business market.[28] A comparable number were being used by students, scientists, and hobbyists. Interestingly, the first Apple II computers produced many of the same annoying features that afflicted the original typewriter. They would create only capital letters; there was no tabulation feature or number pad; the format seen on the screen was not necessarily the format that would be printed out (the "what you see is what you get" of the personal computer appeared in the market only with the introduction of the Macintosh).

The landmark event for the personal computer was the August 1981 introduction of the IBM PC. For a list price of about $3,000, IBM offered a conservatively designed desktop computer based on the Intel 8088 microprocessor. In the judgment of most experts, the IBM PC was no technological breakthrough, but that fact did not stop it from quickly grabbing 30 percent of the business market. In the last three months of 1981 alone, IBM shipped 13,000 of its new machines; over the next two full years 40 times that number would be sold.[29] Despite its technical shortcomings, IBM's machine legitimized the personal computer industry. As Stan Augarten observes in his history of computers, ". . . the PC has had a stabilizing influence on the youthful personal computer industry, providing a focal point for manufacturers and customers alike."[30] IBM's use of an open architecture and policy of making operating system information available to the public created a center of gravity for applications software developers. The fact that it was built largely from nonproprietary components opened the door to many imitators who created "IBM compatible" machines and peripherals. Before long, the vast majority of personal computer users were operating equipment that shared the same operating characteristics as the dominant IBM PC.

Personal computers—of all makes and models—very quickly assumed a form that was recognizable and accepted by consumers. This consisted of a monitor, a standard QWERTY keyboard, an underlying operating system, a processing unit, a disk drive (and eventually an internal hard drive), and a bus-architecture of one or another type.[31] Each of these forms affected the way the user fed data into the machine and how data in the machine was made available to the user. What happened inside the machine—once the user made his keystrokes, or popped her disk into the machine's drive—was a function of microprocessors and software.

Apple Computers remained the sole major holdout from the IBM-driven movement. Apple, too, offered the standard outward features of monitor, keyboard, disk drive, operating system, processing unit, and bus, but its steadfastness in maintaining a closed architecture, proprietary operating system and bus, and reliance on Motorola microprocessors isolated Apple from the larger universe of DOS-based, Intel chip machine users. Despite the greater elegance of the Apple Macintosh machine, the company's share of market in 1993 remained stuck at 13 percent. At the same time, intense price competition within the entire industry cut deeply into its profit margins.

The Brains and the Box

For the typical user, the internal interaction of microprocessors and software was largely transparent and of little concern; what went in and what came out were the things that interested the user. But microprocessors and software very quickly established themselves as the technological soul of the machine, its unique identity, and the source of major improvements in the personal computer industry. In contrast, the business of designing and assembling the machines took on all the characteristics of a commodity business— like television sets and other electronic appliances—commanding lower margins and lower stock valuations. Remarkably, in 1993, the total combined market value of Intel and Microsoft—the two leading vendors of microprocessors and software, respectively— exceeded the market value of the IBM corporation. The suppliers had become more valuable than their customer. They were supplying the brains; IBM and manufacturers of IBM-compatible machines were supplying the boxes the brains were sold in. Clearly, the brains were more highly valued.

Growth of the Personal Computer Industry

The versatility of the personal computer allowed clerical workers and professionals to write and edit text, run spreadsheets, and create graphics—all the things that their typewriters could not do and that the old word processors had failed to accommodate. By 1987, personal computers—of all manufacturers—were outselling word processors by 4.5 times.[32] Unit sales to business in 1991 were projected to reach 20 million. But the growth in sales only led to a great industry shakeout. In 1983, a year in which the market grew by 50 percent, many important competitors exited the industry. Commodore, Atari, and Texas Instruments experienced serious business problems; Timex-Sinclair, Osborne, Coleco, and Mattel vanished from the industry. In 1984, 62 percent of total personal computer sales to business firms went to IBM (49) and Apple (13) alone.[33] T. Modis and A. Debecker point to 1982–1983 as the peak, in terms of numbers of different models and new companies entering the personal computer industry. They cite 125 distinguishable new PCs per year introduced by almost 18 new companies per year. Within five years those rates dropped to 82 new models for 14 companies.[34]

Today, more and more office workers are having personal computers put on their desks at great expense to their employers. It is not at all clear if these are improving the workers' productivity; indeed, many believe that they have simply created more and needless revisions of text and have wasted time on out-of-the-blue spreadsheet forecasts. The one thing that is clear is that employees want them, just as secretaries wanted electric typewriters through the 1960s.

A BACKWARD GLANCE

As a means of putting words on paper, the new computer technology represented a great advance over the crude mechanical instrument that Samuel Clemens and his pal Petroleum Nasby encountered that summer day in 1874. A safe bet is that it in turn will be displaced by something better in the future, as likely as not developed and manufactured by some entity unknown to us today.

The story of the typewriter was not recounted here simply as a quaint tale; rather, the invention of the device, its transformation over time, and the rise and fall of its various manufacturers underscores many of the themes to be developed in detail in this book. Looking back at this business of printed documents, we can see a number of distinct developments:

• *New innovations from old capabilities.* The Sholes typewriter was a synthesis of a number of existing mechanical technologies. Joined together, they created something new. The early electrics likewise joined together familiar components (small electric motors and manual typewriters) to create a new machine. Even the very radical leap to personal computer technology carried with it the old and the familiar: the QWERTY keyboard, typing conventions, and so forth. Although not mentioned here, the personal computer itself was built from available components created by other sectors of the electronics industry: television monitors, printed-circuit boards, memory chips, semiconductors, and the like.

• *Dominant design.* After an initial period of intensive churning of product innovations—different modes of striking the paper (type bar, type wheel, type sleeve), hidden and visible types, dual keyboards versus single boards with shift keys, and so forth—a dominant design emerged in the manual typewriter industry. At that point, experimentation with the fundamental systems of the machine tapered off. Manufacturers and customers had a clear idea in their minds as to what a typewriter should be and how it should operate. No substantial innovation took place until 25 years later, when electric machines began to attract interest. A similar phenomenon is seen in the personal computer industry, in which a tremendous amount of product variety was very quickly crystallized by the emergence of the IBM PC, whose great success enforced a good deal of design and operating uniformity.

• *A shifting ecology of firms.* From the days when only Remington and two or three other firms were in the market, there was an explosion of competing firms followed by an implosion later. We will see in the next chapter that the rapid exit of firms from a young industry is closely related to the emergence of a dominant design. In this case, the emergence of the IBM PC was followed shortly by the exit of many previously important competitors.

• *Waves of technological change.* One hundred and twenty-five years of innovation in typewriters, word processors, and personal computers had one fundamental objective: to put words on paper neatly and efficiently. Over that period we have witnessed the shift from handwriting to manually operated machines, a dramatic shift to electric machines, and the introduction of a radically different technology—digital technology. Each change reflects the fundamental objective, but each represents a different way of achieving it. Each is based on a different technology, which requires in turn a different set of skills on the part of producer firms.

• *Changing leadership at breakpoints in technology.* Remington's monopoly crumbled rapidly with the innovation of visible typing. Underwood, a newcomer, took the lead and held it for the next three decades. When the electric machine came in, a virtual outsider (IBM) rode it to the top while traditional leaders stuck with the old technology and fell on hard times. The leap to digital technology brought in other unknown firms, particularly when word processors were riding high. The regaining of leadership by IBM's personal computer is unusual in this respect, as this firm was a dominant force in both the electric typewriter and PC waves of innovation. Some might argue that IBM was merely the packager or distributor of the truly important innovations underlying the PC industry—software and microprocessors. Here leadership rested in Microsoft, designer of the ubiquitous DOS operating system, and Intel, whose chips were the heart and soul of the machine. Recent developments, particularly the rising fortunes of these two firms and the declining fortunes of IBM, seem to support this argument.

• *The invasion of an alien technology.* Electric typewriters have almost totally displaced manual machines in the workplace, and one might speculate that the same has happened in the home market. The appearance of personal computers in the 1970s represents an invasion by a truly alien technology, and all of its purveyors—hardware, software, printer manufacturers, and so forth—have come from outside the original manual typewriter tradition; only IBM had any position in electrics. As we will see in later chapters, looking for industry-shattering innovation among the current players in an industry might be misdirected effort; most of the important innovations occur in unexpected places, and when they do, the current leaders often react in inappropriate ways and lose their dominant positions in the industry.

There is much to be learned by looking backward through time at industries that have run their full course of birth, growth, maturity, and decline, as we have done here with the typewriter industry. Subsequent chapters continue this method, in each case choosing industries that are familiar and not so complex that they will lose the reader in a thicket of technical details. These case studies are intended to be entertaining as well as enlightening. Looking at a number of innovation-driven industries helps us see common patterns from which a general model can be constructed.

Notes

1. Samuel Clemens's correspondence, cited in Richard Nelson Current, *The Typewriter: And the Men Who Made It* (Champaign, Ill.: University of Illinois Press, 1954), p. 72.
2. George Nichols Engler, *The Typewriter Industry: The Impact of a Significant Technological Innovation*, Ph.D. diss. (Los Angeles: University of California at Los Angeles, 1970), pp. 20–21.
3. Bruce Bliven, *The Wonderful Writing Machine* (New York: Random House, 1954), p. 34.
4. Current, *The Typewriter*, pp. 1–22.
5. Engler, *The Typewriter Industry*, p. 20.
6. Bliven, *The Wonderful Writing Machine*, pp. 55–56.
7. From *The Story of the Typewriter, 1873–1923*, (Herkimer, N.Y.: Herkimer County Historical Society), pp. 74–75.
8. Correspondence cited in Kenneth E. Eble, *Old Clemens and W.D.H.* (Baton Rouge: University of Louisiana Press, 1985), pp. 56 and 81.
9. George Carl Mares, *The History of the Typewriter* (London: Guilbert Pitman, 1909), p. 58.
10. Herkimer County Historical Society, *Story of the Typewriter*, p. 72.
11. Bliven, *The Wonderful Writing Machine*, p. 66.
12. "Penman's Art Journal," 1887, as cited in Current, *The Typewriter*, p. 110.
13. JoAnne Yates, *Control Through Communication: The Rise of System in American Management* (Baltimore: Johns Hopkins University Press, 1989), p. 43.
14. Shoshana Zuboff, *In the Age of the Smart Machine* (New York: Basic Books, 1989), p. 116.
15. Unattributed remarks cited in Current, *The Typewriter*, p. 119.
16. Remington used a type-bar design; Hammond and Hall both used a type wheel; and the Crandell machine used a design called the type sleeve, in which the letters and numbers were arranged on a long, slender cylinder that formed the outer sleeve of the key-driven movement.
17. Philo Remington and his brothers were forced to sell their interests in the typewriter in reorganization proceedings. The early success of their typewriter could not cover their losses from other business lines, and eventually they were bankrupt. The Remington name was sold with the company's interests and manufacturing facilities.
18. Current, *The Typewriter*, p. 112.
19. See *The Evolution of the Typewriter* (New York: The Royal Typewriter Company, 1921), pp. 41–45.
20. Engler, *The Typewriter Industry*, p. 30.
21. Ibid., p. 129.
22. Ibid., pp. 131–133.

23. Tom Forester, *High-Tech Society* (Cambridge, Mass.: MIT Press, 1987), p. 195.

24. "The Revolution in the Office," condensed from *Data Processing*, May 1978, in Tom Forester, ed., *The Microelectronics Revolution* (Cambridge, Mass.: MIT Press, 1981), pp. 232–243.

25. Walter A. Kleinschrod, *Critical Issues in Office Automation* (New York: McGraw-Hill, 1986), p. 8.

26. Paul Freiberger and Michael Swaine, *Fire in the Valley: The Making of the Personal Computer* (Berkeley, Calif.: Osborne/McGraw-Hill, 1984).

27. Stan Augarten, *Bit by Bit: An Illustrated History of Computers* (New York: Ticknor & Fields, 1984), pp. 270–273.

28. Kleinschrod, *Critical Issues,* p. 12.

29. Freiberger and Swaine, *Fire in the Valley,* p. 279.

30. Augarten, *Bit by Bit,* p. 281.

31. Hidetaka Kai, *Competitive Strategy Under Standardization in the Personal Computer Industry and Its Influence on New Entrants,* unpublished S.M. thesis (Cambridge, Mass.: MIT Alfred P. Sloan School of Management), May 1992.

32. "Personal Computers Invade the Office," *Business Week,* August 8, 1983.

33. Survey data cited in James K. Loebbecke and Miklos Vasarhely, *Microcomputers* (Homewood, Ill.: Irwin, 1986), p. 4.

34. T. Modis and A. Debecker, "Innovation in the Computer Industry," *Technological Forecasting and Social Change,* vol. 33 (1988), pp. 267–278.

CHAPTER 2

Dominant Designs and the Survival of Firms

C HAPTER 1 DESCRIBED HOW THE TYPEWRITER INDUSTRY attracted a great number of entrants between 1885 and 1915. With the potential of the new invention made clear through expanding sales, entrepreneurs—many of them renegades from the Remington and Caligraph organizations—appeared with a number of uniquely designed machines. This is fairly typical in new industries of assembled products: a pioneering firm gets the ball rolling with its initial product, a growing market begins to take shape around that product, and new competitors are inspired to enter and either expand the market further or take a chunk of it with their own product versions. At this embryonic stage, no firm has a "lock" on the market. No one's product is really perfected. No single firm has mastered the processes of manufacturing, or achieved unassailable control of the distribution channels. Customers have not yet developed their own sense of the ideal product design or what they want in terms of features or functions. The market and the industry are in a fluid stage of development. Everyone—producers and customers—is learning as they move along.

This environment is conducive to market entry by many firms as long as capital and technical barriers are not too high, as was the case with typewriters in the late nineteenth century. One did not need to be a rocket scientist to develop a new typewriter design. A good hand with mechanical gadgets was what was required, and partners like Remington were around to handle the technical- and capital-intensive business of manufacturing that new design.

At this stage in a product's evolution, both producers and customers are experimenting. Even as new companies enter with uniquely designed products, established firms are busy perfecting their original designs and introducing new models; and customers are not yet so wedded to any particular design or company that they will not experiment with something new. Industry standards at this stage are usually rudimentary, when they exist at all.

Within this rich mixture of experimentation and competition some center of gravity eventually forms in the shape of a *dominant product design*. Once the dominant design emerges, the basis of competition changes radically, and firms are put to tests that very few will pass. Before long, the ecology of competing firms changes from one characterized by many firms and many unique designs, to one of few firms with similar product designs.

This chapter examines that changing ecology of firms and considers 1) the idea of dominant design, 2) the conditions under which it occurs, 3) how the emergence of a dominant design affects the pace of innovation and the structure of an industry, and 4) the extent to which a dominant design can be recognized when it first appears. We consider these issues in terms of several important modern industries.

WHAT IS A DOMINANT DESIGN?

A dominant design in a product class is, by definition, the one that wins the allegiance of the marketplace, the one that competitors and innovators must adhere to if they hope to command significant market following. The dominant design usually takes the form of a new product (or set of features) synthesized from individual technological innovations introduced independently in prior product variants. Looking back over the early history of the typewriter industry, we can see that the Underwood Model 5 did this and emerged as the dominant design. It was enormously well received by the marketplace, and the subsequent introduction of copy-cat models by its major rivals (the Remington Monarch in 1900 and the L.C. & Smith Brothers Model 8 in 1907), both of which trailed Underwood's sales by a wide margin, confirmed its dominance. With its single QWERTY keyboard, visible type, tab feature, shift-key capitalization, carriage cylinder, and so forth, this particular design brought together a number of market-proven innovations into a single machine and very quickly came to command the typewriter industry. It remained the dominant design for decades, defining how the typewriter was *supposed to look and operate* in the minds of both typists and other typewriter producers. Any firm that wanted to offer a keyboard with an innovative arrangement of letters, or that wanted a circular type wheel (like the old Burt design), did so at its peril; it might capture some small niche of the market where those features had demonstrated merit, but it could abandon any hopes of being a mainstream producer with those sorts of designs.

The IBM PC format quickly became the dominant design in its market, and in retrospect we can see how its success followed a pattern similar to that of the Model 5—doing in the digital age what Underwood successfully managed in an age of mechanization. The PC, like the Model 5, offered the market little in the way of breakthrough technology, but it brought together familiar elements that had proven their value to users: a TV monitor, standard disk drive, QWERTY keyboard, the Intel 8088 chip, open architecture, and MS DOS operating system. Together, these elements came to define the *idea* of the personal computer for at least 80 percent of the market. By the early 1990s, software that added a user-friendly interface (Windows™) into this design attempted to bridge that last important chasm between the Apple Macintosh and PC poles of the user market.

A dominant design embodies the requirements of many classes of users of a particular product, even though it may not meet the needs of a particular class to quite the same extent as would a customized design.[1] Nor is a dominant design necessarily the one that embodies the most extreme technical performance. It is a so-called satisficer of many in terms of the interplay of technical possibilities and market choices, instead of an optimizer for a few.

A dominant design drastically reduces the number of performance requirements to be met by a product by making many of those requirements *implicit* in the design itself. Thus, few today would ask if a car had an electric starter and electric windshield wipers, or whether a typewriter could produce upper- and lowercase letters, or whether a personal computer had a built-in disk drive, though these were unique features in models that preceded the dominant design. Today, these features are implicit in designs that the market expects and that all producers find themselves compelled to emulate. They are no longer serious issues nor are they advertised as advantages of one or another manufacturer's product. They are subsumed within the popularly accepted design.

HOW DOES A DOMINANT DESIGN OCCUR?

If the emergence of a dominant design is the landmark event for an industry as hypothesized, then managers need to understand how dominant designs occur. It would be tempting to think that there is some predetermination to the emergence of a dominant design—that automobiles with internal combustion engines were somehow exactly what the gods of transportation always meant for us to have, and that earlier experiments with electric- and steam-powered cars were misguided aberrations destined to go nowhere. The emergence of a dominant design is not necessarily predetermined, but is the result of the interplay between technical and market choices at any particular time. This is easily illustrated by the standard keyboard that found its way into the first Remingtons, the Underwoods, and virtually all successor typewriters, computers, and other keyboards to this day. From a practical standpoint, dozens if not hundreds of different keyboard designs might have been as effective ergonomically. What Sholes, Remington, and hundreds of others settled on was the product of the experiments, technical possibilities, individual choices, proprietary positions, and—to some extent—sheer inertia. Equally, the persistence of dominant designs illustrates the momentum of both established practice and complementary assets such as—in the case of typewriters—typing skills and training.

Indeed, this notion of dominant design as successful evolution can be represented using Kim Clark's design hierarchies approach; a simplified hierarchy drawn from the history of the typewriter is illustrated in Figure 2-1. A "technological trajectory" (two are shown here) is the path of progress established by the choice of a core technical concept at the outset. Decisions about the product, constrained by prior technical choices and by the evolution of customer choices, influence these various trajectories.

FIGURE 2–1. **Design Hierarchies and Dominant Design**

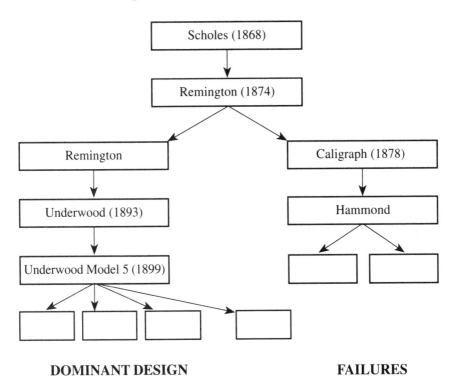

DOMINANT DESIGN   **FAILURES**

The idea of a dominant design is conceptually broader than technical competition and progress. Factors other than technology come into play; chief among these are collateral assets, industry regulation and government intervention, strategic maneuvering by individual firms, and communication between producers and users.

Collateral Assets

Collateral assets—or *co-specialized* assets, as described by Teece[2]—seem to have a two-way relationship with the emergence of a dominant design. A firm in possession of collateral assets such as market channels, brand image, and customer switching costs will have some advantage over its competitors in terms of enforcing its product as the dominant design. The experience of IBM in personal computers is a case in point. There were plenty of firms with PCs on the market in 1981, the year in which IBM first offered its personal computer. To the buying public, the name IBM had tremendous brand value; as a huge firm, its entry meant that replacement parts and service would be available and that applications software would begin to appear, encouraged by industry standards that would conform to IBM's machine.

Industry Regulation and Government Intervention

Industry regulation often has the power to *impose* a standard and thus define a dominant design. For instance, the FCC's approval of the RCA television broadcast standard worked to the advantage of RCA by establishing its design as the standard for the emerging television industry. Today, efforts by governments around the world to define standards for high-definition television—standards that will either favor or undermine the interests of their domestic producers—will certainly have an impact on dominant design in that field.

Strategic Maneuvering at the Firm Level

The product strategy followed by a firm relative to its competitors may determine which firm's product design becomes dominant. This is what Cusumano, Mylonadis, and Rosenbloom have called "strategic maneuvering."[3] In their study of videocassette recorder standards, these researchers determined that one reason the VHS system backed by JVC won market dominance over Sony's Betamax was the different strategies followed by these two firms. While JVC followed a "humble" strategy of establishing alliances first in Japan and then in Europe and the United States, Sony chose to go it alone—stressing its reputation and deliberately avoiding alliances or contracts that would impinge on its vertical integration for this important new market. According to Cusumano et al., it was primarily JVC's strategy, and neither the technological advantages of VHS, the firm's collateral assets, nor government regulation that made VHS the dominant design. In fact, VHS was technically inferior in many ways to its Betamax rival. Apple Computer followed a similar tactic with its Apple II, encouraging many suppliers of compatible peripheral equipment to invest in its growth. With the more exclusive architecture of the Macintosh, Apple abandoned this idea to its detriment.

Communication between Producers and Users

Finally, the way each firm manages communication with its customers many have a significant effect on its ability to impose a dominant design. This is a case of market learning. Staying close to customers makes it possible for producing firms to observe how their evolving products are actually being used, how they are succeeding or failing to satisfy customer requirements, and how design changes might close the gap between product capabilities and user requirements. Close contact with users during the period of experimentation helps firms determine which product features are truly important to customers. Managing this producer-user interface may take the form of close ties to "lead users,"[4] users' associations, and industry groups. Conversely, Christensen has shown that customers for entrenched products can influence a firm not to change when change is called for, increasing their resistance and vulnerability to technological progress.

DOMINANT DESIGN, COMPETITION, AND INDUSTRY STRUCTURE

Economists have been comfortable with the notion that the creative synthesis of a new product innovation by one or a few firms results in a temporary monopoly situation, high unit profit margins and prices, and sales of the innovation in those few market niches where it possesses the greatest performance advantage over competing alternatives. This is in line with Schumpeter's path-breaking "creative destruction" model and subsequent studies on the economics of innovation.[5] As demand and production grow, and as more applications are found for the innovation, many new firms enter the market with variations of the product. For example, early versions of the automobile included steam and electric vehicles as well as the now familiar internal combustion engine; there were literally dozens of these auto producers in the United States alone during the early auto days. Typewriter companies, we recall, entered by the dozens with curved keyboards, double keyboards, and other exotica. There were more than 30 of these companies doing business in the United States during the formative years of the typewriter industry.

Burton Klein suggested a profound connection between industry structure and technological change in his seminal work on dynamic economics.[6] Klein portrayed each firm's investments and product introductions as experiments providing corrective and stimulating feedback about product and market requirements. Thus the earliest period in the development of a product line or industry in which few firms participate would necessarily be a period of relatively slow technical progress and productivity advance. As larger numbers of firms entered the arena, broadening the range of experimentation and the definition of the product technology, Klein expected greater innovation with correspondingly greater technology progress and productivity advance.

Finally, as a few firms came to dominate the industry with superior product technology and productivity, both experimentation and progress would be expected to slow. The renewal or broadening of competition would be required for rapid progress to recur. In reviewing earlier work, Klein found no case in which a major advance, one that established a new and more rapid trajectory for technological progress, came from a major firm in the industry in question (an unsettling point I examine in detail later). From this evidence he concluded that the process of moving from a dynamic organization to a static one, from a period of rapid organizational learning to a period of slow or no progress, appears to be irreversible.

It is common to think of innovative entrants to a young industry as being small firms. This is not entirely the case. Remington was a major industrial company by the standards of the day when it went into the typewriter business. So was IBM in 1981 when it decided to enter the PC business and earlier when it entered the electric typewriter business. This is an important point we will return to in Chapter 9. The appearance of a dominant design shifts the competitive emphasis in favor of those firms—large or small— that are able to achieve greater skills in process innovation and integration and with more highly developed internal technical and engineering skills. Once the dust has settled on the contest for *product* innovation, then competitive engagement shifts to a new battleground: *process* innovation. When the marketplace decides that the QWERTY keyboard, or some other design standard, is what it wants, then innovators start figuring out how to make that peculiar keyboard as efficiently as possible; and some firms will be better able to do that than will others.

Firms that are unable to make the transition toward greater process innovation are unable to compete effectively and very often fail. Ones that possess special resources may successfully merge with the ultimately dominant firms. Overall, the inability to change organizational structure and practices in tandem with the evolution of technology in the industry is a major source of failure.

One might hypothesize that the peak of the total population curve for competition in any assembled product industry will occur within a year or two of the time when a dominant design emerges in that industry. In the course of this chapter, evidence from a number of other industries—old and new—addresses this point. Prior to the appearance of a dominant design, one would expect to see a wave of entering firms with many varied, experimental versions of the product, just as we did with the typewriter, the personal computer, and the early automobile. Following the emergence of the dominant design, the expectation, given this hypothesis, would be a wave of exits by competing firms and a general consolidation of the industry. This is represented in Figure 2-2. Thus the appearance of a dominant design in year 10 would mark an important change in the evolution of an industry, and effective competition would begin to take place on the basis of cost and scale as well as on the basis of product performance.

If this hypothesis is correct, we will have observed a repeatable pattern in the dynamics of innovation and change that is useful for both managers and scholars. The following developments might be hypothesized as gaining strength in the wake of the dominant design.

FIGURE 2–2.   **Dominant Design and Numbers of Competing Firms**

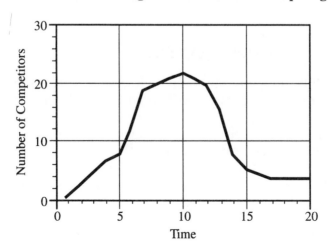

Enforcement of Standards

A dominant design has the effect of enforcing or encouraging standardization so that production or other complementary economies can be sought and perfected. Effective competition then shifts from innovative approaches to product design and features, to competition based on cost and scale as well as on product performance.

Change in the Pace and Direction of Innovation

Once accepted, a design can have a profound impact on both the direction of further technical advance and the rate of that advance. The wide acceptance of the QWERTY keyboard—one component of the dominant typewriter design—made further innovations in keyboard design off-limits. Innovators might tinker with the peripheral keys, or add new keys like the / (slash) or the + (plus), but the rest became untouchable; if keyboard changes were to be made, they would have to be limited to other dimensions of the keyboard just as the hidden mechanisms that controlled its movements were.[7]

The pace at which major innovations find their way into the product slows down considerably after the emergence of the dominant design. Perhaps operating on the adage that you do not take a well person to the surgeon, firms turn their energies away from the innovation of product features and toward the innovations that will lead them to cost or quality advantages on what has become a fairly standardized product. The illustrations that follow make this point clear.

EVIDENCE AND EXAMPLES

We turn now to a discussion of some specific examples that exhibit the waves of change suggested by this model of dominant design and the survival of firms: the manual typewriter industry, the auto industry, the electronic calculator, integrated circuits, television and television picture tubes, Winchester disk drives, and the massively parallel supercomputer. In general, each of these industries exhibits a similar pattern of firm entries and exits.

At the dawn of a new industry, firms (mostly small, entrepreneurial firms) enter at a moderate pace. Later, a rapid wave of entry occurs, raising the number of firms in the industry steeply.

After a dominant design is established, the total number of firms declines steadily until it stabilizes with a few large firms. Very often the successful firms are those that entered the industry in its early stages.

Typewriters Revisited

Growth in the typewriter industry was initially slow, probably because no one had mastered the typing skills needed to capture the full value of the new machine. By 1885, four new competitors had appeared, breaking Remington's monopoly, and the typewriter was gradually accepted by the public. By the turn of the century over 30 firms had machines in the U.S. market, but until that time typewriter manufacturers offered products with few standardized characteristics. Royal appeared in 1904, and by 1909, as seen in Figure 2-3, the number of competing firms had increased to 40. Underwood introduced its Model 5 in 1899. The visible writing of the Model 5 allowed the typist to see what he or she had actually

FIGURE 2–3. **Number of Firms in the U.S. Typewriter Industry**

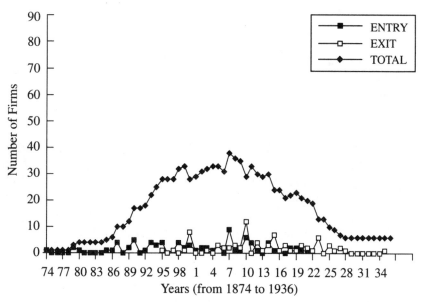

Source: Based on data in George Nichols Engler, *The Typewriter Industry: The Impact of a Significant Technological Innovation* (Los Angeles: University of California at Los Angeles, 1970).

typed as the keys struck the page. It was the first to have a tabu-
lator—making columnar presentations much simpler—and it was
able to cut stencils and make good copies. These valued features
won Underwood a large share of the commercial office market.
And as more people learned to use the Model 5, it formed their
expectations of what a typewriter should be. From that point on,
the essential features of the typewriter were set in the Underwood
machine. It became the dominant design—the model of "typewrit-
erness" that the public expected and that others would eventually
follow.

The introduction of the Underwood Model 5 marked a parting
of the waters in the crowded typewriter industry. As Figure 2–3
indicates, the end of rapid growth in the number of competing firms
occurred shortly after the introduction of the Model 5; after 1907,
the number of firms in the industry began a slow and irreversible
decline. By 1940, only five producers had any standing in the market: Remington, Royal, Smith, and Underwood each with 20 percent market share, and IBM with about 10 percent. Others, mostly
foreign firms, had the remaining 10 percent.[8] More than 90 percent
of the firms that had entered the industry had disappeared, either
through bankruptcy or, in a few cases, merger. Only a few of the
early innovative entrants survived. Except for a variety of embel-
lishing features, little would change in the product or the competitive situation until the introduction of the electric typewriter. Even
then, the electric typewriter represented less of a change for the
user than did the advent of the first manual machine at the turn of
the century. It remained for the development of the personal computer to provide an example of similar broadening of the market.

We can hypothesize that the emergence of a dominant design
very suddenly shifted the basis of competition away from the
development of unique product features to other capabilities such
as low-cost manufacturing, marketing, service, or some other factors; indeed, George Engler, whose study of the industry has been
cited here and in Chapter 1, reached that conclusion.

Automobiles

More than 100 firms entered and participated in the U.S. auto
industry for a period of five years or longer, as presented in Figure
2-4. The wave of entry began in 1894 and continued through 1950;
the wave of exits began in 1923 and peaked only a few years later,
although it has continued until the present day.

FIGURE 2–4.   **Number of Firms in the U.S. Automobile Industry**

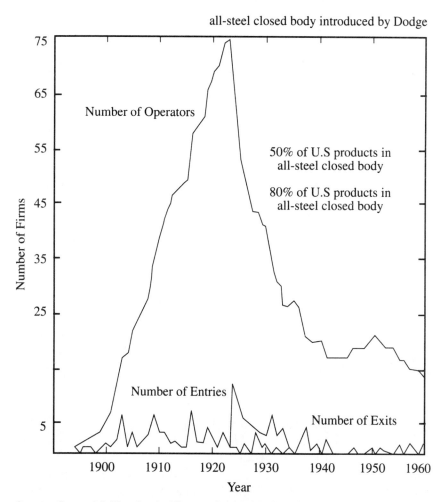

ENTRY AND EXIT OF FIRMS IN THE U.S.
AUTO INDUSTRY: 1894-1962

all-steel closed body introduced by Dodge

Number of Operators

50% of U.S products in
all-steel closed body

80% of U.S products in
all-steel closed body

Number of Entries

Number of Exits

Number of Firms

Year

Source: James M. Utterback, "Innovation and Industrial Evolution in Manufacturing Industries," in Bruce Guile and Harvey Brooks, eds., reprinted with permission from *Technology and Global Industry* (Washington, D.C.: National Academy Press, copyright 1987), based on data from R. Fabris, "Product Innovation in the Automobile Industry," Ph.D. diss., University of Michigan, 1966.

As we would hypothesize, entry of firms into the industry began slowly, but accelerated rapidly after 1900. From 1894 to 1918, 60 firms entered the industry and none left; participation reached a peak of 75 firms in 1923. In the next two years, 23 firms, nearly one-third of the industry, left or merged, and by 1930, 35 firms had exited. During the Great Depression, 20 more firms left. There was a brief flurry of entries and exits immediately following World War II, but the number of U.S. firms in the industry was basically stable between 1940 and 1980, when a number of foreign producers set up production operations in North America.

A number of major product innovations appear within this pattern of entries and exits. We do not have data on innovations for the 1894–1918 period, but we assume that during these formative years product innovations were frequent and substantial. The year 1923, when the number of competing firms reached its peak, was the year that Dodge introduced the all-steel, closed body automobile—an important innovation. This new body format dramatically improved the strength and rigidity of the chassis, and at the same time provided an opportunity for manufacturers to move away from hand forming of exterior body panels to the highly capitalized but efficient process of machine stamping.

By 1925, fully half of U.S. auto production was all-steel, closed, body cars; and by 1926, 80 percent of all automobiles were of this type.[9] Exits from the industry began and picked up speed rapidly around this time, and the number and rate of product innovations declined markedly. New concepts that did come along in product accessories and styling were tested in the low-volume, high-profit luxury automobile. Conversely, incremental innovations were more commonly introduced in lower-priced, higher-volume product lines. General Motors appears to have led in both types of innovations, particularly for major product changes. Between 1919 and 1962, the U.S. auto industry witnessed a declining number of major innovations on an annual basis, a decrease in the number of new entrants, and a steady withdrawal of firms from the business (see Table 2-1).[10]

The Dodge all-steel, closed body design was introduced during the period in which fully half the major innovations took place—1919–1929. While it clearly became the dominant design for the auto body and a major part of the total product package, its influence on the rate of firm exit and entry cannot be established

TABLE 2–1.   **Major Innovations and Firm Entries/Exits from U.S. Auto Industry**

Period	Innovations	New Entrants	Firm Exits
1894–1918	NA	60	0
1919–1929	14	22	43
1930–1941	11	6	29
1946–1962	7	4	8

Source: R. Fabris, *Product Innovation in the Automobile Industry,* Ph.D. diss., University of Michigan, 1966, p. 92.

causally. However, the link between major innovations and the decline of new entrants and increase in exits fortifies our intuition about the linkages here.

Televisions and Television Tubes

Research leading to the appearance of the television started several decades before the first successful results were achieved. RCA entered the industry in 1929 after David Sarnoff, impressed by a demonstration by inventor Vladimir Zworykin, decided to hire Zworykin and put him in charge of RCA's Electronic Research Group in Camden, New Jersey. Several other firms or inventor-entrepreneurs entered the infant industry during the 1930s, and all contributed to the expanding frontier of technical knowledge. Philo Farnsworth, Louis Hazeltine, American Television, and Allen DuMont are some of the most important names in the early years of television.

The industry's commercial birth can be traced back to the 1939–1940 World's Fair in New York, where millions saw television displays for the first time. For the purposes of our analysis, 1939 marks the beginning of the industry. Data in Figure 2-5 start in 1949. The figure clearly shows that the television industry conforms to the hypothesized relationships between dominant design and the peaking of competing firms in the industry. The first decade of the industry obviously witnessed a rapid increase in the number of firms making television sets. The wave of entry most likely peaked in 1950, the first year of our entry data, or one year earlier. The total number of firms steadily increased until 1952, the year in

FIGURE 2–5.   **Number of Firms in the U.S. Television Industry**

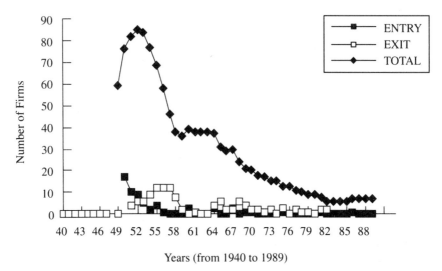

Years (from 1940 to 1989)

Source: James M. Utterback and Fernando Suárez, "Innovation, Competition, and Industry Structure," *Research Policy,* vol. 22, no. 1, January 1993, p. 11.

which it peaked at 85 firms. The wave of exits started to take off in 1951 and peaked around 1956.

Several things happened in the early 1950s television industry that had a significant impact on the pattern of innovation and competition that was to follow. First, the uncertainty about technical standards for color broadcasting (i.e., UHF versus VHF) was resolved by the Supreme Court in 1951. Two years later the FCC approved the National Television Standards Committee (NTSC) system, backed by a group of manufacturers headed by RCA. Several firms that had opposed the RCA technical standards dropped out of the business due to this legal ruling. Second, several features of the television set converged to form a dominant design around 1952. The most important aspect of this design was the size of the screen and therefore the characteristics of the picture tube. The first set produced by RCA had a 10-inch monochrome tube. Almost all tubes produced in the 1940s were smaller than 14 inches. RCA produced its first 21-inch and other large tubes around 1952, and these soon became the market standard. Third, during the early 1950s, RCA started licensing its television technology to other firms. This further reduced competition and supports the idea that RCA held rights to most of the key characteristics of the product at the time.

The story of the TV picture and receiving tubes is closely related to that of the television industry itself. Figure 2-6 depicts a rapid increase in the total number of tube producers from 1949 to 1956, analogous to that previously discussed for the television industry. In 1956, four years after the peak of the television industry curve, the total number of firms in the tube industry reached its peak of 66 firms.

One of RCA's major innovations was the development of the shadow-mask color picture tube. The FCC ruled in favor of the RCA-compatible standard in December 1953, and programs were first broadcast in this format in January of 1954. Hazeltine made major contributions to brightness. Some problems in manufacture constrained the size of the tubes to 16 inches until CBS laboratories learned how to curve the mask. RCA licensed both developments. A problem with the initial tubes was that they were metallic with glass bonded to the front, and this interface proved troublesome, often separating and ruining the tube. The 21-inch, all-glass tube—first black and white, then color—eliminated this problem

FIGURE 2–6.   **Number of U.S. Picture Tube Producers**

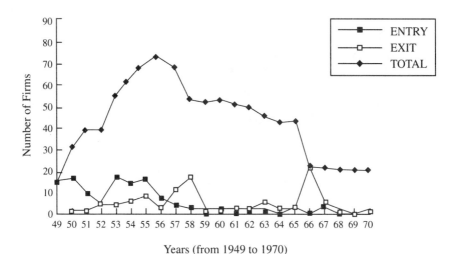

Years (from 1949 to 1970)

and has been by far the biggest seller since the mid-1950s. The first such tube was introduced by RCA late in 1955 and captured a significant portion of the TV tube market during the rest of the decade. The advent of reliable color tubes contributed to the difficulties that many tube producers were experiencing during the late 1950s and fostered concentration in the industry. Indeed, in May 1958, RCA publicly announced the first all-glass 21-inch color picture tube, which was to hold a large share of the color tube market.[11]

The Transistor

According to J.E. Tilton, three firms dominated the receiving vacuum tube business in the United States in 1950: General Electric, Philco Ford, and RCA.[12] Over the ensuing decade these firms spent more on R&D and received more patents than did new firms entering the industry (counting the expenditures and patents of Bell Laboratories), but a cohort of new entrants gained nearly two-thirds of the new and growing transistor market. By 1966, three of these new entrants—Texas Instruments, Motorola, and Fairchild Semiconductor—together accounted for 42 percent of the market, while the vacuum tube manufacturers' share of the transistor market declined to just slightly more than one-fourth of the total. The difference between established firms and new entrants in this business would be even more dramatic if one included IBM's production for its own use (IBM is believed to have entered production in 1961).

Figure 2-7 shows that the total number of firms in the transistor industry began to rise rapidly with its invention in 1948. This increase was virtually halted around 1959, when the planar transistor entered commercial production. Transistors produced through the planar process rapidly became the dominant design in the industry. Introduced by Fairchild Semiconductors, planar transistors presented many advantages over mesa transistor technology. In particular, the planar transistor was flat, which meant that electrical connections could be achieved by depositing an evaporated metal film on appropriate portions of the wafer. This was a great advantage over the mesa transistor, whose irregular surface dictated that electrical connections be done laboriously by hand. The planar transistor prompted a drive to produce low-cost transistors—a phenomenon typical of post-dominant design stages. The

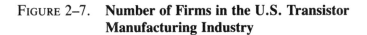

FIGURE 2–7. **Number of Firms in the U.S. Transistor Manufacturing Industry**

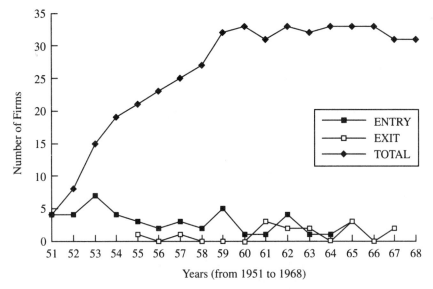

Source: Based on data in E. Braun and S. MacDonald, *Revolution in Miniature: The History and Impact of Semiconductor Electronics* (Cambridge, England: Cambridge University Press, 1978); and J.E. Tilton, *International Diffusion of Technology* (Washington, D.C.: The Brookings Institution, 1971).

reader will note that exits from the industry, almost nil before 1959, became commonplace thereafter.

The Electronic Calculator

The American calculator industry in the early 1960s consisted of five major companies manufacturing the electromechanical machines that controlled nearly 90 percent of the market: Frieden, Monroe, Marchant, Victor, and Olivetti. Frieden, Marchant, and Monroe each had approximately 20 percent of the market, Victor a slightly smaller share, and Olivetti 10 to 15 percent. These companies were almost completely vertically integrated because of the need for a high degree of precision in the manufacture of many specialized parts. There were strong barriers to new-firm entry. By concentrating on specific segments of the market, the major companies avoided intense competition. Extensive distribution and service networks reinforced their market dominance. In addition, the technology of electromechanical calculators had reached a high level. It was proving difficult for any firm to come up with a dramatic breakthrough that would threaten the status quo.

Initially this situation did not change when the electronic calculator entered the market in 1962. The first electronic calculators were extremely complex and expensive machines of more than 2,300 discrete parts aimed at specialized scientific and technical market segments. Figure 2-8 shows that between 1962 and 1970, 11 firms entered the industry, with 10 surviving. This wave of entry peaked in 1972 with the entry of 21 firms in a three-year period. However, exits began in 1971, following the introduction of the calculator chip, a dominant design that made unit assembly a simple matter of piecing together the chip, display device, and keyboard. The entry of semiconductor manufacturers such as Texas Instruments and Rockwell in 1972, and National Semiconductor in 1973, further precipitated the departure of firms that were largely

Figure 2–8.   **Number of Firms in the U.S. Electronic Calculator Industry**

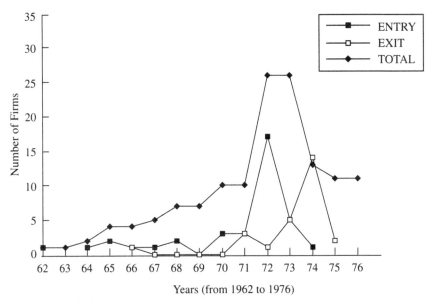

Source: Based on data in B. Majumdar, *Innovations, Product Developments, and Technology Transfer: An Empirical Study of Dynamic Competitive Advantage, The Case of Electronic Calculators,* Ph.D. diss., Case Western Reserve University, Cleveland, Ohio, 1977.

assemblers of purchased components. The industry's structure then appears to stabilize, with a few of the semiconductor makers (e.g., Rockwell) dropping out and a small number of the remaining vertically integrated companies dominating the market. Thus the appearance of a dominant design and the drive toward vertical integration that normally follows its appearance were almost concurrent in this highly compressed example.

The Integrated Circuit

The integrated circuit industry is the only one in the sample that does not clearly conform to the hypothesis regarding a collapse of the number of competitors following the emergence of a dominant product design. In fact, Figure 2-9, displaying data on U.S. firms, shows no clear peak in firms during the data period. Therese Flaherty, who has studied the integrated circuit industry, suggests that no one product of any generation can be easily considered a dominant design. The product has continued to change substantially from generation to generation, which may explain the very

FIGURE 2–9.   **Number of Firms in the U.S. Integrated Circuit Industry**

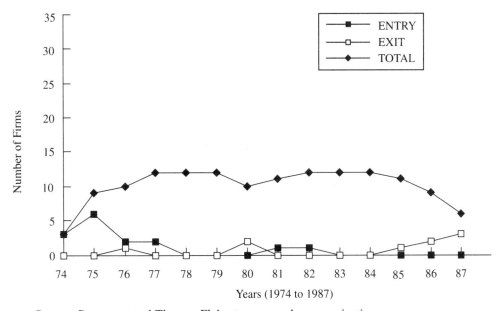

Years (1974 to 1987)

Source: Dataquest and Therese Flaherty, personal communication.

broad plateau observed in total industry participation as many firms both enter and exit the industry.

There have been many generations of integrated circuits. For instance, DRAM (dynamic random access memory), the most important segment of the industry at this time, has already passed through seven generations (1K, 4K, 16K, 64K, 256K, 1MB, 4MB). Competition has been intense within and between generations, and no firm has been able to maintain a leadership position from one generation to another. Based on this industry, Fumio Kodama introduced the concept of "surf riding." If one company leads the race in, say, 4K memories, it will not lead in the 16K generation. Having lost that one, however, it may attempt to strike back in the contest for 64K memories, where the leader of the 16K generation will not likely figure as a prominent competitor. In general, American firms have been losing ground to Japanese entrants. The first three generations were dominated by American firms, but Japanese firms began taking a significant share of the market from the 64K generation onward.

Although a quick look at the integrated circuit industry suggests that the model has limited explanatory power in this case, several issues cast a shadow on such a conclusion. The first is Flaherty's observation that within each generation of integrated circuits the "enter early" strategy was a winner. Second, the production capacity of the major firms has increased relative to market demand through each generation; fewer companies are needed to satisfy demand.

Exits for firms from the American integrated circuit industry began in 1985 and increased steadily for the next two years. As new entries were nil during this period, the total number of American firms declined in 1987 to one of its lowest levels. Today the prevailing industry pattern is higher concentration and larger firms. Finally, although product innovation is still important in later integrated circuit generations, process innovation and production capabilities are increasingly critical as generations pass and greater production volumes are required of participant firms. Such production capabilities form an effective barrier to entry in the industry.

Winchester Disk Drives

The technology for Winchester disk drives was first developed by IBM in 1973 as a high-speed method of storing data. A number of competing firms emerged with similar technology and products. At first these were designed for use with mainframe and minicomputers, but future generations of the product addressed the storage needs of the proliferating base of microcomputers. The Winchester disk drive industry attracted many startup firms, many of which enjoyed success in the early years. Between 1978 and 1983—the year in which the number of firms producing these drives peaked— sales to original equipment manufacturers grew from $27 million to $1.3 billion. Industry analysts were euphorically projecting a tripling of revenues from that level by 1987.[13]

Clayton Christensen identifies five generations of Winchester drives in his data: 14-inch, 8-inch, $5\frac{1}{4}$-, $3\frac{1}{2}$-inch, and $2\frac{1}{2}$-inch drives. In the first two generations the motor was separate, while in the third it was incorporated in the drive spindle. Further important design changes were made in the $3\frac{1}{2}$-inch drives, while the $2\frac{1}{2}$-inch drives are essentially a miniature version of these and have not to date enjoyed important sales growth.[14] Christensen argues persuasively that established firms failed to master each successive generation of Winchester disk drive technology through being too wedded to existing customer demands and not sufficiently attentive to the emerging demands of smaller computer manufacturers.

Smaller drives were much slower and more expensive at first, but they did bring the hard drive to desktop machines. While established firms led the difficult but incremental improvement of components, new firms led with innovative architectures using existing components. The leaders in each generation of drives were different from those in the prior generation, with the exception of the current $2\frac{1}{2}$-inch drives. Christensen claims that the $3\frac{1}{2}$-inch drives incorporate all the features and functions that will be seen in $2\frac{1}{2}$-inch and even smaller drives and thus constitute a dominant design. This is a pleasing conclusion because it perfectly supports the hypothesis with respect to the number of firms remaining in the industry, as shown by our independent analysis of his data in Figure 2-10.

Supercomputers

Supercomputers, the most powerful computational systems at any given time, today achieve speeds in the 100 MFLOPS (million floating operations per second) range. Three major technologies have been used to build these machines: sequential, vector, and parallel processing. Sequential computers, the architecture of which is often referred to as von Neumann, have only one central

Figure 2–10.   **Number of Firms in the U.S. Winchester Disk Drive Industry**

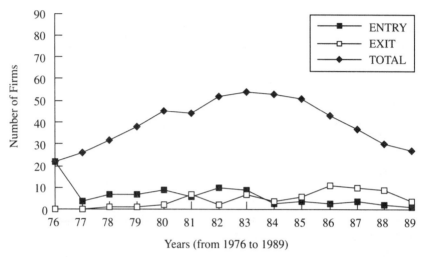

Years (from 1976 to 1989)

Source: Based on data from Christensen (see note 14).

processing unit (CPU); they do one thing at a time. Vector processors allow simultaneous computation for problems with vector-like or matrix-like structures. Parallel processing, or massively parallel processing, is a computer architecture in which hundreds or thousands of processors are put on many jobs simultaneously to finish tasks faster and with greater generality than do more traditional supercomputers. This, however, requires wholly new software.

Traditional supercomputer makers such as Cray, Fujitsu, Hitachi, IBM, and NEC produce mostly sequential machines. A second set of firms, minisupercomputer makers, now use sequential architecture with the incremental innovation of pipelining and vector processing. Massively parallel computer (MPC) makers are the latest entrants in the supercomputer industry, as shown in Figure 2-11. Firms such as Thinking Machines, Intel, Floating Point Systems, and Meiko started production about 1985, while the MPC pioneers (Ametek, Myrias, and Goodyear Aerospace) entered the industry only as far back as 1983.

If the MPC architecture becomes the dominant design, the exit of some traditional firms from the industry would seem likely in the future; firms such as IBM and Cray, which have greater resources, might turn toward this architecture.

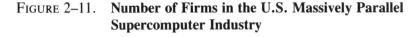

FIGURE 2–11.   **Number of Firms in the U.S. Massively Parallel Supercomputer Industry**

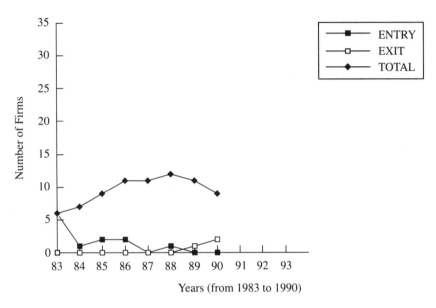

Other Research

Recently, Tushman and Anderson provided further evidence for the hypotheses considered here.[15] They gathered valuable data on the minicomputer, glass, and cement industries and performed tests of the model. Their work not only provides more data to support the concept of the dominant design and its importance in the life cycle of an industry, but also enhances our understanding of this process.

International Comparisons

The previous examples have illustrated how the entry and exit of firms from an industry parallels product innovation within that industry. Most of the examples provided here point to the conclusion that entering early is the most viable strategy. Entering at later stages, although theoretically possible, has proven to be a much riskier strategy and less likely to succeed. All of the evidence presented here, however, is drawn from the U.S. experience. The question arises: Does the pattern found in U.S. industry—that is, great falling off in the number of participating firms subsequent to the appearance of the dominant design—hold outside the United

States? A limited amount of research indicates that with respect to Japan it does not.

The Japanese experience with automobiles, calculators, integrated circuits, and Winchester disk drives shows an opposite pattern—of *more* firms joining these industries after the appearance of the dominant design. The successful late entry of large and highly integrated Japanese firms in some of our examples suggests that late entry, although difficult, is possible. The Japanese pattern would support the popular stereotype of American firms as innovators and creators of new industries and the Japanese as skillful at applying their considerable talents of automated production to product refinement and manufacture. However, the issue of late entry by Japanese firms could bear much further study. Early entry may still prove to be the strategy of choice in the future, even for Japanese firms, now that their research capabilities are world-class and the attention of American firms to excellence in manufacturing has been reawakened. In this sense, the strategies of firms in the two nations may be converging.

Limitations and Caveats

The idea of a dominant design does not seem to hold in industries producing nonassembled products such as rayon, glass, pulp and paper, metals, or industrial gases. Also, product categories such as integrated circuits and photographic film may be difficult to classify, as they share some characteristics of both assembled and non-assembled products.

Because nonassembled products contain fewer materials than assembled products do, there is more concentrated focus of technological effort and experimentation in the production process; periods of variation and experimentation result in what might be called an enabling technology. This enabling technology incorporates many of the elements needed in a continuous production process and allows the focus of technological effort to shift to process improvement rather than process innovation and design.

CAN WE RECOGNIZE A DOMINANT DESIGN WHEN WE SEE IT?

For managers, of course, the important question is whether a dominant design can be seen for what it is when it first appears or is discernible only in retrospect. If the emergence of a dominant design is a signal that an important shift is about to take place with respect to the pace of innovation and the number of competing firms, the ability of managers and industry watchers to receive that signal—or even better, to predict the emergence of a dominant design—should be important with respect to their product designs, R&D, and process development. There are three schools of thought on this question.

First, some believe that dominant designs are the result of chance events. In this sense, their appearance cannot be predicted (though they may be recognized). This school would say that the QWERTY keyboard would be a curiosity piece today had August Dvorak and his ideas for keyboard design been on the scene earlier, during the period of experimentation with the first typewriters. Steel-bodied automobiles, the norm since Dodge's all-steel innovation of the 1920s, may have been dictated by the high cost of aluminum relative to steel at that time. Certainly aluminum, then as now, had tremendous performance advantages over heavier steel. Today, when the cost difference is not as great, the tradition of steel auto bodies is difficult to change.

The second school of thought has a deterministic viewpoint— i.e., something inherent in the technology determines the outcome with respect to the dominant design. The laws of nature, for example, fairly dictate that only a few synthetic materials (nylon, rayon, polyester) have chemical structures that support the spinning of long-fibered material. Thus the technological trajectory accommodates only a few possible candidates for the dominant design.

Third, others suggest that social and organizational factors work together to determine dominant design. Here again come into play arguments such as the early success of the QWERTY keyboard having created an investment in particular typing skills and barriers to other designs. The same may apply to the IBM PC; IBM's stature can be said to have led to an industry standard around which small competitors and software writers naturally gravitated.

Neither of these three schools of thought is entirely right or entirely wrong. Each, in fact, contributes to our understanding of the facts. But no matter how a dominant design is determined, it is doubtful that it can be recognized except in retrospect. Attempting to define or anticipate the appearance of a dominant design simply by mapping features and functions of the product alone is doomed to frustration. However, design simplicity and so-called technological elegance are clearly characteristic of many dominant designs, the DC-3 aircraft being a notable example.

Our inability to immediately perceive a dominant design for what it is in no way diminishes its impact on the evolution of innovation and competition in an industry. For assembled products, as later chapters will show clearly, the appearance of a dominant design ushers in a period in which the rate of product innovation slows and the rate of process innovation increases.

DOMINANT DESIGNS AND THE COURSE
OF FUTURE INNOVATION

A dominant design has other implications for business and R&D decision makers. As we have seen in the case of the typewriter, and as we will see in other case histories presented throughout this book, a dominant design has a powerful impact on the development of future technological innovations within the same industry. Discussion of the typewriter in the preceding chapter noted the extent to which this one innovation—a mechanical device for putting words on paper—altered life in the business workplace, with respect to both how work was done and who did it. An army of new workers emerged to handle the growing requirements for business letters, reports, and so forth. It is doubtful that the inventors of the typewriter anticipated this development. The standardization of typewriter design and the development of widespread QWERTY keyboarding skills created a market momentum that future innovations in typing, word processing, and personal computers were forced to recognize.

As new waves of innovation occurred—electric typewriters, stand-alone word processors, and personal computers—they did so within constraints of habits, skills, and user expectations set in place by the original innovation—the manual, QWERTY, Model 5-style typewriter. User acceptance of the dominant design of the original innovation created certain boundaries within which subsequent waves of innovation wisely developed. Thus IBM successfully sought to enhance performance of its electric typewriters through electromechanical applications only. Whether it would have enjoyed much market success if an improved keyboard configuration had been introduced at the same time—even if the keyboard was demonstrably more efficient—is doubtful. Likewise, firms introducing new personal computers today must minimize their meddling with features in which current users have substantial investments: QWERTY keyboards, 3½-inch disk drives, operating systems, and so forth. Successful innovations in personal computers more often than not are transparent to users.

Later chapters will make it clear how the same phenomenon has occurred in other industries. For example, we will see in the next chapter how the displacement of gas lighting by incandescent lighting was advanced by Edison's running wires through the very same pipes that once brought illuminating gas into consumers' homes. Electric lamp sockets were cleverly adapted to former gas burners. Once the innovation of electric lighting established itself with users, subsequent technological innovations in lighting (fluorescent) and in electric appliances had to be made with the contraints imposed by the initial innovation (current, voltage, power grid, socket sizes, and so forth).

The lesson for technology managers and business strategists is straightforward: understand the constraints of systems, user learning, habits, and collateral assets already imposed by the existing dominant design if there is one. And as you develop innovative products, consider how these products will fit with current constraints.

ANTICIPATING MAJOR TECHNOLOGICAL CHANGES AND COMPETITIVE CHALLENGES

The preponderance of managers' external intelligence, thought, and action is usually directed toward competitors making products like their own that are similar in size, market approach, and competitive strategy. But as has been noted, the most threatening challenges are often those that come from outside the traditional definition of the industry and its products. Data presented in previous chapters suggest that architectural product innovations are often produced by new entrants—not only new firms, but also large enterprises entering a new area of business or spin-offs of established competitors formed to exploit a new idea. The formation of new firms is highly visible, and this suggests that their commitments to product introductions may be one of the most fruitful sources of early information about technological innovation in progress. One of the clear advantages of analyzing new firm activities is that there are far fewer of them than there are patents, technical papers, or variations of existing products—there is simply less noise to worry about in reaching a conclusion. This is the one sure approach that anyone could have used to identify the early implementation of xerography or of instant photography.

Twenty years ago computer memory was a wholly captive market, with a few large firms producing magnetic core memories for use in their own products. A survey conducted in 1970 by one of my students showed that all but five of 31 established computer companies were concentrating their resources on the manufacture of core memories. Twelve manufacturers outside the United States had a similar preponderance of magnetic core technology. However, eight newly formed firms exhibited a much different pattern. None were involved with magnetic core memories, while seven—including a struggling new company called Intel—were investing in development of the semiconductor memory chip. At least three of the new firms—Intel, Signetics, and Cogar—were spin-offs from larger firms and concentrated on more advanced technology than did their parents. Significantly, AT&T and IBM were among the larger firms also exploring the then-new memory chip idea. Analysis of the computer memory market as it unfolded provided a clear insight into the shape and direction that computer memory technology would take.

Monitoring new firm formation would have signaled clearly the vigor of the calculator and personal computer industries, the transistor and today's semiconductor memory chips, hard disk drives, and flash memories. The same would be true for the manual typewriter, the electric typewriter, and the word processor, as well as for minicomputers, fault-tolerant computers, supercomputers and massively parallel computers. This is not to say that new firms will be more successful financially than their established competitors. Being on the cutting edge of technology may be an extremely vulnerable position. As we have seen, many entrants in the race to start a new industry fail. The important point is that this is often the position taken by a newly formed firm.

A fascinating point to note in Table 2.2 is that older technologies may prefigure the most contemporary ideas. So-called flash memories, the new memory cards for portable computers, are present-day versions of the magnetic film memories first tried in the 1970s. Similarly, ceramic fibers used to insulate the space shuttle (among other applications) are in some respects an extension of the technology first tried in the production of ceramic filaments for gas lamps. Vacuum-tube design principles have been used to create a new system for spraying agricultural chemicals, reducing to one-tenth the chemicals earlier required and performing the job with inexpensive, small-scale equipment. And some of the current efforts to eliminate chlorofluorocarbons may benefit from knowledge of alternatives that were explored but abandoned earlier in favor of refrigerants now thought to be harmful to the earth's atmosphere. Thus looking at the evolution of technologies may help not only in anticipating possible directions of change, but also in thinking creatively about the design of new technologies.

During the past ten years scores of new firms have been formed to exploit findings in biotechnology, and new resource commitments are exceeding a billion dollars annually. With such widespread support and experimentation, one might anticipate almost the equivalent of a revolution in the fortunes of not only medicine and pharmaceutical firms, but also agriculture and the chemical and materials industries. Each innovation in biotechnology will be seen in terms of increasingly refined, enlarged, and more effective material forms long before it achieves widespread usage. The technical potentials in this area, though, will be much easier to assess than will be the business winners and losers. To anticipate com-

TABLE 2–2.   **U.S. Computer Memory Manufacturers' Product Offerings in 1970**

Memory Technology	Established Firms	New Firms
Core memory	26	0
Plated wire	8	
Thin magnetic film	5	1
Semiconductor chips	6	7
Number of firms	31	8

Source: Compiled by the author from James M. Utterback and James W. Brown, *Business Horizons,* vol. 15 (October 1972).

mercial outcomes, one must look for indicators of combinations of economic and technical events as well as the political and social forces that may create either demand for or resistance to a new product or process—a far more complex task.

Notes

1. David Teece, "Profiting from Technological Innovation," *Research Policy* 15, no. 6 (1986). As Teece and others have noted, the dominant design model is better suited to mass markets, where consumer tastes are relatively homogeneous. Also, representations here about the dominant design extend only to assembled manufacturing industries. Among nonassembled products such as rayon or glass, innovation in the production process—not the emergence of a dominant product design—is a more powerful theme. (See Chapter 5 for further discussion.)
2. Teece, "Profiting from Technological Innovation."
3. Michael Cusumano, Y. Mylonadis, and R. Rosenbloom, "Strategic Maneuvering and Mass-Market Dynamics: The Triumph of VHS over Beta." *Business History Review,* vol. 66 (Spring 1992), 51–94.
4. Eric von Hippel, *The Sources of Innovation* (Oxford, England: Oxford University Press, 1988).
5. Joseph Schumpeter, *Business Cycles: A Theoretical, Historical, and Statistical Analysis of the Capitalist Process* (New York: McGraw Hill, 1939).
6. Burton Klein, *Dynamic Economics* (Cambridge, Mass.: Harvard University Press, 1977).
7. In fact, Edward B. Hess improved greatly on this aspect of keyboard mechanics by reversing the linkage between the key and the type bar, giving the machine a lighter touch and greater strike power for more even impressions.
8. George Nichols Engler, *The Typewriter Industry: The Impact of a Significant Technological Innovation,* Ph.D. diss. (Los Angeles: University of California at Los Angeles, 1970).
9. William J. Abernathy, *The Productivity Dilemma* (Baltimore, Md.: Johns Hopkins University Press, 1978), pp. 18–19.
10. R. Fabris, *Product Innovation in the Automobile Industry,* Ph.D. diss. (Ann Arbor: University of Michigan, 1966), pp. 85–93. These data are biased by the fact that Fabris counts only firms that produced automobiles for five years or more. Other, more comprehensive sources show massive entries and exits in the industry prior to 1923, though not all of the firms counted actually produced many cars.
11. I am grateful to John Rydz, a participant in the early RCA developments, for the information given here.
12. J.E. Tilton, *International Diffusion of Technology: The Case of Semiconductors* (Washington D.C.: The Brookings Institution, 1971).
13. William D. Bygrave and Jeffry A. Timmons, *Venture Capital at the Crossroads* (Boston: Harvard Business School Press, 1992), pp. 126–127. Fuller discussion of the skyrocketing growth and eventual implosion of the Winchester drive industry can be found in a case study by William A. Sahlman

and Howard H. Stevenson, "Capital Market Myopia," 288–055 (Boston: Harvard Business School, 1987).

14. Clayton Christensen, *The Innovator's Challenge: Understanding the Influence of Market Environment on Processes of Technology Development in the Rigid Disk Drive Industry,* DBA diss. (Boston: Harvard Business School, 1992), pp. 42–73; also discussion with the author.

15. Michael Tushman and Philip Anderson, "Technological Discontinuities and Organizational Environment," *Administrative Science Quarterly* 31 (1986), 439–456.

CHAPTER 3

Product Innovation as a Creative Force

I have struck a big bonanza.
Thomas Edison on the incandescent lamp, 1878

IN 1878, A YELLOW FEVER EPIDEMIC swept through the southern United States, claiming an estimated 14,000 lives. Renegade Indians in Idaho raided ranches and small villages for sheep and horses. The city of New Haven, Connecticut, issued the world's first telephone directory; and up in Hartford Albert Pope converted his sewing machine plant to produce a new-fangled device called the bicycle. Out in Cincinnati the Procter & Gamble Company introduced a product called White Soap for lack of a better name.

Unknown to the general public at the time, a high-stakes race was in progress on both sides of the Atlantic to develop a practical "electric candle." Inventors in England, Germany, and the United States all were trying to be first to introduce an incandescent lamp. Thomas A. Edison was one of them.

People in America and Europe already had a passing familiarity with electricity. Man-made electricity had been used since the 1840s to power the telegraph and for the process of electroplating. Electric fire alarm boxes had been installed in Boston in 1852. The newly introduced telephone relied on generated electricity. In Europe the individuals involved with electricity were, for the most part, members of the scientific community; in America they were mostly nonacademic experimenters.

By 1877 a few commercial areas were being illuminated by arc lamps, devices in which a continuous arc of electricity leaped between two electrodes, producing an intensely bright light. But arc lighting was too eye dazzling for home use; it required its own generator and needed frequent replacement of the electrode tips, which burned out rapidly. Popular since the early part of the century, when a method was found for distilling gas from wood and coal, gas lighting was the preferred technology of the day. Back in 1816, Baltimore was the first U.S. city to install gas street lamps; New York and Boston quickly followed suit.

As a lighting technology, gas was demonstrably superior to candles, kerosene, and whale oil, providing roughly five times as much light. By mid-century the business of distilling, distributing, and burning gas was developed to the point where 30 companies were producing and distributing gas through networks of pipes to homes and workplaces in America. By 1860 the companies numbered 211, and by 1870 the number of gas firms reached 350.[1]

While candles and oil lamps prevailed in the dwellings of rural America, the warm glow of burning gas lamps lighted the parlors and kitchens of a growing number of urban homes. But just as the gas industry was making its greatest advances, European experimenters and a few Yankee tinkerers were developing a technology that would cause it to dim and sputter.

THE LIGHT GOES ON FOR EDISON

One day in 1878, Thomas Edison visited the workshop of William Wallace in Ansonia, Connecticut. Wallace had developed a powerful electric generator to power an arc light system, and Edison wanted to see it for himself. A news reporter described Edison's amazement at Wallace's blazing display:

> Mr. Edison was enraptured . . . eight electric lights were kept ablaze at one time, each being equal to 4,000 candles. . . . This filled up Mr. Edison's cup with joy. . . . He calculated the power of the instrument and of the lights, the probable loss of power in transmission, the amount of coal the instrument would save in a day, a week, a month, a year, and the results of such savings on manufacturing.[2]

Edison saw at once the commercial potential in electric lighting, and in no time at all was reckoning that it would be feasible to
light up all of lower Manhattan with Wallace's dynamo and one
500-horsepower engine. He envisioned electric wires under the
streets of New York, snaked through existing gas tubing into shops
and homes.[3] Straight away Edison ordered one of Wallace's dyna-
mos for his workshop at Menlo Park, New Jersey and dove into
the work of concocting an electric lamp that would be effective and
long-lived. He knew that others were in the race to do the same,
and well ahead of him; but Edison was characteristically sure of
himself. "I saw," he said later, "that the thing had not gone so far
but that I had a chance."

Edison's Invention Factory

Today we are used to the idea of corporate and university
research centers—well-equipped and funded laboratories
where teams of scientists and technicians conduct research
and development on tomorrow's breakthrough products.
Nothing like this existed before Edison's time.

In 1876, Thomas Edison set up his own R&D center at
Menlo Park, New Jersey with the express purpose of developing technologies and inventions with high potential for
commercial success. This was something entirely new. If a
project did not have the look and feel of something he could
commercialize, Edison generally steered clear of it. That
attitude paid off repeatedly. During his lifetime, Thomas Edison was awarded no less than 1,043 patents and became
known as the Wizard of Menlo Park.

Like successful entrepreneurs today, Edison's track record
with commercially successful inventions drew money to him
like a magnet. His invention of the stock ticker in the late
1860s at the age of 22 had made him famous. Best of all, it
had made him famous with the right people—the money men
of Wall Street and the telegraphy business.

Using his earnings from previous inventions and capital
from investors, Edison set up his Menlo Park workshops in
1876. They consisted of a long two-story clapboard building,
a smaller brick mechanical shop, some small sheds, and a
farmhouse that was used as a library—not exactly the Xerox

Palo Alto Research Center, but remarkable for the times. These facilities were stocked with machining equipment, laboratory instruments, electrical testing devices, chemicals, and staffed with more than 40 capable mechanics and technicians.

By the time Edison began his work on electric lighting, this facility had already churned out a number of important inventions, including the carbon transmitter that complemented the Bell telephone (1877), the first phonograph (1877), and the tasimeter, a supersensitive heat-measuring device.

So powerful was Edison's public reputation at the time, that within weeks of announcing his intention to develop electric lighting, his business representative, Grosvenor P. Lowrey, was already working with financiers to set up the Edison Electric Light Company. As word of this got out, gas company stocks plummeted.

Within four years Edison's enterprise had outgrown Menlo Park, and he opened a new research and manufacturing facility in nearby West Orange, New Jersey. By 1882, the Menlo Park laboratory had produced 400 patented inventions.

Many oars were already in the water when Edison entered the race for the electric lamp. The most advanced lamp design at the time was that of an Englishman, Joseph W. Swan. Swan had tinkered off and on with incandescent lamps since 1860, and his 1877 design featuring a carbonized paper filament inside a glass vacuum bulb was not fundamentally different from the one Edison would succeed with in the near future. Swan's design produced a working lamp, but one that burned out quickly. By 1879, using improved methods of evacuating air from the bulb while he heated the filament, Swan was producing a much more satisfactory result.[4] In 1880, he substituted a slender carbon rod for his carbonized paper filament. But by this time, the Wizard of Menlo Park had already stolen the march on him.

Edison entered the race for incandescent lighting with both feet in September 1878, believing that the technology had not developed so far that he could still make a big impact. As historians Robert Friedel and Paul Israel tell us, "For Edison, the search for a practical incandescent light was a bold, even foolhardy, plunge into the unknown, guided at first more by over-confidence and a few half-baked ideas than by science or system."[5]

Like everyone else then working on incandescent lamps, Edison knew that passing a current through a wire (or other filament) would make it glow brightly. Two other things he knew: A denser filament could take a higher voltage, and the higher voltage would cause the filament to burn up. The challenge, then, was to find a way to make a filament glow brightly from high voltage without quickly burning up.

From that point Edison took a wrong turn. Taking a cue from his earlier work in telegraphy, he installed a regulator that would automatically reduce the current when the filament became too hot. After much experimentation, he gave up on this idea and got down to working with different filaments. Edison and his assistants immersed themselves in a variety of promising materials. A letter from arc-lighting pioneer Moses Farmer suggested that they use a carbon filament inside a vacuum, an approach that Swan and other experimenters as early as 1850 had already explored.

Although today we associate Edison with the electric light bulb, the impact of his mind and hand on the larger *system* of electric lighting is largely overlooked. Even in late 1878, when the race was moving quickly, Edison was much more than a bench scientist with an intense but limited focus; he was a systematic thinker. From the very beginning he envisioned how electric lighting might be developed and distributed on a wide basis. He was intent, he told the *New York Times,* "in finding a candle that will give a pleasant light, not too intense, which can be turned on or off as easily as gas," and at "a trifling cost compared with that of gas."[6] The system of gas illumination, it seems, was for Edison a useful model; according to Robert P. Rogers, he hoped to identify and keep its best features while eliminating its worst.[7] In his notes he wrote, "Object: E. to effect exact imitation of all done by gas, to replace lighting by gas with lighting by electricity."[8] This, he already knew, would require more than just a lamp—it would require efficient electrical generation, wiring, metered distribution, sockets, fuses, and fixtures. All of these separate parts, in Edison's words, "form one machine."

Thus, while his assistants experimented with filaments of chromium, aluminum, iridium, platinum, ruthenium, silicon, carbon, and tungsten, Edison directed work on improvements to the electric generator that would be needed if large-scale electric lighting were to succeed. And before long he and his crew had engineered a 90 percent efficient dynamo. Edison was also thinking ahead to the problem of wiring electrical service on a broad scale. He would need to find a way to minimize the requirements for expensive copper if his system were to be cost-competitive with gas lighting. In developing his own incandescent lamp prototype, therefore, he immediately went to high voltage, knowing that if his system ran on much lower voltage—as did those of other lighting experimenters—much larger-gauge and consequently more expensive copper wires would be needed.

On October 19, 1879, slightly over a year after beginning their experiments, Edison and his staff at Menlo Park found a filament that did the trick. After trying filaments in hundreds of forms, they carbonized a piece of common cotton thread in a vacuum (so that it would not oxidize), bent it into the shape of a horseshoe, connected it to an electrical current, and mounted it in an exhausted glass bulb. Flipping on the switch, they were delighted with its glowing incandescence, which lasted through one hour, then into the night and the next day. To their great delight, the carbon filament kept burning for almost two days. Edison now had his workable "electric candle." He also had an experienced staff to perfect it, the capital to take it into production, and the basics of an underlying system for generating and selling electricity.

In the months that followed, Edison and associates worked at improving their filament and produced a lamp with a 179-hour life using a carbonized paper filament. A filament of Japanese bamboo did even better, and this remained the Edison standard design for the next 14 years.[9]

COMMERCIAL DEVELOPMENT

Workers at the Edison laboratory and the residents of Menlo Park became the guinea pigs for the first incandescent lighting system. Lamps hung from overhead wires lighted the workshops, the streets around the invention factory, and even a few residences. In the week after Christmas in 1879, Edison and his staff put on a public display of their new invention, and thousands of curiosity seekers—and a few competitors—tramped through the little commune and its buildings to see "progress on the march." Among the crowd were employees of the gas lighting industry, who later declared that Edison's invention was a big disappointment and that none of the 40 "burners" on display produced as much light as a single gas light.[10] Edison later recounted how the gas people had tried to sabotage this first public exhibition of electric lighting:

> I remember the visit of one expert, a well-known electrician, then representing a Baltimore gas company. . . . This man had a length of insulated No. 10 wire around his sleeve and back, so that his hands would conceal the ends, and no one would know he had it. His idea, of course, was to put this across the ends of the supplying circuit and short-circuit the whole thing—putting it all out of business without being detected. . . . He did not know that we had already worked out the safety fuse and that every little group of lights was protected independently. He slyly put this jumper in contact with the wires—and just four lamps went out in the section he tampered with. [Laboratory workers] saw him do it, however, and got hold of him, and just led him out of the place with language that made the recording angels jump to their typewriters.[11]

When he had gotten his "system" ready, Edison made his first commercial installation aboard the steamship *S.S. Columbia* in May 1880. Edison sold the shipowners a stand-alone, turnkey system: generator, wiring, and 115 lamps to light its staterooms and saloons. He supervised the installation himself. An electric system was seen by the owners as an important improvement over open-flame lighting in this application, as the electric lamps would not produce smoke or fumes in the closed, confined spaces of the ship. The newly constructed *Columbia* departed for its maiden voyage to California via Cape Horn, and as it steamed down Delaware Bay toward the open sea by night, its shining Edison lights are said to have given it a brilliant appearance. This lighting system proved so effective that it was not replaced with more modern equipment for another 15 years.

Edison's next system was sold to a New York lithography workshop in January 1881. Many of the first users of the Edison system were upscale institutions, the real pacesetters in society. These included the Chicago Academy of Music and the Palmer House Hotel, England's House of Commons, *Magasins du Bon Marche* in Paris, Milan's *La Scala* Opera House, and Rome's School of Fine Arts.[12] In February 1881, Edison moved from Menlo Park to oversee the installation of what, for him, was the first test of his vision—the lighting of lower Manhattan from a central generating station on Pearl Street. This was a success, and

TABLE 3–1.   **Expansion of Edison Installations and Lamps**

Year	Installations	Lamps in Operation
1881	NA	5,122
1882	153	29,192
1883	NA	64,856
1884	NA	92,020
1885	520	132,875
1886	702	181,463

Source: Arthur A. Bright, Jr., based on Edison Manufacturing Company data, *The Electric Lamp Industry: Technological Change and Economic Development from 1800 to 1947* (New York: Macmillan, 1949), p. 71.

from then on business expanded briskly as stores, homes, and factories bought Edison's lighting system (Table 3-1).

America was taking to the new lighting technology, which was accounted to be cleaner, safer, and more convenient than competing technologies. And Edison was not alone in expanding the business. By 1885, eight other firms were competing for some if not all aspects of the incandescent lighting market. Some firms had made the transition from the arc lighting industry; others, like George Westinghouse and his Union Switch & Signal Company, had expanded into lighting from earlier work making electric generators for the railroads. Swan Lamp Manufacturing bore the name of the Englishman who had pioneered incandescent lamps long before Edison's work got off the ground.

Despite these competitors, Edison held the lion's share of the market, controlled most of the important patents, and employed most of the highly skilled workers needed to manufacture lamps on a large scale. The Edison lamp won top honors over its rivals, including Swan's, at the Paris Electrical Exposition. In 1884, it took the top award at the London Crystal Palace competition.

The Gas Industry under Siege

The many local companies that produced and distributed illuminating gas around the country enjoyed a comfortable monopoly up until the 1880s. Candles and various lamp fuels were their only competitors. In cities, at least, gas had definite advantages over these: cost, brightness, and convenience. Even the appearance of arc lamps in the late 1870s was not a serious threat: their harsh light was useful only for street lighting.

The gas industry very quickly recognized the potential threat of incandescent lighting and acted to thwart its progress. The gas "monopoly" (as Edison called it) publicly belittled the significance of electric lighting, exaggerated its dangers, and used political influence with regard to safety standards and municipal charges for power distribution in ways that would impede its progress. In New York City, for example, gas proponents tried to persuade city aldermen to charge a fee of $1,000 per mile of underground power distribution, a fee that did not apply to their gas lines.

Some improvements were made in the efficiencies of producing and distributing gas over the decades, but next to nothing had improved in the illuminating effectiveness of gas. Arthur A. Bright, Jr. tells us that the industry conducted virtually no research in the modern sense. The general application of one major improvement was, in fact, ignored. In the 1820s, someone used a tablet of calcium oxide to improve the brightness of gas lamps illuminating theater stages—the *laterna magica*. The tablet glowed intensely when heated by burning gas, and the term "limelight" entered the vocabulary.

It was not until gas illumination was up against the potentially lethal challenge from electric lighting that real product improvements were made and diffused. The electric lamp, in fact, seems to have provided the model for the most important of these improvements.

If a filament of carbon heated by electricity could be used to give steady and efficient illumination, why would a filament of metal oxide heated in a gas flame not produce a similar result? It is likely that such reasoning led Austrian inventor Carl von Welsbach to the creation of the gas mantle in 1883. The Welsbach mantle was a structure of filaments of cerium and thorium oxides that glowed brightly when heated, producing in one stroke a five-fold improvement in gas lighting efficiency. Its fragility and expense impeded widespread use, but by the early 1890s the mantle was much more serviceable and reduced the cost of gas lighting by almost two-thirds.[1] This single improvement and its variations threatened to sink the nascent electric lighting industry and explains why it took Edison 12 years to turn a profit from his fast-expanding electric lighting business.

After the turn of the century, the gas men had exhausted their supply of serious improvements, while the electric industry continued to make incremental product and process improvements at a steady pace. Gas as a form of urban commercial and residential lighting was doomed. It was the good fortune of the gas industry that it found and developed a new market for its product—space heat and manufacturing process heat—even as the market for illuminating gas was being snuffed out by electric lighting.

The phenomenon of industries making meaningful and dramatic product improvements when directly threatened by a new technology is a common pattern, explored in detail in Chapter 7.

Note

1. Arthur A. Bright, Jr., The Electric Lamp Industry: Technological Change and Economic Development from 1800 to 1947 (New York: Macmillan, 1949), p. 212.

There is little doubt that Edison's success in getting patent protection for his carbon filament lamps and many other systems components—and his tenacity in successfully defending those patents in court—was instrumental in his incandescent light bulb becoming the dominant device in the industry. By late 1883 Edison Electric Light Company had 215 patents and another 307 pending.[13] By 1885 it was producing 75 percent (300,000) of all the electric lamps made in the United States.

THE DOMINANT DESIGN EMERGES

A dominant design in incandescent lamps emerged quickly. In 1884, Edison Electric Light Company issued a lamp that, except for its glass tip, had all the features that would persist over the coming years. Arthur Bright, Jr., describes the period between its introduction and 1893 as one in which there was a "freezing of design."[14] "By 1884 . . . the greatest progress had been made, and no further improvements in carbon resulted for twenty years. Lamp manufacturers were busy with manufacturing and promotion. . . ."[15] The 1884 lamp had the modern "Edison base," the standard screw-in metal base still used today (inspired by the screw cap on kerosene cans of the time). Its carbonized bamboo filament was joined to a glass stem, and the whole assembly was sealed to a pear-shaped glass vacuum bulb at the base. As we will see, this was followed by a period of incremental product innovation, a surge of process innovation, and a decline in the number of producers through consolidation and failures. As Bright describes it, "Once a practical incandescent lamp had been developed and placed on the market, engineering attention shifted largely from the basic characteristics of the lamp and the filament to other aspects of the lighting system."[16]

The superiority of the Edison filament in combination with an exhausted and sealed glass bulb with platinum lead-in wires led to its swift imitation by a number of other companies. In 1885, the Edison Electric Light Company decided to sue its imitators for patent infringement, a course of action it doggedly pursued in the courts until 1892, when it prevailed and its opponents' appeals were denied. Thus the dominant design developed through a combination of technical and legal circumstances. As the data in Figure

FIGURE 3–1. **U.S. Incandescent Lamp Industry, Number of Competing Firms at Year's End, 1880–1896**

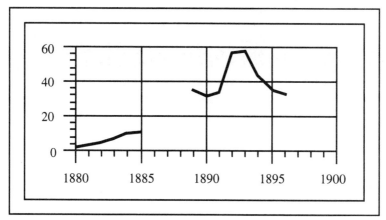

Note: No figures available for 1886, 1887, and 1888.

Source: From data in Arthur A. Bright, Jr., *The Electric Lamp Industry* (see note 4), pp. 73, 92.

TABLE 3–2.   **Improvements to Incandescent Lamp Design and Performance**

Year	Carbon Filament	Metallic Filament	Lumens[a]	Life (hours)
1881	Carbonized bamboo		1.68	600
1884	Flashed cellulose		3.4	400
1888	Asphalted carbonized bamboo		3.0	600
1897		Refractory oxides	5.0	300 or 800[b]
1899		Osmium	5.5	1,000
1902		Tantalum	5.0	250 or 700[b]
1904	GEM (metallized carbon)		4.0	600
1904		Nonductile tungsten	7.85	800
1910		Ductile tungsten	10.0	1,000

[a]Lumens represent efficiency per watt and are applied here to the lamp sizes most commonly used.
[b]The smaller figure applies when lamp used with direct current; the larger figure when used with alternating current.
Source: Franklin Institute, *Incandescent Electric Lamps,* 1885; Schroeder, *The History of the Incandescent Lamp,* 1927; and Schroeder, *History of Electric Light,* 1923. All as cited in Robert P. Rogers, *Staff Report on the Development and Structure of the Electric Lamp Industry* (Washington, D.C.: U.S. Government Printing Office, February 1980), p. 13.

3-1 indicate, the number of lamp producers began to diminish thereafter.

It would be a mistake, however, to believe that the dominance of the Edison lamp design at this time was dictated solely by the artificial constraints of patent law. Edison Electric Light Company sued its competitors—and won—because their lamps were essentially me-too products.

THE SHIFT TO INCREMENTAL INNOVATION AND PROCESS IMPROVEMENT

With the general acceptance of Edison's design, the energies and attention of the industry shifted away from product innovation. The Wizard himself turned to other pursuits. Only when Edison's original patents started to expire in the 1890s was vigorous innovation observable, and this was aimed less at the design of the product than at its performance characteristics. Over a period of years, manufacturers improved their filaments—but very slowly—and eventually moved away from carbon entirely in favor of ductile tungsten. The more important improvements in the period 1881–1910 are shown in Table 3-2.

Gas-filled bulbs that added to operating life appeared in 1913. Frosted bulbs were developed to diffuse light more evenly; they were introduced in 1925. Many of the important lamp improvements were made by firms outside the circle of leading producers, a phenomenon encountered fairly regularly. As Bright has observed:

> It is significant that established lamp manufacturers did not produce the first important innovations; rather, individuals outside the industry were quicker to seize the opportunity to develop new types of filaments which led to large jumps in efficiency. The carbon filament lamp superficially appeared to have reached its limits, for no fundamental improvements had been made in it following 1884.
>
> The sources of the technological advances in lighting from 1897 to 1912 represent one of the most interesting and significant phases of the industry's development. Until around the turn of the century, most of the leading electric lamp producers in the United States and abroad made no genuine effort to achieve fundamental improvements in incandescent lamps or to develop entirely new and superior light sources. The big companies, particularly in this

country, were lulled into a feeling of security by the continuing supremacy of the carbon filaments and the carbon arc and by their own financial supremacy. In the United States the lack of competition within the industry retarded new product development. In Europe, market competition was keener, yet even there the big companies were not responsible for the first important innovations.[17]

Metal filament lamps were introduced first in Europe, where electric rates were much higher, and the efficiency of lamps a greater concern than their initial cost. Because Europeans correctly identified the inefficient carbon filament as a costly element of the lighting system, research was done to produce a metal filament bulb. The superiority of metal filaments was to prove itself in the first years of the new century. General Electric Company, successor to Edison's firm, at first resisted the improved metal filament design, perhaps because its founder had tried and rejected so many experimental metal filaments in the early days at Menlo Park. Instead, it made heroic efforts to increase the efficiency of its traditional carbon technology. Eventually the superiority of the new metal filament bulbs developed by Europeans could no longer be ignored, and General Electric caved in and adopted them through very costly licensing agreements. In subsequent years General Electric did the pioneering work that led to the use of ductile tungsten, which represented a substantial leap in efficiency per watt and useful life (Figure 3-2). It had roughly three times the efficiency of the earlier carbon design and about twice that of General Electric's last best effort with carbon (the GEM lamp).[18] It is fair to say that the ductile tungsten lamp represented the ultimate innovation in the incandescent bulb and that subsequent changes to the lamp were incremental improvements.

The next big improvements took place in the factories that manufactured lamps for the burgeoning commercial market. Fol-

FIGURE 3–2.   **Waves of Improvement in Lighting**

Gas flame or kerosene lamp	7 candlepower
Welsbach gas burner	250 candlepower
Tungsten filament lamp	1,500 candlepower

Source: David E. Nye, *Electrifying America: Social Meanings of a New Technology, 1880–1940* (Cambridge, Mass.: MIT Press, 1991), p. 17.

lowing the appearance of the ductile tungsten lamp, production in the lamp industry jumped from around 15 million units in 1914 to close to 200 million units in 1925. This could not have been accomplished without fundamental process innovations.

All of the lamps for Edison's initial installations were made essentially by hand in the Menlo Park laboratory. Subsequent lamps were produced by the Edison Lamp Company in a nearby factory. Until 1893, the business of putting together a light bulb was laborious handwork of more than 200 steps[19]: glassblowers created the delicate bulbs; skilled workers constructed the even more delicate filaments on stems, sealed them to the base, and used a vacuum device to extract the air from the bulb as it was sealed. Until 1885, the vacuum process alone could take up to five hours. But a string of process innovations would dramatically reduce production times, reduce the skill and experience needed by labor, and introduce a number of lamp-making machines that together would cause the price of the standard electric lamp to drop precipitously. The high points of this series of innovations are presented in Figure 3-3.

Together, the course of process innovation and refinement of the original Edison design led to better and better lamps at lower and lower cost. As Bright described it, "The improvements in man-

FIGURE 3–3. **Major Process Innovations in Electric Lamp Manufacturing**

1885   The Sprengel mercury pump reduced the time needed to exhaust air from a bulb from five hours to 30 minutes.

1894   Michael Owens of Libbey Glass replaced hand-blown bulbs with a semi-automated "paste mold" blowing machine.

1895   Buckeye Incandescent Lamp Co. of Cleveland introduced a machine to seal in the wired lamp base.

1896   GE imported and improved a European method of adding a drop of phosphorous (a "getter") to absorb the last oxygen molecules from the bulb.

1901   GE developed a stem-making machine to assemble glass stem lead-in wires and filament supports.

1903   GE tubulating machine improved the process of exhausting air from the bulb during manufacture.

Source: Data from Arthur A. Bright, Jr., *The Electric Lamp Industry* (see note 4).

ufacturing methods from 1894–1896, when added to the advances from the preceding fourteen years, produced a lamp considerably cheaper and better than that of 1880, *even though it was essentially the same in design* [my emphasis]."[21] Thus there was plenty of room for continual improvement in the modern sense, long after the dominant design had been established. The decline in lamp prices is reflected in Figure 3-4.

By the 1930s, the incandescent lighting industry was already half a century old; it was now a mature technology, and very little was being done to improve the product. The innovators focused their attention on the creation of specialized lamps for photography, aviation, motor vehicles, floodlighting, and so forth.

But just as the typewriter industry was gradually infiltrated by the electric machine, the incandescent lighting industry suddenly found itself with a new competitor on its flank: the fluorescent lamp. The two industry leaders, GE and Westinghouse, had developed the first commercial fluorescent through a collaborative research program. The new lamp was introduced in 1938, but neither company pushed the new technology for fear of alienating the power utilities that purchased their lamps, generators, and other

FIGURE 3–4.   **Price of Carbon Filament Electric Lamps,[a]
1880–1896**

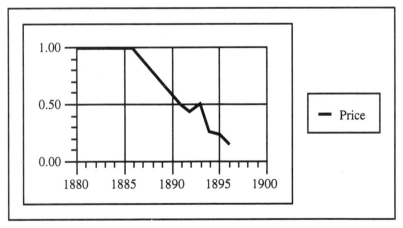

[a]For 16 candlepower lamp, average.

Source: Data from Arthur A. Bright, Jr., *The Electric Lamp Industry* (see note 4), pp. 93 and 134.

electrical equipment. The energy efficiency of the new technology was well understood, and the utilities were not anxious to see power demand reduced through the widespread use of fluorescent lamps. Sylvania, a bit player in the lighting industry at the time with only 5.5 percent of lamp sales and no prospects for expansion, had no concerns about offending the power utilities and went into fluorescents aggressively, eventually capturing 20 percent of the new and growing market.[21]

Fluorescents encroached on the incandescent market first in the workplace, just as electric typewriters had first displaced manual machines from the office before spreading to home and student markets. In the 1990s, as public concern for energy costs and consumption proliferates, we can see fluorescents moving from commercial applications to residential use. The long, ceiling-mounted tubes that traditionally characterized fluorescents have been redesigned to a shape that can replace the incandescent bulb in most residential fixtures. Even the power utilities, whose interests are now bent on reducing the need to site and build more power stations, are coming full circle on conservation issues, and many are subsidizing the high initial cost of residential fluorescent lamps to their customers as a means of reducing energy demand and the costly prospect of financing billion-dollar generating plants.

Fluorescent lighting provides an excellent example of how waves of product innovation can periodically wash through an industry. As we saw in the typewriter industry—with its major product innovations in manual, electric, and computer-based typing—lighting has experienced three major waves of innovation in the past 150 years: gas illumination, incandescent lighting, and fluorescent. A fourth may be waiting in the wings.

In the spring of 1992, Intersource Technologies, a small California firm, announced what it termed the biggest breakthrough in lighting since Edison's original invention. The company called a national press conference to demonstrate its prototype of a new kind of light bulb that it claimed would produce the same number of lumens as an incandescent bulb using one-fourth the energy. Further, the company estimated lamp life at 15,000 to 20,000 operating hours, as opposed to 750 to 1,500 hours for a conventional filament bulb. The new device has a standard Edison screw-in base; it generates radio waves from a magnetic coil, and these radio waves excite gases in the lamp, causing the phosphorous coated interior surface of the glass to glow. The base and electronic parts of the new lamps are a permanent fixture. Only the glass envelope containing the gas and fluorescent coating is changed if the lamp fails, an interesting product "architecture," which in itself should extend product life and reduce operating cost.

Whether this lighting innovation actually delivers on its developer's representations remains to be seen. If it does, it will be a radical departure in lighting technology and a possible substitute for the time-honored incandescent and fluorescent lamps.

This case points up a number of important lessons about the development and diffusion of technological innovations:

- *Outsiders as innovators.* Each wave of lighting innovation has been originated and carried forward by industry outsiders. Edison had absolutely no standing in the lighting industry of his day; Sylvania was a fringe producer when it pioneered the fluorescent lamp; and the innovators of the new radio wave lamp are outsiders.
- *Social as well as technical factors need to be considered.* At least with respect to consumer products, narrowing the outward appearances between a new technology and those of the old and familiar can be helpful in creating market success. Edison seemed to understand this very well. In his efforts to sell his system to gas customers, he spoke of his electric "burners"—the term used in gas systems. He routed his wires through existing gas conduit and mounted electric lamps in gas wall sconces. He spoke of electric "mains" in the street and used a similar metering system to sell to his customers.[22]
- *Defensive innovation by established technology.* An established technology that has not previously been challenged may be capable of creating tremendous improvements when seriously threatened. The great increase in lighting efficiency caused by the Welsbach mantle is a prime example. Newcomers with radical innovations should assume that entrenched competitors with financial resources will respond vigorously with innovations of their own.

Some entrenched competitors defend their turfs in the legal system, through regulation, and in the court of public opinion. Thomas Edison—America's icon of innovation and progress— once he represented the established technology, threw up his own set of defenses when challenged by innovators in electrical generation. Edison's system had adopted direct electrical current as its standard, even though alternating current was generally understood at the time. George Westinghouse recognized the potential technical superiority of alternating current and worked hard to overcome both the problem of its generation and transmission and the safety issues inherent in its high voltage.

By 1886, Edison viewed alternating current as a dangerous rival and tried frantically to subvert inroads made by Westinghouse and his system on a number of fronts. In this "battle of the systems" Edison was not above throwing up legal impediments and using a number of dirty tricks, including the macabre executions of stray dogs and cats by alternating current, all for the purpose of showing newspaper reporters the rival technology's dangers to the public.[23] Paul David, in his "Thomas Edison and the 'Battle of the Systems' Reconsidered," describes how Edison and his so-named West Orange Gang of assistants convinced the state of New York in 1888 to switch from hanging to electrocution by alternating current as its official form of execution; the great Wizard himself testified to its lethal effectiveness before the legislature. Two years later, an ax murderer named William Kemmler became the first to die in an "electric chair" wired to one of Westinghouse's AC generators.[24]

It is not clear to what extent Edison's public relations campaign associated alternating current with questions of safety in the public mind, or to what degree his own direct current system was given a longer life, but this story does indicate the extent to which even a progressive innovator like Edison will resist change. Paul David quotes Harold Passer's description of Edison: "In 1879, Edison was a bold and couragous innovator. In 1889, he was a cautious and conservative defender of the status quo."[25] Some commentators see in Edison's actions a fear that alternating current would render his heavy investment in generating and distribution capacity and equipment obsolete. Paul David presents evidence suggesting that Edison correctly perceived "the precarious, unstable nature of a competitive situation that was unfolding with unexpected speed," and that his actions were intended to buy time until he could extricate himself from the industry and pursue other interests with the least financial damage.[26]

PRODUCT AND PROCESS EVOLUTION

A central point in the story of the development of the incandescent lamp is the way in which its design and the attendant production process coevolved. The process for producing lamps, which started with over 200 steps involving nearly an hour of labor, was ultimately reduced to 20 steps requiring 20 seconds of labor—a nearly 200:1 reduction. The Sprengel pump similarly reduced evacuation time from hours to minutes, and later improvements spelled further reduction. Similar improvements were recounted in glass forming and sealing. Major product innovations were seen to be concentrated in the years prior to 1884. Major process innovations were seen to occur in a wave from 1885 through the early 1900s. A subsequent wave of more modest product and process innovations occurred with the introduction of the ductile tungsten filament in 1910. Throughout the entire period, lamp performance in terms of efficiency and life in use improved constantly through a series of increasingly refined and sophisticated, though incremental, innovations.[27]

Changes in product design seem initially to shape the course taken in the development of the production process. Later the early choices made in process technology may constrain further developments in the product. When both product and process design are highly elaborated, they may become so intertwined and codependent that neither can change without deeply influencing the other. This fact is often echoed in organizational structure and supplier-buyer relationships as well. The general evolutionary course taken by product and process innovation, organizational and market structure, and relationships with competitors and other firms is the subject of the next chapter.

Notes

1. U.S. Bureau of the Census, *Twelfth Census of the United States,* 1890, vol. X, p. 702.
2. *The Mail,* September 10, 1878, Batchelor Scrapbook, Cat. 1241. Cited by Robert Friedel and Paul Israel, *Edison's Electric Light: Biography of an Invention* (New Brunswick, N.J.: Rutgers University Press, 1986), pp. 9–10.
3. Friedel and Israel, *Edison's Electric Light,* pp. 13–14.
4. Arthur A. Bright, Jr., *The Electric Lamp Industry: Technological Change and Economic Development from 1800 to 1947* (New York: Macmillan, 1949), p. 54. Note: Bright's outstanding book was the second industry study sponsored by MIT in its Studies of Innovation series.
5. Friedel and Israel, *Edison's Electric Light,* p. xii.
6. *New York Times,* September 28, 1878, p. 4. Cited by Friedel and Israel, ibid.

7. Robert P. Rogers, *Staff Report on the Development and Structure of the Electric Lamp Industry* (Washington, D.C.: U.S. Government Printing Office, February 1980), pp. 4–5.

8. Thomas A. Edison, Laboratory Notebook No. 184, "Electricity vs. Gas," 1878, ELA. Cited in Matthew Josephson, *Edison: A Biography* (New York: McGraw-Hill, 1959), p. 181.

9. Bright, *The Electric Lamp Industry,* p. 65. Bright mentions that a Japanese farmer was Edison's exclusive supplier of the special variety of bamboo for a number of years.

10. Josephson, *Edison: A Biography,* p. 225.

11. T.C. Martin, *Forty Years of Edison Service* (New York, 1922), pp. 21–22. Cited in Josephson, *Edison: A Biography,* p. 226.

12. David E. Nye, *Electrifying America: Social Meanings of a New Technology, 1880–1940* (Cambridge, Mass.: MIT Press, 1991), p. 32.

13. Bright, *The Electric Lamp Industry,* p. 84.

14. Ibid., p. 115.

15. Ibid.

16. Ibid.

17. Ibid., pp. 230–231.

18. The GEM (General Electric Metallized) lamp was an effort by General Electric to perfect its carbon filament technology in the face of the invasion of the functionally superior metal filament lamps developed in Europe. GEM filaments stem from experiments conducted by an MIT professor, Willis R. Whitney, who was hired as first director of the General Electric Research Laboratory. Whitney developed a new type of high-temperature furnace in which he heated untreated carbon filaments to 3500°C. in an atmosphere saturated with carbon. His process drove off the normal impurities found in the carbon, producing a filament that behaved more like a metal.

19. Warren Scoville, *Revolution in Glassmaking* (Cambridge, Mass.: Harvard University Press, 1948). Scoville comments that workers "fashioned the entire output of incandescent light bulbs before 1985; in 1920 they made about 40 percent" with machines doing the rest. The remainder of skilled labor is described by Scoville as resulting from "the unwillingness of manufacturers to invest additional capital in a decadent industry" (p. 79).

20. Ibid., pp. 133–134.

21. Robert P. Rogers, *Staff Report,* pp. 25–26.

22. I am indebted to James R. Bright for this insight.

23. Josephson, *Edison: A Biography,* p. 347.

24. Paul A. David, "Heroes, Herds and Hysteresis in Technology History: Thomas Edison and 'The Battle of the Systems' Revisited," *Industrial and Corporate Change,* vol. 1, no. 1 (1992), pp. 151–152.

25. H.C. Passer, *The Electrical Manufacturers: 1875–1900* (New York: Arno Press, 1972), p. 74.

26. David, "Heroes, Herds and Hysteresis," pp. 159–160.

27. Some scholars have termed such an evolutionary path a technological trajectory. For example, see Giovanni Dosi, "Technological Paradigms and Technological Trajectories: a Suggested Interpretation of the Determinants and

Directions of Technical Change," *Research Policy,* vol. 11 (1982), pp. 147–162; and Devendra Sahal, "Technological Guideposts and Innovation Avenues," *Research Policy,* vol. 14 (1985), pp. 61–82. For our purposes this seems a bit too deterministic, though once such a path is initially chosen it does in some respects seem to follow an internal logic dictated by physical laws, characteristics of materials, and so on.

CHAPTER 4

Innovation and
Industrial Evolution

INNOVATION IN THE TYPEWRITER INDUSTRY, in the electric lighting industry, and in those industries profiled in Chapter 2 suggests a dynamic relationship among product innovation, the marketplace, and the firms that emerge and compete on the basis of particular innovations.

In examining the early life of the typewriter it is impossible to separate interactions between producing firms, ongoing experiments with machine designs and features, and the growing cadre of typists. The first decades of incandescent lighting present a similar web of relationships. Edison was more than just a clever inventor working in isolation from other technologists and potential customers. He drew heavily from the work of others in his bid to create a practical incandescent bulb, and the market dimensions of the project were never far from his mind. Even his great moment of success—when the first incandescent lamp burned through the night at Menlo Park—was just one more step in a long process of innovation that emerged with arc lighting, with Wallace's powerful generator, with the development of insulated copper wire, and with dozens of other supporting technologies. As incandescent lighting was accepted in the lighting industry, the focus of innovation in Edison's company and in the companies of his competitors changed as well, but the links among competition, customers, and the innovative process were never shaken loose.

These dynamic relationships remain a part of the innovative process in industry today. For example, even though the dust has far from settled in the personal computer industry, it is clear that the pace and direction of innovation has been heavily determined by a complex web of interrelated events taking place among integrated circuit producers, software companies, disk drive manufacturers, and others. And their progress has not been made in isolation from the market, but has had to factor in the work habits, skills, and expectations of millions of users—many of whom formed their habits and skills in the age of the typewriter.

Unfortunately, academic studies and models of innovation have failed to capture the richness of this system. Instead, we have seen it in fairly linear terms—as something that begins with a company possessing a certain technology, investing in that technology and accompanying ideas, and implementing them in the market. This approach assumes that all innovations occur in the same way in all companies; it misses the important differences and powerful interactions between the subjects of study; and it generally disregards the fact that organizations change throughout their lifetimes. Earlier research also failed to distinguish between product and process innovations, each of which follows a different path yet affects the other. In short, the interaction of technological change, organizations, and the competitive marketplace is much more complex and dynamic than most models describe.

The model presented in this chapter attempts to capture those important dynamic relationships. It describes how change in product and process innovation and in organizational structure occurs in patterns that are observable across industries and sectors. The model incorporates marketplace realities and allows consideration of the different conditions required for rapid innovation and for high levels of output and productivity. This model is based on historical studies of innovations in their organizational, technical, and economic settings. The data gathered from such studies—particularly those of more contemporary industries—are necessarily incomplete, but they nevertheless add to the richness of our insights.

THE DYNAMICS OF INNOVATION

This model has its origins in work begun in 1974 in collaboration with the late William Abernathy at the Harvard Business

School and continued over the years. As a result, it is more familiar to many scholars than to the industrial managers who have the most to gain from it. Bill Abernathy was one of those rare people who successfully bridged the chasm between the academy and industry. This fact, along with his energy and creativity, inspired a new generation of researchers whose work in the areas of technological change, innovation, and industrial management today enriches the tradition of inquiry of which Abernathy was a true pioneer. Some of their important contributions to this tradition are discussed later in the chapter.

The model describes the changing rates of product and process innovation, and considers in connection with these the business-oriented characteristics that mark their ebbs and flows.

Product Innovation

We have already observed the richness of product innovation that prevailed in the early years of the typewriter, the personal computer, and electric lighting industries. Unencumbered by universal technical standards or by uniform product expectations in the marketplace, the early participants in these new industries experimented freely with new forms and materials. This same sense of pioneering prevailed in the early, pre-Model-A years of the auto industry, when any number of uniquely designed vehicles emerged from hundreds of American and European workshops.

We also observed that this flurry of radical product innovation eventually ends with the emergence of a dominant design. With the marketplace forming its expectations for a product in terms of features, form, and capabilities, the bases on which product innovation can take place become much fewer, and the focus of R&D narrows to incremental innovations on existing features. A good example of this was seen in the case of the incandescent lamp. Once the ensemble of necessary features for a commercially effective lamp was introduced by Edison, product innovation downshifted dramatically. The same was observed with the introduction of the Underwood Model 5 and a number of other products mentioned in Chapter 2. Figure 4-1 is a representation of this phenomenon.

Several studies have shown that somewhere along the product innovation curve the performance criteria that serve as a primary basis for competition change from ill defined and uncertain to well articulated.[1] At the same time, forces that reduce the rate of prod-

FIGURE 4–1.   **The Rate of Product Innovation**

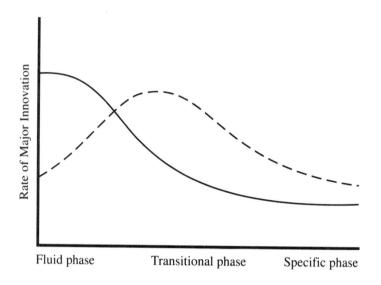

Fluid phase   Transitional phase   Specific phase

uct change and innovation begin to build up. As obvious improvements are introduced, it becomes increasingly difficult to better past performance; users develop loyalties and preferences, and the practicalities of marketing, distribution, maintenance, and so forth demand greater standardization. Innovations leading to better product performance become less likely unless they are easy for the customer to evaluate and compare. Firms attempt to maximize their sales and market shares by defining their development initiatives in terms that clearly matter to potential customers.

But even as the energies that characterize the period of greatest product innovation begin to fade, other creative activities awaken and assume their place.

Process Innovation

During the formative period of a new product technology, the processes used to produce it are usually crude, inefficient, and based on a mixture of skilled labor and general-purpose machinery and tools. Thus, in the first few years of commercially produced incandescent lamps, Edison's products were made by laborious processes in a building adjacent to the laboratory in which they were first conceived. There were no specialized tools, machines, or dedicated craft traditions for incandescent bulb making. It was the product itself, at this point, that mattered to innovators and to those customers venturesome enough to try it out.

But product innovation and process innovation are interdependent; as the rate of product innovation decreases, it is common to observe a growing rate of process innovation (Figure 4-2). In the case of incandescent lighting we noted the innovation of specialized glass-blowing equipment, high-capacity vacuum pumps, and other manufacturing improvements. The number of steps in the manufacturing process dropped from 200 to 30 between 1880 and 1920. Skilled labor using common tools gave way to specialized equipment operated by workers who were less skilled. Lamp production moved from the making of individual units, to batches, to semicontinuous production.

Organizational Change

Essentially, the organization of a firm formed around an innovation goes through the familiar transformation that entrepreneurial organizations experience as they become successful and shift their focus from innovative products to larger-scale production of standardized offerings. This transformation is characterized by the following:

FIGURE 4–2. **Rate of Process Innovation**

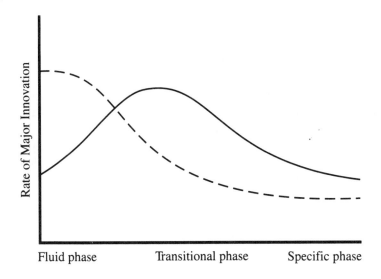

- Informal control gives way to an emphasis on structure, goals, and rules.
- Structure become hierarchical and rigid, and tasks become formal.
- Major innovations—once the life-blood of the firm—are less and less encouraged; continuous incremental improvements become the order of the day.

Not only do changes in products and processes occur in the systematic pattern described earlier, but organizational requirements may also be expected to vary according to a similar pattern. During periods of high market and technical uncertainty, a productive unit must be focused to make progress; for a group to be successful in an uncertain environment, individuals in the organization must act together. This type of structure is called *organic*[2] and emphasizes, among other things, frequent adjustment and redefinition of tasks, limited hierarchy, and high lateral communication. An organic firm is appropriate to uncertain environments because of its increased potential for gathering and processing information for decision making.

The relative power of individuals in the organic firm is related to their assumption of entrepreneurial roles. The rewards for radical product innovation in these firms are substantial and are generally valued by the entrepreneur to a much greater degree than are salary rewards. Realization of potential rewards depends on the survival and growth of the firm, which in turn depends largely on the ability of the entrepreneur to generate a superior product and to capture a share of an emerging market. The innovative capacity of such an organization is high.[3]

As the firm loses its organic character, the relative power of individuals begins to shift from those with entrepreneurial ability to those with management skills. A different set of skills is required for the growth and structuring of the organization. Often the original entrepreneur or entrepreneurial group departs (as did Steve Jobs of Apple, Robert Noyce of Fairchild, and Henry Kloss of Acoustic Research) to start other, smaller enterprises (Next, Intel, and KLH and Advent, respectively). As the transition away from a high rate of product innovation begins, individuals and units in the firm lose their organic connections and become more sequentially interdependent; coordination and control becomes correspondingly more important. Thus, during the transition, organizations are often structured according to products or regions, each division replicating in some respects the earlier entrepreneurial form.

As a dominant design emerges and production operations expand rapidly in response to increased demand, the focus of rewards shifts to those who are able to expand production operations, marketing functions, and so forth. Rewards may be provided in more traditional terms of bonuses, stock options, and other managerial perquisites.

These changes will cause moderation of the innovative capacity of an organization. As a product becomes more standardized and is produced in a more systematic process, interdependence among organizational subunits gradually increases, making it more difficult and costly to incorporate radical innovations.

Once a production process and a set of market relationships and expectations become highly developed with respect to a specified and standardized product, organizational control is provided through structure, goals, and rules. When the business environment is better known and operations become routine, it is seen as necessary to provide more rigid coordination that establishes consistent routines and rules to minimize inefficiency and costs in operations. This type of structure is known as *mechanistic*.

The power and influence of individuals who show administrative ability increases in a mechanistic organization. When the technical and market environment becomes stable—and when growth of a productive unit relies more on stretching existing products and processes—the ability to hold a steady and consistent course is highly valued. Rewards in a stable environment are centered on financial results and on predictable, incremental performance in product and process change that builds on past investments. Ideas that threaten to disrupt the stability of the existing process will be discouraged, and ideas that extend the life of existing products and technology will be encouraged and rewarded, probably in a highly structured manner.

The innovation capacity of such a productive unit tends to be low. When production processes are highly integrated within a system, and a high degree of interdependence exists among subprocesses, the disruption and cost associated with major changes becomes a primary concern. Innovation and change—prized in the organic firm—are a threat and expensive nuisance in the mechanistic firm.

Market Characteristics

When a technology is in its infancy and many producers are rushing to join the industry the market shares of each firm are highly unstable. For example, Klein has shown that between the inception of the auto industry at the beginning of the century and the appearance of its dominant design in 1923, market shares varied rapidly. Klein concludes that "on the basis of 1903 sales it would have been impossible to pick the top ten in 1924," and further that "the positions of the leading makes oscillated greatly during this period."[4] Conversely, during periods of primarily incremental change a chart of market shares consists of mostly horizontal lines with little fluctuation.[5] At the same time, one would expect market feedback to be rapid during this fluid period of inception, and expect performance, features, and functionality of the product to be much more important than price to its demanding "lead users."[6] Perhaps a better way to phrase this is to say that price is more influenced by value in use than by direct cost of production. Both development efforts and costs and profit margins may be relatively high.

After a dominant design or standard is determined, products are likely to become more commoditylike and undifferentiated in terms of function and features. The key functions required of a car, a typewriter, a personal computer, or a light bulb will be widely agreed, and not to have the full set of features and functions means not to be competitive in most of the market. Stable market shares will generally imply the existence of only a few significant and dominant producers. Market feedback will tend to be slow, and direct contact with customers relatively less compared to analysis of statistics and industry information. Price, performance, features, and service will tend to be at parity over the long run with small changes serving as stimuli to take marginal market share from rivals. Incremental changes in products made by competitors will tend to be copied rapidly. The emphasis of innovation, however, will tend to be process improvements that are less easily copied. Price and quality will strongly influence competitiveness, and price will depend heavily on direct manufacturing costs. It is important to note that the rigid situation described here is probably as much or more the result of managerial attitudes and organizational factors as it is to technical factors. Klein contends that "when firms begin to act on the assumption of a lower rate of progress there is likely to be both an increase in the degree of organization and a decline in the degree of competitive interaction."[7]

The Competitive Environment

As this process of decreasing product innovation and increasing process innovation moves forward, it is not uncommon to observe important changes in the competitive environment.

We have already seen how the absence of consensus on product capabilities and features introduces tremendous uncertainty for both customers and producers. Once consensus crystallizes around a particular product, however, that product can enjoy large market share for an extended period. The case of the DC-3 aircraft provides an example of how that consensus can be achieved in one product. The DC-3 is not the most familiar example to readers who have grown up in the jet age, but this aircraft was a culmination of previous innovations and it set the standard for commercial aircraft for two decades.[8] It was not the largest, or the fastest, or the longest-range aircraft to fly when it was introduced, but it was simply the *only* economical, large, fast plane able to fly long distances. The DC-3 satisfied combined market needs so well, in fact, that it provided the basic concepts of commercial aircraft design from the time of its introduction in the mid-1930s until jet-powered aircraft appeared in the late 1950s. Some design concepts introduced in the DC-3 continue in use today.

But as product capabilities and features are crystallized through the emergence of a dominant design, competition between rival firms stabilizes. The number of competitors drops off quickly after this landmark event for the industry, and the bases of competition shift to refinements in product features, reliability, and cost. From this crystallization, a set of efficient producers usually emerges.

The appearance of a dominant design shifts the competitive emphasis to favor those firms with a greater skill in process innovation and process integration and with more highly developed technical and engineering skills. When this happens, many firms are unable to compete and effectively fail. Others may possess special resources and thus merge successfully with the ultimately dominant firms. Weaker firms may merge and still fail.

Eventually the competitive environment reaches a point of stability in which there are only a few firms—four or five is a typical number from the evidence reviewed to date—producing standardized or slightly differentiated products with stable sales and market shares. A number of small firms may remain in the industry serving specialized market segments, but compared with the small firms entering special segments early in the industry, they have little growth potential. Thus it is important to distinguish between small surviving firms and small firms that are new entrants, and to keep in mind that the term "new entrants" includes existing larger firms moving from their established market or technological base into a new product area.

Mueller and Tilton were among the first to present this hypothesis in its entirety.[9] They contend that a new industry is created by the occurrence of a major process or product innovation and develops technologically as less radical innovations are introduced. They further argue that the large corporation seldom provides its people with incentives to introduce a development of radical importance; thus these changes tend to be developed by new entrants without an established stake in a product market segment. In their words, neither large absolute size nor market power is a necessary condition for successful competitive development of most major innovations.

Mueller and Tilton further contend that once a major innovation is established, a rush of firms enters the newly formed industry or adopts a new process innovation. They hold that during the early period of entry and experimentation immediately after a major innovation, the science and technology on which it depends are often only crudely understood and that this reduces the advantage of large firms. However:

> As the number of firms entering the industry increases and more and more R&D is undertaken on the innovation, the scientific and technological frontiers of the new technology expand rapidly. Research becomes increasingly specialized and sophisticated and the technology is broken down into its component parts with individual investigations focusing on improvements in small elements of the technology[10]

Clearly, the situation Mueller and Tilton describe works to the advantage of larger firms in the expanding industry and to the disadvantage of smaller entrants. Reese Jenkins studied this explicitly in the case of photography and found that as the product became standardized, smaller firms consolidated and the industry went through a phase of large and small firms fighting for market share, followed by a phase dominated by an oligopoly of large firms.[11]

Staples, Baker, and Sweeney have summarized several clear parallels between our model and Mueller and Tilton's hypotheses:

> The Utterback and Abernathy model holds implications for organizational structure, just as Mueller and Tilton's does for the composition of an industry. A comparison of the two will show a number of similarities. Both describe a continuum. The stages roughly correspond. Both emphasize the shift of the basis of competition from performance and technological characteristics to price and cost considerations. In both, the evolution is accompanied by an expanding market, increasing importance of production process investment, and a progression from radical to incremental product and process innovation. In general, they describe a progression from a state of flux with rapid technological progress to an ordered situation with cumulative incremental changes. Although they emphasize different aspects of innovation from different perspectives, the models are consistent.[12]

Both this work and that of Mueller and Tilton contend that as an industry stabilizes—that is, as technological progress slows down and production techniques become standardized—barriers to entry increase. The most attractive market segments will already be occupied. As process integration moves forward, the cost of production equipment usually rises dramatically. Product prices fall concurrently, so that firms with the largest market shares are the ones to benefit from further expansion. Product differentiation usually forms around the technical strengths and R&D organization of the existing firms. Strong patent positions established by earlier entering firms become difficult for later entrants to circumvent. Finally, an existing distribution network may also be a powerful barrier to entry, particularly to foreign firms.

Another hallmark of stability is the emergence of a set of captive suppliers of equipment and components. Although such suppliers can be an initial source of innovation and growth, they may ultimately become a conservative force, further stabilizing the competition and change within the product market segment and creating yet another barrier to entry.

A final characteristic of the evolution toward stability is a concerted drive among the surviving firms toward vertical integration from materials production to sales. Integration may take various forms. Firms producing the product can reach backward to furnish more of their own components, subassemblies, and raw materials; or firms producing components can reach forward to do more of the assembly and production of final goods for the market. Such dramatic changes have ripple effects on firms that buy from or sell to the evolving set of productive units. It is just at the point of stability where firms get locked into narrow positions that they also ultimately increase their vulnerability. An existing distribution network can suddenly be threatened by a new technology that requires sharply reduced servicing or maintenance, or by the entrance of a large product line. An existing patent may expire. Although Mueller and Tilton contend that industries become stable when patent positions expire, this seems more likely to be a period of invasion of the industry by a new wave of product and process change—or, in a few cases, the revitalization of the dominant technology itself.

In the early days of an industry, when products are unique in design and capabilities, competition has more to do with winning over customers to the new technology embodied in an unrefined product than in crossing swords with rival innovators. Thus innovators compete as much against their own product inadequacies and market skepticism as against their rivals. This explains the great optimism that spread among companies such as Apple and Tandy when IBM first entered the personal computer field. Far from trembling out of fear for Big Blue's clout as a potential rival, these firms understood that the real enemy was public skepticism about the value of personal computers; they understood clearly that IBM's entry to the field would give the industry the credibility it was struggling to engender with the general population.

THE MODEL SUMMARIZED

We might summarize the model thus far as exhibiting interdependent rates of product and process innovation over time, and these in turn are linked to important transformations in the characteristics of product, process, competition, and organization. These relationships are combined in Figure 4-3.

FIGURE 4–3. **The Dynamics of Innovation**

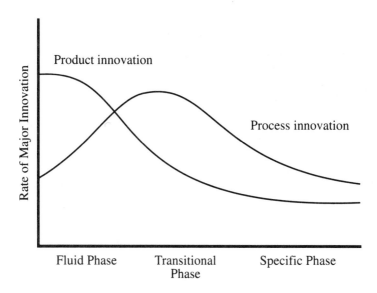

Product	From high variety, to dominant design, to incremental innovation on standardized products
Process	Manufacturing progresses from heavy reliance on skilled labor and general-purpose equipment to specialized equipment tended by low-skilled labor
Organization	From entrepreneurial *organic* firm to hierarchical *mechanistic* firm with defined tasks and procedures and few rewards for radical innovation
Market	From fragmented and unstable with diverse products and rapid feedback to commodity-like with largely undifferentiated products
Competition	From many small firms with unique products to an oligopoly of firms with similar products

PHASES WITHIN THE MODEL OF INNOVATION DYNAMICS

This model attempts to capture the dynamic processes that take place both within an industry and within its member firms over time. It is a model that attempts to cut through two dimensions: 1) the components of product innovation, process innovation, the competitive environment, and organizations; and 2) the life cycle of the industry itself. It is toward this second dimension that we now turn.

Social and natural scientists often segment the subjects of their analyses into chronological or developmental periods. European historians have the Dark Ages, the Middle Ages, the Renaissance, and modern times; developmental psychologists have early childhood, adolescence, adulthood, and old age. These are largely categories of convenience that facilitate discussion and generalization, even though specific cases stubbornly fail to fall into these categories. They also help us to understand patterns and implications for action.

Developmental phases are also used in this model of industrial innovation, if only as a matter of analytical convenience. These phases are here called *fluid, transitional,* and *specific.* Because this is a dynamic model, these phases are associated with both the rate of innovation and the underlying dimensions of product, process, competition, and organization. In effect, these phases slice the model a different way, each cutting across those dimensions.

Significant characteristics in each of the three phases—as they apply to product, process, competition and organization—are briefly stated in Figure 4-4. While this listing is by no means complete, it does nevertheless give a sense of what is going on within an industry as it passes through three stages of development.

The Fluid Phase

The fluid phase is one in which a great deal of change is happening at once and in which outcomes are highly uncertain in terms of product, process, competitive leadership, and the structure and management of firms.

In the fluid phase of a technology's evolution, the rate of product change is expected to be rapid. The new product technology is often crude, expensive, and unreliable, but it is able to fill a function in a way that is highly desirable in some niche markets. In the batch of examples presented through Chapter 3, the Remington No. 1 typewriter was just such an expensive and inelegant contraption. Mark Twain's complaints about his infernal new machine did not overshadow his need to churn out text at a rapid pace—which even this early typewriter successfully accomplished. Likewise, the high initial cost and experimental nature of incandescent lighting did not inhibit the builders and owners of the *S.S. Columbia* from installing Edison's first system. Its unique benefits for lighting in closed spaces where fumes and fire dangers were important considerations made it preferable to the existing technologies of gas and oil lamps. The first personal computers were also crude and relatively expensive versions of what would emerge over the following decade, but dedicated lead users were undeterred by these drawbacks and stayed with the new technology through its many early forms.

Product innovation in the fluid phase proceeds in the face of both *target* and *technical* uncertainties. Target uncertainty refers to the fact that most early innovations do not enjoy an established market. Markets, in fact, tend to grow around these innovations. The emergence of an entirely new market and occupation—like typist—testifies to the power of technological innovations to create markets; discussion in Chapter 8 of George Eastman's innovation of roll film and the subsequent rise of amateur photography will help to reinforce this point. But in the early years, it is not always clear who the target market is or what product features will best serve its interests.

Technical uncertainty results from the diffused focus of research and development during the fluid phase. When the technology is in a state of flux, firms have no clear idea where to place their R&D bets. Many, in fact, concentrate on product technologies that ultimately will be ignored by the marketplace in favor of others. Custom designs and user-adapted designs are common during the fluid phase, and we see them essentially as experiments in the marketplace.

To reiterate, process innovation generally takes a back seat to product innovation in this early fluid stage. Frequent and major changes in product design and specifications impede the development of linked process innovation. The inputs in terms of materials are off the shelf; manufacturing uses general-purpose equipment and skilled labor and is conducted in small-scale plants, generally located close to the source of the technology. While this is not effi-

FIGURE 4-4. **Significant Characteristics in the Three Phases of Industrial Innovation**

	Fluid phase
Innovation	Frequent major product changes
Source of innovation	Industry pioneers; product users
Products	Diverse designs, often customized
Production processes	Flexible and inefficient, major changes easily accommodated
R&D	Focus unspecified because of high degree of technical uncertainty
Equipment	General-purpose, requiring skilled labor
Plant	Small-scale, located near user or source of innovation
Cost of process change	Low
Competitors	Few, but growing in numbers with widely fluctuating market shares
Basis of competition	Functional product performance
Organizational control	Informal and entrepreneurial
Vulnerabilities of industry leaders	To imitators, and patent challenges; to successful product breakthroughs

cient in terms of modern production standards, it does make the cost of process flexibility low; and process change is frequent at this stage owing to the rapid evolution in product technology.

Functional product performance is the basis for competition during the fluid phase. Since most producers are unknown quantities, brand names count for little. As we observed in Chapter 2, the number of competitors is small at this stage, but rises as the product technology gains a market that encourages new entrants

Transitional phase	Specific phase
Major process changes required by rising demand	Incremental for product and with cumulative improvements in productivity and quality
Manufacturers; users	Often suppliers
At least one product design, stable enough to have significant production volume	Mostly undifferentiated, standard products
Becoming more rigid, with changes occurring in major steps	Efficient, capital intensive, and rigid; cost of change high
Focus on specific product features once dominant design emerges	Focus on incremental product technologies; emphasis on process technology
Some subprocesses automated, creating islands of automation	Special-purpose, mostly automatic, with labor focused on tending and monitoring equipment
General-purpose with specialized sections	Large-scale, highly specific to particular products
Moderate	High
Many, but declining in numbers after emergence of dominant design	Few; classic oligopoly with stable market shares
Product variation; fitness for use	Price
Through project and task groups	Structure, rules, and goals
To more efficient and higher-quality producers	To technological innovations that present superior product substitutes

with different approaches to lifting technical constraints. Fluid phase firms retain their entrepreneurial character and often reflect the personalities of their founders, who are generally technical entrepreneurs.[13] Among the set of competitors are, inevitably, one or more imitators. Both Sholes and Edison—and, as we will see later Eastman—worked feverishly to acquire and protect patents to their innovations to assure their technological superiority against a field of imitators.

The Transitional Phase

If the market for a new product grows, the industry may enter what could be termed a transitional phase. Market acceptance of a product innovation and the emergence of a dominant design are its hallmarks. Competitive emphasis in this phase is on producing products for more specific users as the needs of those users become more clearly understood. The focus of firms begins to shift from the inventor's workbench to the factory floor, where the large-scale production of innovative products must be worked out.

It is in this phase that product and process innovations start to become more tightly linked. Materials become more specialized; expensive specialized equipment is brought into the manufacturing plant; islands of automation begin to appear; managerial controls are suddenly seen as important. The growing rigidity of these aspects of operations means that changes in the product can be accommodated only at increasingly greater cost.

The Specific Phase

The term "specific" rather than "mature" is used here because the manufacturing of assembled products aims over time at producing a very specific product at a high level of efficiency. Here, the value ratio of quality to cost becomes the basis of competition. Products in the specific phase become highly defined, and the differences between products of competitors are often fewer than the similarities. Even automobiles, very complex products, tend to follow very similar design and manufacturing protocols, having essentially the same aerodynamic shape, similar engines, interiors, and so forth.

The linkages between product and process are now extremely close. Any small change in either product or process is likely to be difficult and expensive and require a corresponding change in the other. Even what may seem like a small change—such as shifting production from manual to electric typewriters—is viewed as revolutionary by manufacturing, which by now has fully automated operations geared to highly efficient, low-unit-cost production of highly specified products.

Organizationally, the day of the inventor has given way in the specific phase to the tenders—that is, those who monitor and control the smooth working of the production system. This term does not refer exclusively to laborers but to managers and engineers as well, people whose jobs and skills tend to mirror those of labor and whose roles are equally altered by technological change.[14]

BREAKING OUT OF THE SPECIFIC PHASE

In terms of this model, the firm that produces in the specific phase has entered a final state from which only a radical departure in product or process can liberate it. In his landmark study of the U.S. automobile industry up to the early 1970s, William Abernathy documented the extent to which product and process innovations—over time—led that industry into a trade-off between technological innovation and production efficiency,[15] a situation in which innovation had come in a distant second. At the time Abernathy conducted his study and published his findings, complex production methods and specialized machinery had reduced the direct labor hours required to produce a car from some 4,600 hours (roughly the time required to build an average house) to less than 100.[16] This amazing progress, however, was shown to be accompanied by overwhelming standardization and uniformity among producers, prompting one auto executive to comment that the last important automotive innovation had been the automatic transmission—a feature introduced in the 1930s.

Abernathy's Productivity Dilemma

Looking at auto engine plants during a long period extending through 1973, William Abernathy made the following observations:

- An overall reduction in mechanical novelty occurred; while auto options proliferated, variety decreased.
- Major innovations were self-limiting, reducing the need for future innovations.
- While product line diversity had increased, for individual plants diversity had actually decreased.
- The tasks and skills of labor had evolved with the evolution in equipment "from craft skills to operative skills to systems-monitoring skills."

Abernathy's study of the auto industry included a focused look at the Ford Motor Company. There he found that innovation, evolution, and competitive factors had been respon-

sible for creating two different environments: an engine plant
that was so highly automated that response to change was
extremely difficult; and an assembly plant much less complete that demonstrated a course of evolution from fluid to
specific phase and was still more dependent on large
amounts of manual labor than on specific machinery because
of its annual struggle to accommodate model changes.

Thus a single industry, indeed a single company, can support productive units in distinctly different phases of industrial evolution. As Abernathy said of the Ford assembly
plant he studied and observed to move toward the specific
stage under pressure from foreign producers, "The long
period in which the stage of development remained flexible
shows that a productive unit need not progress toward either
extreme [fluid or specific] unless the overall competitive
environment requires a change."

Source: William J. Abernathy, *The Productivity Dilemma: Roadblock to
Innovation in the Automobile Industry* (Baltimore and London: The Johns
Hopkins University Press, 1978), pp. 112–113, 145.

Is the specific phase of production the "end of history" for an
industry? Is there a way to break out of this highly capitalized,
highly controlled, and generally uninnovative mode of production?
Recent innovations in flexible manufacturing by Japanese auto
manufacturers have enabled them to defy the iron rule of mass production: that long production runs of standard products and low
unit costs are necessarily bound together. As James Womack, Daniel Jones, and Daniel Roos have documented in *The Machine That
Changed The World,*[17] Japanese auto companies can retain low unit
cost while producing greater variety in smaller runs. Their unique
capability to produce small lots makes this possible. This brand of
flexible manufacturing acts as an enabler for a business strategy
based on a high level of product variety and near custom-tailoring
of products to the specification of individual customers. Joe Pine
has described this strategy in *Mass Customization: The Next Frontier of Business Competition.*[18] The strategy of mass customization
uses both flexible manufacturing and the creation of unique products from standard platforms to satisfy customer requirements
more fully. Among the examples of firms already following this
strategy, Pine cites National Bicycle Company of Japan, which has

made it possible for a customer to order a bicycle with any of over 11 million configurations of model, color, frame size, and components, and receive it at the local bike shop within ten days.

Flexible manufacturing and the strategy of mass customization seem to offer an escape hatch from the innovative dead end of the specific phase. Just as the quality revolution has exploded the idea that quality and low cost are mutually exclusive characteristics that must be traded off, these new notions seem to break the mutually exclusive ends of product variety and low production costs. However, flexible manufacturing and mass customization may also be a trap resulting in products with little commercial potential and in unwanted product variety. For example, Abernathy and Clark have shown this may be true for highly specialized auto engines, and White has shown that it may be true more generally.[19]

THE NEXT WAVE OF INNOVATION

Most technology-based innovations are in fact part of a continuum of change. We have already seen how the typing of documents has gone through waves of innovation; the same happened in lighting and will be found to have happened in many other industries. How, then, does this model accommodate these waves of innovation?

Experience with a number of industries supports the notion that each wave of innovation repeats the pattern of interlinking product and process innovation and the importance of dominant design on the number of firms that the industry can support at one time. Each new wave of innovation has its fluid, transitional, and specific phases; each sees the rate of product innovation peak more or less early and experiences a surge of process innovation even as product innovation declines; each is characterized by a peak in the number of competing firms sometime around the emergence of the dominant design, with a decline thereafter.

Figure 4-5 illustrates these familiar patterns, but adds something new. In the top two quadrants are the product and process innovation curves for two waves of innovation at the level of the firm. In both cases the rate of product innovation reaches a high point very early. The dominant design appears around this time. The rate of process innovation continues to increase, but it too declines as the innovation and the firm enter the specific phase.

FIGURE 4–5. **Model Extended to the Next Wave of Innovation**

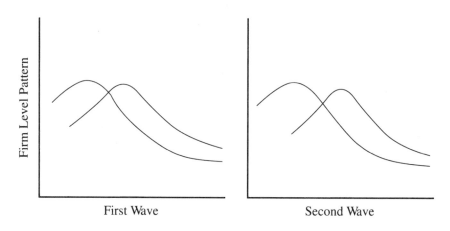

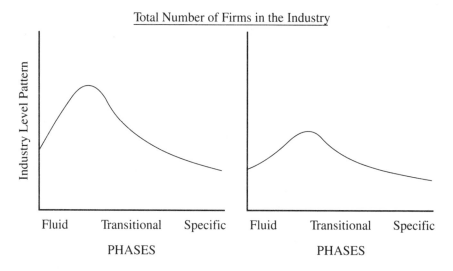

The lower quadrants relate the innovative activities of firms to the number of firms participating. In both cases, the number of firms reaches a zenith around the time that the dominant design first appears and drops rapidly thereafter. What is worth noting here is the overall lower number of firms participating in the second wave of innovation. Thus, while there might be many firms making incandescent lamps (the first wave in electric lighting), there would be fewer trying to break into the fluorescent lamp business (the second wave).

We could speculate that this pattern would repeat itself in any subsequent wave of lighting technology. It should be mentioned that this point is intuitive and not based on empirical findings. Still, the pattern rings true with experience: we know that there were many more manual typewriter makers than there were electric typewriter firms; there were many more incandescent lamp firms than there were fluorescent lamp makers; more competitors were in the dry-emulsion photographic plate business than were in the succeeding celluloid roll-film industry (treated in Chapter 8). When and if automobiles powered by noninternal combustion engines take the roads in larger numbers, we would expect that far fewer than the hundred firms that emerged in the United States during the first auto age will vie for dominance in the new industry.

The reason for this drop-off in the number of competing firms in later waves is no doubt related to the fact that markets are often well defined by the first wave of innovation, and established firms develop the distribution channels and production facilities to serve these markets, limiting the number of possible firms that can reform the industry—even with a superior technology.

This hypothesis does not hold up when the new wave of innovation substantially broadens or alters the market. The innovation of computer-based typing, for example, so altered the way this mundane task was accomplished that barriers to new firms tumbled, and dozens of computer and software firms entered the industry. These last points will be treated in greater detail in Chapter 9, though they are speculative and need a good deal more research.

Notes

1. J.S. Frischmuth and T.J. Allen, "A Model for the Description of Technical Problem Solving," *IEEE Transactions on Engineering Management,* May 1969, pp. 79–86.
2. See T. Burns and G.M. Stalker, *The Management of Innovation* (London: Tavistock, 1961).
3. For an excellent discussion of the background, personality, and motivation of the entrepreneur, see Edward B. Roberts, *Entrepreneurs in High Technology* (New York: Oxford University Press, 1991), in particular pp. 251–259.
4. Burton H. Klein, *Dynamic Economics* (Cambridge, Mass.: Harvard University Press, 1977), pp. 100–101.
5. Ibid., p. 108.
6. See for example, Eric von Hippel, *The Sources of Innovation* (Oxford: Oxford University Press, 1988).
7. Klein, *Dynamic Economics,* p. 108.

8. See Almarin Phillips, *Technology and Market Structure: A Study of the Aircraft Industry* (Lexington, Mass.: Lexington Books, 1971).

9. D.C. Mueller and J.E. Tilton, "R&D Cost as a Barrier to Entry," *Canadian Journal of Economics,* vol. 2 (November 1969), p. 576.

10. Ibid.

11. Reese V. Jenkins, *Images & Enterprise: Technology and the American Photographic Industry, 1839–1925* (Baltimore & London: The Johns Hopkins University Press, 1975).

12. E.P. Staples, N.R. Baker, and D.J. Sweeney, "Market Structure and Technological Innovation: A Step Towards a Unifying Theory," Final Technical Report," NSF Grant RDA 75-17332, November 1977, p. 12.

13. Edward B. Roberts, *Entrepreneurs in High Technology* (Oxford: Oxford University Press, 1991).

14. See James R. Bright, *Automation and Management* (Boston, Mass.: Division of Research, Harvard Business School, 1958) for a thorough discussion of this generally overlooked relationship.

15. William J. Abernathy, *The Productivity Dilemma: Roadblock to Innovation in the Automobile Industry* (Baltimore and London: The Johns Hopkins University Press, 1978), p. 112.

16. By 1990, this had shrunk to 20 hours per vehicle in the leading plants, or even less in a few instances. See James P. Womack, Daniel Jones, and Daniel Roos, *The Machine That Changed the World* (New York: Rawson Associates, 1990).

17. Ibid.

18. B. Joseph Pine II, *Mass Customization: The Next Frontier of Business Competition* (Boston: Harvard Business School Press, 1993).

19. William J. Abernathy and Kim B. Clark, "Mapping the Winds of Creative Destruction," *Research Policy,* vol. 14, no. 1 (January 1985), pp. 3–22; and M. Abdelkader Dagfous and George R. White, "Information and Innovation," *Research Policy* (forthcoming).

CHAPTER 5

Innovation in Nonassembled Products

M OST OF US THINK OF "products" as assembled goods of many parts: televisions, washing machines, food processors, automobiles, Maine hunting boots, and so forth. This is only natural, as the most obvious items around us tend to be assembled goods, and this class of product gets the lion's share of public attention. In the office workplace the eye is naturally drawn to products like computers, desks, file cabinets, felt-tipped pens, telephones, and so forth. It looks right past the carpeting and floor tile, the paint on the walls, and the steel in the desk drawer. Like the glass panes in the windows, these are nonassembled products and their presence is just as transparent to us. An engineer working for a paint manufacturer would not see the world this way; neither would a petroleum refiner, a textile executive, nor a glass manufacturer. Theirs are nonassembled products composed of only one or a few materials—and these are as important to our economy and modern way of life as assembled goods.

The concept of dominant design discussed in Chapter 2 and the model of product and process innovation outlined in Chapter 4 were derived from studies of assembled products. William Abernathy, who so greatly contributed to both, did much of his research in the auto industry. The question arises as to whether the idea of dominant design and the interrelationship between product and process innovation shown in the model apply also to nonassembled products such as petrochemicals, copper wire, synthetic fibers, and the thousands of other homogeneous products. Abernathy himself expressed his doubts when he wrote the following:

> The model applies most directly to a productive unit in which multiple inputs are combined and transformed through a complex production process that yields a highly valued product whose characteristics may be varied. . . . In cases where the product or productive unit is definitionally standardized (for example, sulfuric acid, nylon, or copper), the prospect of radical product innovation is definitionally limited, if not practically impossible.[1]

This chapter and the next, however, will show that the model does in fact apply, if in a slightly altered form.

Further, do the processes that manufacture these products pass through fluid, transitional, and specific states? Before addressing these issues, it would be useful to consider an extended example of one nonassembled product—plate glass—and the process innovations that have made it inexpensive and ubiquitous in our society. Like rayon, steel, gasoline, and any of numerous other nonassembled products, glass illustrates many important issues that bear on the model and on our understanding of industrial innovation.

EVOLUTION OF AN INDUSTRY

As a simple product made from the melting of sand (silica), lime (calcium oxide), and soda (sodium oxide), glass was probably discovered in the remains of fires; the secrets of its making were undoubtedly deduced. Molten glass being malleable, creative people learned to shape it into artistic forms, and to color it through the introduction of common minerals.

Glass has been a part of civilization for an estimated 3,000 years. The ancient Syrians are thought to have been the first masters of glassmaking, and from them the art spread to the Egyptians, Phoenicians, and others. Artisans in fourth-century Alexandria and elsewhere in the Roman world developed the art of creating colored and mosaic decorative glassware; they even pioneered methods of casting and pressing glass into flat sheets. Like that of all useful crafts, knowledge of glassmaking was spread by traveling artisans and trade contacts. In England, for example, there is evidence that the small forest glassworks in the Surrey and Sussex Wealden areas were medieval enterprises started by French immigrants.[2] In British America, the Virginia Company of London sent six Dutchmen to Yorktown in 1608 to instruct its colonists in the art of making glass. (Like the Dutch glassmen, my ancestors were part of a group of German artisans who came to America to start an ironworks in what is now Germantown, Virginia.) In 1639, the town of Salem, Massachusetts "granted to the glassemen severall acres of ground adjoyning to their howses" and the sum of 30 pounds for the purpose of building a glassworks.

The modern glass industry is divided into two major segments, flat glass and blown glass, and our concern in this chapter is with the former. Until the 1880s, the flat glass industry was made up of small producers employing highly skilled artisans. Almost all of the technological innovations were made in England, France, and Germany. Because of the need for high and sustained levels of heat, glass manufacturing has always been concentrated near adequate fuel sources: first forests, then coal fields, and after the late 1800s, near sources of natural gas.

The first flat glass was made through the crown-glass method— an entirely by-hand operation. With the end of a metal rod, the glassmaker pulled a clump of molten glass out of the furnace pot. The rod was then spun rapidly so that centrifugal force shaped the still-molten glass into a large flat disk. Panes were cut from the outer surface of this disk (see Figure 5-1), and the maximum dimensions of a piece were 34" × 22." The center of the disk, with part of the original clump remaining, was more translucent than transparent and of very little value; it became the "bull's-eye" glass that is seen today over the doorways of seventeenth- and eighteenth-century homes in the eastern United States.

Crown glass was replaced with sheets of flat glass produced by blowing molten glass into the shape of a long cylinder. The glassmaker cut off both rounded ends, slit the cylinder down its length, and, using tongs, folded it open to become a flat piece. Cylinder glass represented an enormous advance both in productivity and quality, though the glass remained wavy and had many imperfections. This method became even more efficient and less costly in 1903, when the American Window Glass Company developed a cylinder-blowing machine that eliminated the need for many highly skilled workers.[3]

Other methods of producing sheet glass eventually replaced the cylinder method, each improving efficiency and product uniformity and reducing cost. The last was made possible by the Col-

FIGURE 5–1. **Window Panes Cut from a Disk of Crown Glass**

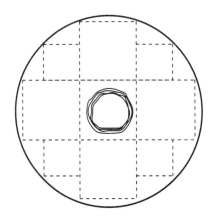

burn sheet-drawing machine, which appeared in 1917. This pulled a continuous sheet of glass, still in a taffy-like state, out of the furnace pot and sent it on its way to the annealing and cutting steps. Incremental improvements made to this method over the next five decades continued to lower unit costs and further reduce the need for skilled labor. Capital costs and constraints on product variation increased proportionately. Flat glass made by any of these more modern methods was by nature thin and troubled by distortions.

A great deal more could be written here about these methods of making sheet glass, but our purpose of understanding the innovation process in nonassembled products is better served by focusing on another, and now dominant, form of flat glass—plate glass—and the evolution of process technologies that supported its large-scale production.

PLATE GLASSMAKING

Plate glass has different product characteristics than do crown and sheet glass. Traditionally it has been thicker and stronger, made in larger dimensions, its surfaces ground and polished, and it has been produced by different methods.

Louis XIV, France's "Sun King," dazzled all of Europe with his military strength, the opulence of his court, and the remarkable palace he built for himself and his successors at Versailles. Versailles was the great showcase of Louis' reign, and a marvel of architecture and the decorative arts as well. One of the palace's novel interior features was the use of very large pieces of plate glass in the *Galerie des Glaces* (Hall of Mirrors). Never before had single pieces of glass of such large dimensions and in such quantities been produced. Louis' mirrors were manufactured by the mixing, melting, casting, annealing, grinding, and polishing represented in Figure 5-2. This is how plate glass was first manufactured in the late 1600s, and it remained a sequence of discrete steps for some time.

In this process, sand, lime, soda, and cullet (bits of old broken glass) were mixed together in a clay pot. The pot was then placed in a wood-fired (later coal-fired) furnace of 1,200°–1,500° centigrade, at which temperature the ingredients would liquefy. A scum of dirt, air bubbles, and impurities accumulated on the surface and was skimmed off. This done, the molten glass was poured onto large table molds with raised edges. Workers with heavy copper rollers smoothed the glass to a uniform thickness, and the molds were carted off to a beehive annealing oven where they remained for several days.

The annealing step was necessary if the finished plates were to have the strength to withstand the grinding and polishing that followed. In detail, all materials are nonuniform, and molten glass is no exception. In its casting, different thicknesses and different rates of cooling produced strains in the glass, which made the plate weak at particular points and easily shattered. Holding the glass in an annealing oven at high temperatures, and reducing its temperature very gradually, allowed these strains to dissipate. The finished product was a thick plate of glass with perfectly flat surfaces that could be used for windows or made into mirrors to reflect the glory of Europe's most extravagant nobleman.[4]

Early production processes were flexible but inefficient. All glassmaking until about 1880 relied heavily on skilled labor in all phases of production, and glass artisans were among the highest-paid workers. Warren Scoville, who wrote the definitive history of

FIGURE 5–2. **The Original Plate Glass Process**

MIX => MELT => CAST => ANNEAL => GRIND => POLISH

glassmaking in America,[5] estimates that glass workers in the late 1800s earned up to one-third more than did craftspeople in other industries. Wages, in fact, accounted for about 40 percent of the value of all glass produced at that time.[6] It was a classic seller's market for skilled glassmakers and American producers recruited them from the glass houses of England and the Continent, offering wage premiums and free passage to obtain their services. Plate glassmaking was even more reliant on artisans, and employed roughly three times as much labor per unit of output than did blown and cylinder glass. In 1879, records indicate that American plate glass was also six times more capital-intensive.[7]

Each phase of the production process was discontinuous; that is, each step was performed separately, glass being moved from one step to another with some element of delay and nonproductive physical handling in between. Special-purpose equipment played a minor role. It was a classic example of what was defined in Chapter 4 as the fluid phase. Between the making of the *Galerie des Glaces* and the building of modern, glass-clad skyscrapers, the entire history of plate glassmaking can be viewed as an evolution toward highly specific production in which all manufacturing steps are united into a continuum, equipment is expensive and made to order, and the use of craft labor is virtually eliminated. That evolution took place between the 1800s and the present and provides a useful analogy to the more general experience of nonassembled products.

The evolution in plate glassmaking followed five steps.

Step 1. Continuous Mixing and Melting

Dramatic improvements to the difficult front end of flat glass manufacturing were made by the Siemens brothers of Germany. In 1861, the first gas-fired Siemens furnace was installed in an English sheet glass factory.[8] The Siemens furnace preheated gas and air before they entered the fire chamber. Athough it was designed as a way to improve thermal efficiency, the fact that the new furnace used gas instead of solid fuel was its real virtue. The cleaner-burning fuel eliminated the smoke and ash that wood and coal furnaces allowed to contaminate the melting pot and gave glassmakers far greater control over furnaces.

By 1880, Siemens furnaces were equipped with an even more important innovation, continuous melting tanks (or tank furnaces), which represented a true integration of process steps. This innovation allowed workers to add ingredients to one end of the melting tank even as molten glass was taken out of the other end for casting. This was a tremendous productivity advance over the traditional method of mixing and melting at night in "day tanks" so that glass could be poured and worked during the day.

As Figure 5-3 illustrates, the new tank furnace had a baffle dividing it into two chambers. Ingredients were poured into the melted glass on one side of the baffle. Impurities and debris floated to the top of that side. Clear molten glass was drawn off on the other side, and as it was, pure molten glass passed under the baffle to replace it.

While the old process required two distinct steps—mixing and melting—here they were combined. Better still, the fact that molten glass could continuously be drawn off for casting eliminated the traditional waiting for that part of the cycle to be repeated. It was a major process improvement: quality improved; capacity increased to twice the level of that allowed by furnace pots; efficiency increased dramatically; and fewer and less-skilled workers were required to tend and charge the furnace. As Table 5-1 makes clear, continuous tank furnaces proliferated in the United States during the first four decades following their introduction, rapidly replacing the old pot furnaces.

This progress, however, carried a price tag. The continuous tank was much more costly than pots, thus requiring higher capital investment. Only continuous production could recoup these higher

FIGURE 5–3. **The Siemens Tank Furnace**

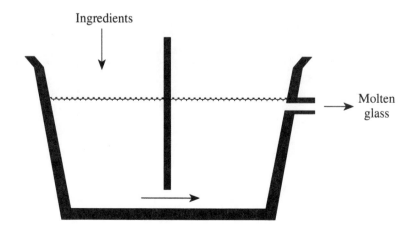

TABLE 5–1. **Number of Melting Furnaces in All U.S. Glassworks, 1879–1919**

	1879	1899	1904	1909	1914	1919
Pot furnaces	280	391	349	370	328	289
Tank furnaces	1	192	340	369	454	598

Source: Warren C. Scoville, *Revolution in Glassmaking* (Cambridge, Mass.: Harvard University Press, 1948), p. 77.

capital costs, and this in turn reduced production flexibility. Changes in color or composition, for example, greatly disrupted operations.

Step 2. Continuous Annealing

Plate glass continued to be cast onto metal tables, held in an annealing kiln for days, and then ground and polished. In this respect, not much had changed in the two centuries since the making of Louis XIV's mirrors. In the 1880s, the idea of using a tunnel annealing kiln, or "lehr," was introduced. As plate was cast onto tables, the tables were hooked together to form a train and rolled through a long tunnel in which the temperature was kept high at the front end, and gradually reduced on the far end. The tunnel kiln converted annealing from a batch process to a continuous subprocess. Better still, it did the job much more quickly: traditional annealing ovens typically took days, whereas tunnel kilns kept at constant, staged temperatures completed the annealing process in a matter of hours. A brief comparison of the steps required in each of the two processes shows why:

	Annealing Oven Steps	Tunnel Kiln Steps
Stack trays of cast glass in oven	x	
Seal the oven	x	
Heat the oven	x	
Anneal the glass	x	x
Allow oven to cool down to the point that workers can enter	x	
Unseal the oven	x	
Remove trays of glass	x	

Only one of the seven steps in the use of the traditional annealing oven added any value to the glass. The tunnel kiln allowed glassmakers to skip every one of the unproductive steps.

Step 3. Continuous Casting

The production of plate glass now had two islands of automation—mixing/melting and annealing—with hand casting in between and a grinding and polishing operation at the end. These remained bottlenecks to the production process until the 1920s. The key eliminating one of these impediments eventually came not from the world of glassmakers but from the young and growing automobile industry.

The first innovation in plate casting was the Bicheroux process, which combined casting and rolling to cut production time and produce more uniform thickness. Molten glass was cast between two rollers, resulting in flatter, more uniform plates that required less grinding.[9] It is suspected that this technique had been tried by English glassmakers without success as early as 1849, prompting a Massachusetts glass man to remark that "I believe it to be an impossibility to make sheets by passing the smelted glass between two rollers, and anyone practically acquainted with the manufacture of glass would, I have no doubt, agree with me."[10] Fortunately, the innovators of the Bicheroux process either failed to hear this remark or failed to heed it.

The second innovation came in 1922, when the Ford Motor Company—by then the world's largest user of plate glass—sought to ensure itself a large supply of high-quality glass for the newly fashionable enclosed automobile.[11] Lack of experience in operating a continuous tank caused problems that Pilkington Brothers, an established U.K. glass firm, helped Ford solve. The Ford/Pilkington process provided casting of a continuous ribbon of plate glass through rollers onto a conveyor that passed through the tunnel kiln. This linked together two formerly separate islands of automation (casting and annealing). The entire process from mixing, melting, casting, and annealing was now continuous. Tangible evidence of just how much more productive plate glassmaking had become is provided by Pearce Davis, whose history of the industry indicates how a sheet of polished plate glass that took ten days to produce in 1889 could be produced in just three days in 1923.[12] Only grinding and polishing remained as a discontinuous step in the production process, and this defect was partly remedied when Pilkington developed machinery that could grind and polish both sides of a continuous glass ribbon simultaneously.

Step 4. The Float Process

For decades, the Pilkington company made plate glass by the Ford/ Pilkington method, introducing process innovations on an incremental basis; the foremost of these was the development of continuous grinding and polishing. In 1952, however, Alastair Pilkington inspired a course of research and development that would lead the company to a revolutionary new method. The float process, as it was called, allowed molten glass from the furnace to form on the perfectly flat surface of molten tin—a substance that, being more dense, would support glass yet be nonreactive with it.[13]

It took the Pilkington company millions of pounds, five years, and some 100,000 tons of scrapped glass to develop the float process and build a pilot plant to make it work. (Fortunately, glassmaking feeds on its own scrap). Another 14 months of operations were required before any salable glass could be produced. In the new process a continuous ribbon of molten glass was carefully drawn from the furnace tank onto a long pool of melted tin. The pool was enclosed in a controlled-atmosphere chamber of nitrogen and a small amount of hydrogen to prevent oxidation of the tin. Heat applied from above the glass ribbon as it entered the tin pool kept it in a melted state to ensure its perfectly smooth and parallel surfaces. As the ribbon progressed through the tin bath chamber, the temperature was progressively dropped, allowing the glass to cool and solidify while still in contact with nothing but the liquid metal. After passing across the tin bath, the glass was conveyed on rollers through the annealing tunnel. Since the surface of the tin was perfectly smooth, the annealed plate needed no grinding or polishing—in fact, the surfaces of this plate glass were smoother than anything grinding and polishing had ever achieved. The resulting product was what plate glassmakers had been working toward for centuries: lustrously smooth glass of uniform thickness straight from the oven.

Besides improved product quality, the new process produced a remarkable set of production efficiencies:

- Elimination of the need to grind and polish reduced the length of the production line by more than half (to 640 feet).
- Grinding and polishing had reduced the volume of finished

glass by 15 to 25 percent, required tons of costly abrasives, and produced process wastes that had to be removed at considerable expense. All of this was eliminated.

- Labor costs were reduced by 80 percent and energy by 50 percent.[14] Capital costs were similarly reduced.

Large panels of plate glass for windows, mirrors, display cases, and other applications were now affordable to commoners as well as princes.

Figure 5-4 is a representation of the float glass process. It shows schematically how molten glass from the tank furnace poured onto the tin bath, proceeded down its length (gradually cooling), and was then carried by rollers through the annealing tunnel from which it emerged ready to be cut and stacked.

The Pilkington float glass plant linked together all the islands of automation into one continuous process, and in so doing took the last big step in turning plate glassmaking from a labor-intensive craft into a highly efficient and automated industry.[15] After the first few years the problems in the process were ironed out and float glassmaking became remarkably trouble free. Sir Alastair Pilkington reported running a plant for 24 months without a major stop.[16] As the company said of its own innovation: "The revolution in glassmaking by this process enabled glassmakers to concentrate more on the properties of glass, and on cutting, shaping, strengthening and installing glass, and less on the process of manufacture."[17]

Float glass operations are much more capital intensive than other forms of flat glassmaking, but their efficiencies are such that

FIGURE 5–4.   **The Float Glass Process**

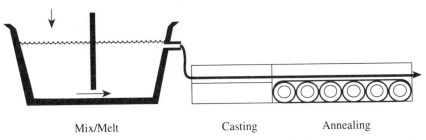

Mix/Melt   Casting   Annealing

Note: Not to scale. Each element of this process is very long. The furnace tank is typically about 80 meters, and the annealing kiln about 400 meters.

they have driven out other forms of production and now account for more than 90 percent of the plate and sheet glass manufactured. Only in developing countries where capital is scarce and markets limited do older technologies still survive.[18]

Innovative Competition within Pilkington Brothers Ltd.

Three decades before its breakthrough with the float glass technology, the Pilkington company recognized that the grind/polish operation posed a serious bottleneck in an otherwise continuous manufacturing process. In 1923, it introduced a grinding and polishing machine that moved cut plates of glass on tables past machines that finished their surfaces, one side at a time.

The next logical step was to finish both sides at once. What Pilkington engineers came up with was the "twin grinder," a series of round, flat, rotating steel tables, or disks, between which the continuously cast glass ribbon would pass. A solution of water and abrasives was injected between the spinning disks and the glass. The coarseness of the abrasives decreased gradually from the first disks to the last, so that the very last disks were polishing out the fine scratches left by the grinding process.

This new high-speed process was expensive to develop and difficult to operate. The slightest misalignment of only one of the disks would shatter the glass and cause a production stoppage. Nevertheless, Pilkington put its first twin grinder into service at its Doncaster works in 1935, and this gave the firm world technological leadership in large-scale plate manufacturing. Glass wastage and high capital and operating costs were the twin grinder's major weaknesses.[1]

The development of the float glass process in the 1950s and 1960s was an obvious technological threat to the twin grinder and to the "barons" of that part of the plate-making operation, even those working for Pilkington. As we will observe in a later chapter devoted to this phenomenon, the appearance of a new technology—a radical innovation—often stimulates those who manage the old and threatened technology to perfect their assets and methods through a number of incremental improvements. Faced with the development of float glass, the Pilkington staff responsible for the grind/polish process was successful in improving it to the point of tripling its productivity through a series of incremental process improvements.

In the end, grinding and polishing, no matter how improved, could not match the float glass process and was totally eliminated from plate glassmaking. But like many other technologies, it went out with a bang, not with a whimper.

Note

1. Sir Alastair Pilkington, "The Float Glass Process," Proceedings, Royal Society of London, 1969. A. 314, 1–25, p. 11.

FIGURE 5–5. **Evolution of Plate Glassmaking Processes**

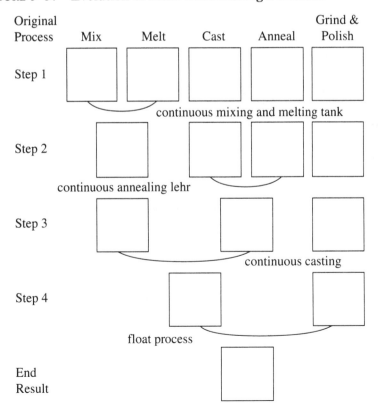

While innovations in this industry will surely appear in the years ahead, the course of process innovation has brought the business of glassmaking to a highly specific state, one in which all the important production steps have been automated and linked together into a continuous system. Figure 5-5 summarizes this evolution.[19]

DISCONTINUOUS CHANGE IN PROCESS ARCHITECTURE

Each of the several production methods for making plate glass, from those of the seventeenth-century workshops at Versailles to those of the latest float glass factory, involved a combination or elimination of earlier steps, each resulting in dramatic productivity gains and lower unit costs. Each combination represents, in effect, a change in process architecture. The same can be said of instances in which a new process technology is being used—as in the change from crown glass to cylinder glassmaking. New process architecture represents a discontinuous productivity advance—in the first case because of the entire elimination of a process step; in the second case because the new production technology is inherently more efficient.

Since each new process architecture results in lower unit costs, the relationship between time, unit cost, and process architectures looks like a downward staircase, each step representing a change in process architecture. Mixing and melting of glass ingredients is combined into one step and unit costs drop; time passes before continuous annealing is introduced, but when it is, costs drop again; and so it goes for continuous casting and for float glass.

Although changes in process architecture are usually few and far between, progress toward improved productivity is not frozen between their occurrences; in reality, major discontinuous changes are usually followed by a number of small, incremental improvements (represented in Figure 5-6). Thus we see a major drop in unit costs caused by process architecture change followed by a number of small drops resulting from incremental improvements. The sum of the two equals the long-term productivity gain.

Other scholars have commented on this pattern of change. Joseph Schumpeter noted the periodic occurrence of industrial innovations that "command a decisive cost or quality advantage and that strike not at the margins of the profits and the outputs of

FIGURE 5–6. **Long-term Productivity Gains**

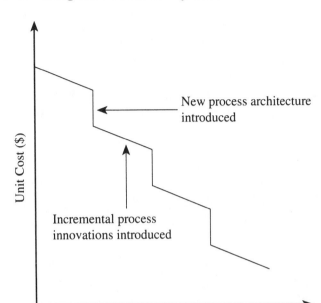

the existing firms, but at their foundations and their very lives."[20] Philip Anderson and Michael Tushman describe a "technological cycle" in which a technological discontinuity is followed by an era of ferment from which a dominant design emerges; this is followed by an era of incremental change during which the dominant design is elaborated.[21] In discussing nonassembled products such as glass, we might easily substitute the term "enabling technology" for dominant design.[22] Here the process of making crown glass, the Ford/Pilkington method of continuous casting, and the float glass process were all enabling technologies that appeared in a rush and were refined incrementally in ensuing years.

When compared to process improvements in the production of complex assembled products (automobiles and television sets, for example), process innovations such as the Siemens furnace tank, the tunnel kiln, and the float process have a more profound impact on productivity and costs. The latter represent truly fundamental improvements, whereas the former are essentially incremental. We do not see single process changes that cut the assembly cost of automobiles in half, for instance; even if we did, the cost of the final product would not dramatically decrease due to the high cost of plant, product development, and component parts. Both fixed and variable costs would remain high.

The essential difference in the productivity gains from process innovations may, in the final analysis, come down to the fact that complex assembled products have many more process steps than do nonassembled products. William Abernathy found, for example, that the production process for an automobile engine (just the engine!) had 130 steps: drill, turn, drill, grind, attach component, transfer to next station, and so forth. The combination of two or three of these steps into one has only a limited effect; the engine maker still faces 128 or 129 steps. Advances in the field of "design for manufacturability" have led to important step reductions, particularly in the automobile industry. The original Ford Taurus (1986), for example, was the first American automobile design in recent memory to be scrutinized in detail with an eye toward assembly process shortcuts. Before the car went into production, Ford engineers and assembly crews found hundreds of ways to reduce production steps: the number of side and door panels was reduced from nine to two; unnecessary bolts were designed out; screw sizes were made uniform so that crews would not have to change torquing heads; the number of component parts was reduced.[23] While the number of assembly process steps for the Taurus was a great improvement over competing U.S. models, and Ford's assembly costs were substantially better, even these Herculean efforts did not result in an order-of-magnitude change in total unit costs. The most archaic plate glassmaking process, by contrast, had only basic five production steps. And combining these steps has resulted in order-of-magnitude efficiencies.

THE HIGH COST OF INTRODUCING PROCESS INNOVATIONS

It should not be construed that these giant leaps in productivity are obtained without cost or risk. Technological discontinuities produce abrupt improvements but often involve tremendous investments in research and new plant and equipment. Sir Alastair Pilkington once remarked that had he and his directors known the full extent of the cost of developing float glass technology, they might never have tried it. Despite its immediate success once the process was humming, the company invested royally, and would not break even on cash flows for 12 years. According to the British glassmaker: "If you went to an accountant and said, 'I've got a great idea to create a massive negative cash flow for certain, and it may—if it's a great success—break even in its cash flows in 12 years,' you wouldn't find many accountants who'd say 'that's exactly what I want.' "[24]

Pilkington had, in effect, bet the company on the float glass process. It was a private firm at the time, with wealthy owners who did not need to concern themselves with annual cash dividends or the ups and downs of their stock price. Today it is a public firm, and during a speech to an audience at MIT, former chief scientist Dennis Oliver remarked that under the constraints of public ownership, no such gamble would have been taken.

SUMMARY

Richard Nelson has suggested that to describe and understand the complexities of the innovation process, one should attempt to define a number of internally consistent categories of technologies and industries.[25] His guess is that five to eight categories would be the minimum number required. In defining just two extreme groups we have certainly ridden roughshod over many subtle distinctions and differences; yet this still seems a useful beginning in terms of both the similarities and the differences suggested between analysis of the flat glass case and the case of assembled products presented earlier.[26]

Michael Porter has drawn a similar conclusion in his explorations of a research agenda for understanding the determinants of the international success or failure of firms. Taking the industry as his unit of analysis, Porter divides these into factor-driven industries, roughly analogous to the present nonassembled category, and knowledge- and skill-intensive industries, roughly analogous to our assembled products category. Porter concludes that in the case of factor-driven industries: "basic factors determine success: the firm must optimize within constraints; and success shifts with factor shifts." For the case of knowledge- and skill-intensive industries: "exogenous change is significant and ongoing; ability to shift constraints is high; important factors are created or attracted; and the firm's ability to deploy factors is paramount."[27]

This work is congruent with Porter's ideas about the sources of change, and we will see that enabling process innovations such as float glass seem to be more likely to emerge from within an industry than do radical product changes such as the electric typewriter, word processor or personal computer, or fluorescent lighting, which tend to come from new entrants or other marginal "outsiders." In the following three chapters we will look at other aspects and cases of innovation in nonassembled products to try to extend and enrich the insights afforded by the flat glass case. Let us begin by taking a broader cut at other studies of innovation in nonassembled products in Chapter 6.

Notes

1. William J. Abernathy, *The Productivity Dilemma: Roadblocks to Innovation in the Automobile Industry* (Baltimore and London: Johns Hopkins University Press, 1978), pp. 83–84.
2. For discussion of glassmaking methods in thirteenth- to seventeenth-century England, see G.H. Kenyon, *The Glass Industry of the Weald* (Leicester, England: Leicester University Press, 1967).
3. Warren C. Scoville, *Revolution in Glassmaking: Entrepreneurship and Technological Change in the American Industry, 1880–1920* (Cambridge, Mass.: Harvard University Press, 1948), pp. 116–117.
4. Unlike the contemporary product, plate glass that required grinding and polishing was slightly clouded by the tiny pits and scratches caused by that process. By contrast, window glass produced by the blown cylinder process was much clearer but somewhat wavy.
5. Scoville's work was prepared under the direction of the Committee on Research in Economic History, Social Science Research in Economic History, Social Science Research Council, in collaboration with the Committee on Technological Change at MIT.
6. Scoville, *Revolution in Glassmaking*, pp. 31–32.
7. Ibid., p. 12.
8. Ibid., p. 24.
9. Pearce Davis, *The Development of the American Glass Industry* (Cambridge, Mass.: Harvard University Press, 1948), p. 158.
10. George F. Neale of Lenox Rough Plate Glass Company, as quoted in Scoville, *Revolution in Glassmaking*, p. 168.
11. Auto glass at that time had to conform to closer thickness tolerances to prevent rattles. Later, shatterproof, tinted, and reflective glasses would be needed in enormous quantities.
12. Davis, *The Development of the American Glass Industry*, p. 254.
13. The discovery of the float glass process was apparently quite accidental. Alastair Pilkington had been working on a problem with the firm's traditional method of melt, cast, anneal, grind, and polish. It was observed that whenever the temperature within the plant dropped by even a few degrees because of an open door or some other simple change, irregularities occurred in the

casting. To eliminate temperature fluctuations in the short space where the molten glass poured from the furnace and entered the annealing kiln, Pilkington introduced an open vat of molten tin. Sitting under the space between furnace and kiln, its thermal mass would keep the air temperature constant.

One day, a malfunction in the take-up mechanism that pulled the glass into the kiln caused the molten glass, still pouring from the furnace, to drop directly onto the liquified tin. The line was shut down and the mess was cleaned up. It was then that someone noticed the flawless surface of the scrap glass that had been in contact with the molten tin. This inspired Alastair Pilkington to experiment further with the process.

14. Presentation at MIT by Dr. Dennis Oliver, then chief scientist and a director of Pilkington.

15. Pilkington ACI Limited, *Ribbons of Glass* (Sydney, Australia, 1989), pp. 6 and 31.

16. Sir Alastair Pilkington, "The Float Glass Process," Proceedings, Royal Society of London, 1969. A. 314, 1–25, pp. 6–8, and personal conversation with the author.

17. Pilkington ACI Limited, *Ribbons of Glass,* p. 31.

18. The last, largest, and most modern plant ever built to manufacture plate glass by the traditional method never even opened its doors. Built by Saint-Gobain-Pont-a-Mousson, the continental glass giant, the plant was rendered obsolete by the Pilkington float glass method before it went into production.

19. I am grateful to Teresa C. Nolet for her work in researching the flat glass case and in suggesting the analysis in Figure 5-5. See James M. Utterback and Teresa C. Nolet, "Product and Process Change in Non-Assembled Product Industries," (Cambridge, Mass.: MIT Center for Policy Alternatives working paper 78-12, September 18, 1978).

20. Joseph Schumpeter, *Capitalism, Socialism, and Democracy* (New York: Harper & Brothers, 1942), p. 84.

21. Philip Anderson and Michael L. Tushman, "Technological Discontinuities and Dominant Designs: A Cyclical Model of Technological Change," *Administrative Science Quarterly,* 35 (1990), p. 606.

22. I am grateful to Teresa C. Nolet for suggesting this idea.

23. Eric Taub, *Taurus: The Making of the Car that Saved Ford* (New York: E.P. Dutton, 1991), p. 205.

24. Sir Alastair Pilkington, interviewed by James Brian Quinn, "Pilkington Brothers, Ltd.," Case Study B.P. 78–0148, The Amos Tuck School of Business Administration, Dartmouth College, 1978.

25. Comments on my presentation, "Innovation, Competition and Industry Structure," Sloan Foundation Seminar on Competitiveness, Harvard Business School, October 17, 1991.

26. Adam Smith implied that technologies were of two different types with different effects for industry structure and the division of labor. In the case of the pin factory, sequential operations prevailed—forming of wire, cutting to length, shaping the bead and point—and were best carried out under one roof. In the watch factory, parallel operations prevailed—making various gears, springs and fasteners, pieces of the case, hands, and so on—necessarily coming together only in final assembly. Parallel operations suggest a very different

industry structure, leading to constant shifts in networks of supplies and assemblers and a wider variety of finished watches. This still seems like a simple and sensible starting point in defining a set of categories. Adam Smith, *An Inquiry into the Nature and Causes of the Wealth of Nations* (New York: Modern Library, 1937). Originally published in 1776.

27. Comments at a Strategic Management Society conference on *Fundamental Issues in Strategy,* Napa, California, November 1990.

CHAPTER 6

Differences in Innovations for Assembled and Nonassembled Products

THUS FAR WE HAVE considered innovation for assembled products and, in Chapter 4, developed a model to think about its patterns. Chapter 5 described innovation in nonassembled (homogeneous) products, using the plate glass industry as an example. This chapter will show how patterns of innovation are similar and how they differ for these two product classes.

It would be useful if we could classify products and technologies into sensible groups, between which patterns and details could be observed. Unfortunately, scholarship has not provided any such meaningful and simple classification, so the approach here is to look at the two extremes: complex assembled products on the one extreme, and homogeneous, nonassembled products on the other. Recognizing the patterns of innovation for these will perhaps provide insights into others that fall between.

Certainly these product "classes" are neither inclusive nor easily defined. Products such as glass, rayon, and petroleum might be viewed as nonassembled, and complex products such as mainframe computers and airliners might be classified as assembled; but there is a broad middle ground of products that have some characteristics of both. Modern color photographic film, for example, is by all appearances a nonassembled product, but closer inspection reveals a material that is no longer a simple, emulsion-coated strip of celluloid. Today's color film has up to twelve different coatings put together in very complex ways. Integrated circuits, which under magnification seem dazzlingly complex, are coming to have in their manufacture many of the characteristics of nonassembled products.

THE MODEL OF PRODUCT AND PROCESS INNOVATION

Chapter 4 presented a model of the relationship between product and process change over time. That model was devised with assembled products in mind, and is repeated here in Figure 6-1. Many of the patterns of product and process innovation carry over to nonassembled products, and this is supported by scholarship on a number of unrelated industries. The differences will be highlighted later in this chapter.

Major Product Change Precedes Major Process Change

In Figure 6-1, we note that product development enjoys an early wave of innovation, but that its rate subsides and gives way to a growing rate of process innovation. We observed this to be the case in the incandescent lamp industry. We expect the crest of the prod-

FIGURE 6–1. **Model of Product and Process Innovation**

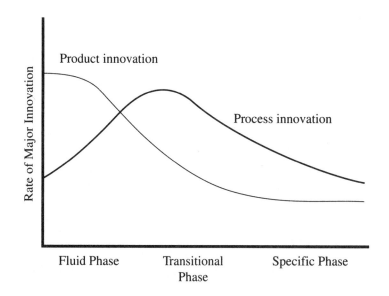

uct innovation wave among nonassembled products to tend to sub-side earlier—that is, a dominant form of the product to appear somewhat earlier. Even nonassembled "products" such as gener-ated electricity go through some form of change before the benefits of process innovation begin to appear. Electricity, for example, was first generated in direct and then in alternating forms, with different phase characteristics and at many different voltages before the standard we accept today was achieved and produced on a massive scale. Major process innovations—the transformer, AC-DC converter, turbine generator and, later, turbines operating at super-critical steam conditions—occurred in concert with the appearance of a dominant form of the product. Process integration, incremental change, and growth in scale followed, with emphasis on productivity-enhancing process innovations.

As observed earlier with respect to assembled products, a dominant product design incorporating many of the performance requirements of the marketplace is usually reached after a period of experimentation in both the manufacture and use of the product. A dominant design shifts the focus of technological effort onto the improvement and differentiation of the product. This idea appears to hold as well for nonassembled products. However, because non-assembled products contain a smaller number of different mate-rials, very early on there is a more concentrated focus of techno-logical effort and experimentation in the production process, which goes through similar periods of variation and experimentation, resulting in a so-called enabling technology. This enabling technol-ogy incorporates many of the elements needed in a continuous pro-duction process and allows the focus of technological effort to shift to process improvement from product innovation and design.

Robert Stobaugh of the Harvard Business School, in a study of the petrochemical industry, calls the firm that introduces a new product the *product innovator* and the firm that develops a new commercial process to make that same product the *process inno-vator*. Looking at the experience of nine product innovators in the petrochemical industry, Stobaugh found that the average time lag between the year of the product innovation and its initial produc-tion by a process innovator was 5.7 years.[1] Stobaugh's research also confirmed a rising level of process innovation in the early years after a new product innovation, followed by a decreasing incidence of process innovation over time. This conforms to the product and process innovation curves in the model.

Major Process Change Diminishes over Time

Stobaugh determined the number of new processes developed around nine product innovations, by decade, over an extended period. The total number of new processes for manufacturing the product increased in each of the first three decades, but the number of "major" innovations within this total number was highest in the first decade and on the decline from that point onward (see Figure 6-2). Minor process innovations commanded an increasing percentage of the total over time. Further, Stobaugh provided evidence that the likelihood of subsequent new processes being major innovations decreased with the passage of time. Thus the chance that the next process change for a particular product will represent a major innovation becomes increasingly slim (see Figure 6-3).[2]

Markets Are Specialized at First, but Often Broaden over Time

Assembled products like electric arc and incandescent lamps first served specialized markets: ships, retail establishments, and cul-

FIGURE 6–2. **Number of New Processes Developed in Each Decade of Product's Life, Average for Nine Products**

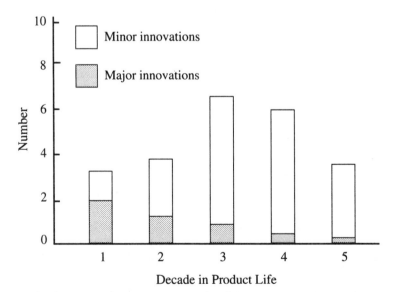

Source: Robert Stobaugh, *Innovation and Competition: The Global Management of Petrochemical Products* (Boston: Harvard Business School Press, 1988), p. 26. With permission.

FIGURE 6–3. **Probability of Next New Process Representing a Major Innovation**

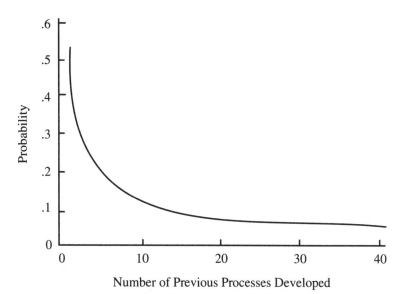

Number of Previous Processes Developed

Source: Robert Stobaugh, *Innovation and Competition: The Global Management of Petrochemical Products* (Boston: Harvard Business School Press, 1988), p. 27. With permission.

tural institutions. Photographic cameras were originally intended for a small cadre of professional portrait takers. The innovators of the typewriter first saw their market as the telegraphic industry. Early automobiles were the playthings of the wealthy few. A study of the market for digital computers conducted for IBM in the 1950s determined the total demand for all types of computers to be limited to $2–$3 billion, essentially for massive processing operations.[3] In each of these cases, however, a larger market developed as innovations made the products increasingly plentiful and inexpensive. Today, electric lamps, cameras, typewriters, automobiles, and computers surround our lives.

A similar pattern exists among many nonassembled products, and the best example is perhaps found in J.A. Allen's study of the polyethylene industry (called polythene in the United Kingdom and some European countries). First made in a laboratory of Imperial Chemical Industries Ltd. in 1933, polyethylene found its first use as a replacement for *gutta percha,* a natural tropical material used to insulate underwater electrical transmission cables. The new material was extremely expensive, owning to the difficulty of its manufacture. The first commercial plant was not built until 1939. Expansion followed World War II, and in North America, where leading chemical firms were licensed to produce it, many new applications were found and production rose rapidly. In the early 1950s, three new processes were introduced for making polyethylene of higher densities (the Ziegler process; the Standard Oil of Indiana process; and the Phillips Petroleum process).[4] Today, world polyethylene production is larger than that of any other polymer, and the product is so cheap and plentiful that it is used for throwaway bags and milk bottles.

Outsiders Play a Role

The importance of industry outsiders to product innovation of assembled products is very widely observed, as the work of Eric von Hippel has made clear. User knowledge of the subtleties of application, he points out, is often the key to product innovation. Either on their own, or in conjunction with manufacturers, users of assembled products are shown to be an important source of innovation.[5] For example, Bell Laboratories and Texas Instruments were users of electronic components, but not producers of vacuum tubes, when they produced the initial innovations in transistors and integrated circuits.

We see evidence of the same for nonassembled products, though on a reduced scale. In his exceptional history of the petroleum refining industry, John Enos makes it clear that the creative changes in the refining process came from outside the industry itself, though some of the innovators were closely related to it.[6] The same holds, as will be revealed more fully in Chapter 7, for the nineteenth-century ice industry—a hotel keeper having developed many of the important process innovations. The role of Ford Motor Company in glassmaking improvements has already been noted.

Insiders play a much larger innovative role however in nonassembled product industries, particularly in the processes by which they are manufactured. Here, knowledge of the subtleties of manufacturing practices among process equipment makers, or the producers themselves, provide a fertile environment for innovation.

Other Similarities to the Assembled Products Model

Nonassembled products industries share many other patterns with assembled goods. The scale of operations increases dramatically (assuming the market success of the product) as process innovation comes into play. Steelmaking, textiles, and glassmaking are just three of the industries that illustrate. Operations become less entrepreneurial and more bureaucratic; the development of special-purpose equipment and more specific product focus makes product variation more costly and difficult to manage. The industry itself comes to be dominated by a handful of firms, competing on the bases of price and their ability to deliver in quantity.[7]

OBSERVABLE DIFFERENCES

While common patterns of process and product innovation exist between assembled and nonassembled products, striking differences remain and merit attention here.

Greater and Earlier Focus on Process Innovation

The heavy emphasis on process innovation for nonassembled products gives manufacturers and the process equipment makers with whom they deal the greatest incentive to create improvements. As we have seen, plate glass is an old product, and while it has experienced some important physical improvements over the centuries, today's plate glass is much the same in functional terms as the plate glass of 200 years ago. On the other hand, the functionality of an assembled product such as the Boeing 747 is tremendously different from that of commercial aircraft of the 1930s. Glass, like many homogeneous products, has remained very much the same as a product; what has changed is the process by which it is made; it is the process that accounts for today's uniformly high-quality glass in great quantities at low prices. The same phenomenon is observable in oil refining, chemicals, aluminum, steel, ice and refrigeration, textiles, and countless other industries. The patterns of innovation for assembled and nonassembled products are thus different in the sense that the rate of process innovation quickly outstrips the rate of product innovation among nonassembled goods, and process innovation dominates the industry as it passes through the transitional and into the specific phases of its evolution (see Figure 6-4).

FIGURE 6–4. **Patterns of Innovation for Assembled and Nonassembled Products**

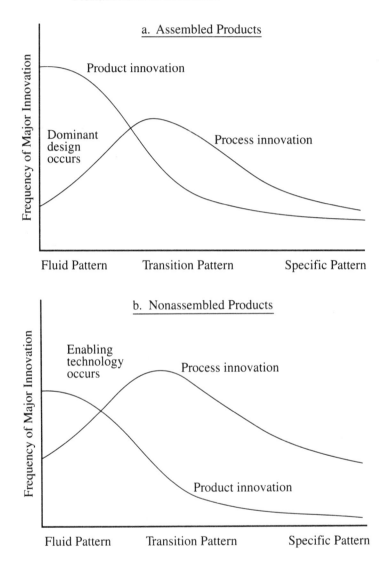

a. Assembled Products

Frequency of Major Innovation

Product innovation

Dominant design occurs

Process innovation

Fluid Pattern   Transition Pattern   Specific Pattern

b. Nonassembled Products

Frequency of Major Innovation

Enabling technology occurs

Process innovation

Product innovation

Fluid Pattern   Transition Pattern   Specific Pattern

Process Innovations: Infrequent Large Steps, Incremental Improvements

In his study of the petroleum refining industry, John Enos found that since the first commercially successful method of "cracking" heavy hydrocarbons into gasoline components was introduced in

1913, there have been three waves of process innovation: one in the early 1920s, another in 1936, and the final one in the 1940s. Each successive wave yielded improved processes, displacing those of earlier waves.[8] Enos attributes each of these waves of innovation to a different motive cause: to extract more gasoline out of increasingly scarce crude oil; to reduce refining cost; and to improve quality. As he remarked:

> These inventions and innovations . . . permitted the manufacture
> of products of higher qualities and greater yields at successively
> lower costs. The processes . . . were initially noncontinuous and
> subsequently continuous in operation. In almost all cases the
> inventions were made by men close to the oil industry but not
> attached to the major firms.[9]

As in the plate glassmaking industry, where each major process innovation led to very large productivity gains, Enos showed the astonishing productivity gains from three waves of innovation (Table 6-1). These innovations resulted in the sizable gains in raw material, capital, labor, and energy productivity seen in the first two columns of numbers in the table. Incremental improvements to the last innovation—the fluid process—between its original installation and what Enos describes as its "present installation" (about 1961) accounts for still more productivity gains.

These are the "process discontinuities" that researchers Anderson and Tushman describe as

TABLE 6–1. **Productivity Gains in Petroleum Cracking**

| Inputs | *Consumption of Inputs Per 100 Gallons of Gasoline* | | |
	Burton Process	*Fluid Process, Original Installation*	*Fluid Process, Present Installation*
Raw materials (gallons)	396	238	170
Capital (1939 dollars)	3.6	0.82	0.52
Labor (man hours)	1.61	0.09	0.02
Energy (million BTUs)	8.4	3.2	1.1

Source: John Enos, *Petroleum Progress and Profits: A History of Process Innovation* (Cambridge, Mass.: MIT Press, 1962), p. 224. With permission.

. . . fundamentally different ways of making a product that are reflected in order-of-magnitude improvements in the cost or quality of the product. They include the Bessemer furnace in steel production, catalytic cracking of petroleum, electronic imaging (vs. light-lens copying), genetic engineering using restriction enzymes, and dry gelatin photographic processes.[10]

While a good portion of the great increases in refining capabilities were won through small, incremental process improvements, others came in large chunks (with introductions of the Burton process in 1914, and the fluid process in 1955).

Johan Gullichsen's study of chemical wood-pulping operations reveals a similar pattern. Gullichsen explains that wood pulping was once a batch process of cooking, bleaching, washing, and pulping wood chips, but is now a continuous operation. The first major process improvement was the elimination of multistage washers and their appetites for abundant water and process time in favor of a single step. Further technological advance in 1964 by

FIGURE 6–5A. **Conventional Wood Pulping Operation (pre-1976)**

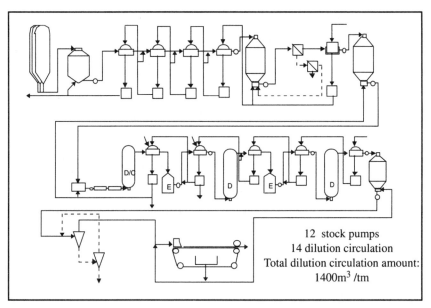

Source: Johan E. Gullichsen, "Innovations Through Exploration of Fibre-Water Interactions," *Innovations for Survival* (Falun, Sweden: The Marcus Wallenberg Foundation, 1986), pp. 45–46. With permission.

FIGURE 6–5B.   **Continuous Wood Pulping Operation**

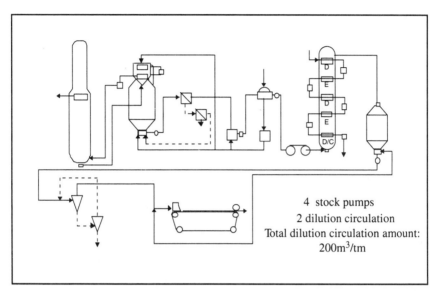

4 stock pumps
2 dilution circulation
Total dilution circulation amount:
200m^3/tm

Source: Johan E. Gullichsen, "Innovations Through Exploration of Fibre-Water Interactions," *Innovations for Survival* (Falun, Sweden: The Marcus Wallenberg Foundation, 1986), pp. 45–46. With permission.

Howard Rapson and Bertil Andersson led to a process in which all the many bleaching stages were carried out in one reactor. The reactor itself was smaller than any of the many pieces of equipment it displaced and further reduced water requirements. Figure 6-5A represents the conventional batch cooking, drum washing and drum washer bleaching process. Figure 6-5B is the continuous cooking, diffuser washing, displacement bleaching technology that appeared in Scandinavia in the late 1970s. This technology reduced the number of process steps and water requirements each by a factor of seven times. Gullichsen, one of the signal contributors to the continuous pulp process, anticipated similar step reductions in the years ahead.[11]

These and other studies affirm what was seen in the case of plate glassmaking—that process innovations for nonassembled products are often characterized by infrequent but major productivity improvements—breakthrough innovations—between which incremental improvements are made. Figure 5-6 (Long-Term Productivity Gains) illustrated this phenomenon.

Managerial Perspective on Breakthrough versus Incremental Innovation

There is evidence from a number of sources that overall technological and productivity advances are a combination of both incremental and major innovations—the proportions being an area of scholarly disagreement. Enos's study of petroleum refining led him to the conclusion that the two forms of innovation were essentially equal: "In an industry where startling innovations are relatively infrequent, accumulated improvements tend to contribute just as much to technological progress."[1] Daniel Hollander conducted detailed research at five rayon plants operated by DuPont, attempting to determine the sources of increased efficiency. His conclusion was that "technical change was of overwhelming significance in explaining the reduction in unit factory costs." Seventy-seven percent of these technology-based cost reductions, according to Hollander, were attributable to "minor" technical changes—gradual process improvements that could not be identified with formal projects or changes.[2]

Although it has not been studied formally, at least an equal share of the productivity benefits brought about by the Pilkington float glass technology described in Chapter 5 may be attributable to incremental improvements made to the basic process during its first years of operations.

Scholars may argue about the relative contributions of breakthrough and incremental technological innovation to commercial progress, and those contributions must surely vary widely among different industries. Some have decried what they see as a dangerous tendency by U.S. companies to base their strategic research on breakthrough technical innovations, while their Japanese competitors pursue a strategy of relentless incremental innovation. To use a baseball analogy, the Japanese game plan is to win market dominance on the basis of many and frequent singles, walks, and doubles, while their American rivals look to occasional home runs to carry the day. The American strategy, of course, is viewed as risky and expensive.[3]

The picture of American firms as breakthrough innovators and Japanese firms as incremental improvers, with success going to the latter, fails on two counts. First, there is plenty of evidence that these national stereotypes do not hold: American firms, particularly in nonassembled product industries such as chemicals, synthetic textiles, refining, and even steel, have historically been leaders at making incremental innovations; and such Japanese firms as Toyota, with its lean production system, have demonstrated their ability to come up with truly breakthough product and process innovations. Second, neither strategy—by itself—leads to market dominance; all the evidence points to the need to innovate *both* with breakthrough products and processes and with regular incremental improvements. Any firm that plans to win the race to commercial success by being either a steady plodding tortoise or a swift-footed hare will find itself outpaced by firms that have developed the virtues of both.

Notes

1. John Enos, *Petroleum Process and Profits: A History of Process Innovation* (Cambridge, Mass.: MIT Press, 1962), p. ix.
2. Daniel Hollander, *The Sources of Increased Efficiency* (Cambridge, Mass.: MIT Press, 1965), pp. 117–119.
3. See for example, Steven Wheelwright and Kim B. Clark, *Product Development Performance* (New York: The Free Press, 1990).

Like the emergence of a dominant design, the emergence of a major change in process architecture—a discontinuous change—is not always apparent. Recognition of an emerging dominant design is difficult except in retrospect, but with a new process architecture, several obvious signs can alert us. First, as Anderson and Tushman have stated, there are order-of-magnitude cost and quality improvements. It might be fair to restate this as a great increase in output relative to the same level of input. But even here, greater output or greater quality from a new architecture may not be so obvious; major new processes are usually riddled with technical problems that are worked out only over time. The Pilkington float glass process is a perfect example. The second sign is the number of process steps. As discussed in Chapter 5, the combination or elimination of steps, or success in making batch processes continuous, is usually a clear indicator of a change in process architecture.

The commercial development of rayon fiber provides an excellent parallel to the case of plate glass.

THE CASE OF RAYON

Rayon resulted from the desire to produce a man-made substitute for silk.[12] As early as 1855, a French inventor, George Audemars, had found a means of producing filaments by drawing a needle through a solution of collodion. Threads solidified in the air as he did so, and these were wound onto a spool. This process was patented but was commercially a dead end. Successor techniques drew the fiber from long pipettes. An important innovation appeared in 1862 with the "spinneret"—a glass device similar to a nozzle, containing a hole through which a cellulose solution was pumped to form a long filament.

Count Hilaire de Chardonnet patented a process for the production of rayon in 1884. He built a plant soon after, but did not begin production until 1891. Acetate rayon was patented in 1894, but its small volume did not interfere with the success of viscose rayon, which emerged in the early twentieth century as the dominant product design.

The enabling technology for the rayon industry encompassed a set of innovations that included an improved spinneret, the spinning solution of properly treated cellulose, equipment for filtering and mixing the solution and pumping it through the spinneret to form fibers, and finally a device for collecting the filaments and twisting them into yarn. The spinneret evolved from one of glass that contained a single hole to one of platinum that contained many holes. It was easier to make precision holes in platinum, and the platinum spinnerets made it possible to spin several fibers at once, which when twisted together formed a yarn.[13] This innovation made possible tremendous productivity gains.

The viscose solution patented by C.F. Cross and E.J. Bevan in 1892 consisted of cellulose treated with caustic soda and carbon disulfide and dissolved in water or diluted caustic soda solution. Charles Topham discovered the importance of aging the solution and developed the equipment needed for spinning it into yarn. His system used the multihole platinum spinneret, a filter and a mixer to improve the quality of the spinning solution, and a pump for even yarn thickness (denier). His most noted innovation was the development of the spinning box, which gathered the filaments emerging from the bath and twisted them together into yarn that formed a "cake" against the inside walls of the box. This eliminated the step of rewinding and twisting required when rayon was spun onto a bobbin; thus Topham moved rayon production one step closer to a continuous process.[14] Viscose rayon could have been produced without the spinning box (previous types of rayon and later some viscose rayon were spun onto a bobbin), but the spinning box contributed significantly to commercial production.

Over time rayon production progressed, as did plate glass, toward a continuous, flow-like processing. A thread-advancing reel was patented in 1906 and went into preliminary production in 1913. This device made possible the continuous flow of rayon fiber from spinneret and spinning bath through all the purifying and drying processes. However, its use was discontinued because of development cutbacks during World War I, the lack of good construction materials for the reel, and the availability of cheap labor (compared to the purchase and upkeep of new equipment). The continuous spinning process was finally fully implemented in the United States in the 1930s, after the old technology (box and bobbin processes) had been more fully played out and volume had increased. Figure 6-6 provides a summary of the process of development.

The literature (especially the work of Daniel Hollander) provides data on the many technology-based changes in the rayon industry that cumulatively resulted in increased productivity and reduced cost. Increased spinning speed, compensation spinning, and the cake-to-cone process are a few examples. Emphasis was on improved materials handling at every step of the process. Stronger yarn, faster equipment, elimination of unnecessary transfers and processing steps, improved control over the process, and monitoring capability—all added up to efficient, effective materials handling. Automatic control of solution preparation equipment, spinning apparatus, and washing, drying, bleaching, and dyeing equipment were islands of automation connected by manual transfer operations. Eventually, the thread-advancing reel was used to link the islands into a continuous process.

The locus of innovation in the rayon industry was largely the manufacturer, but users and suppliers both made contributions. For example, the direct winding of rayon onto beams instead

FIGURE 6–6. **Major Stages in Rayon Process Improvement**

Solution preparation	Combined steeping tank/press built, eliminating material transfer.
	Autocontrol mechanisms and larger units make continuous processing possible and reduce cycle time.
	Raw material recovery systems incorporated, conserving materials.
	Viscosity monitoring system improves process control and dyeing properties of material.
Spinning	Double piston pump to force cellulose through the spinneret increases control.
	Spinning speed increased through introduction of toothed-wheel pumps.
	Acid bath replaces iron sulfate, making yarn stronger and easier to handle.
	Compound added to prevent clogging of spinneret.
	DuPont converts to "all-active" spinning; each spinneret nozzle feeds one bobbin, increasing capacity.
	Improvements to the Topham spinning box, introduction of electric spindles make faster spinning possible.
Post-spinning	Reeling machine with measurement capabilities increases process control and reduces breaking.
	Compensating spinning allows take-up reel to adjust as material builds up, contributing to productivity.
	Motors, stabilizers, traverse mechanisms improved.
Finishing	Elimination of the rewinding step results in large increase in productivity.
	"Flat wrap" process eliminates the skeining step.
	Improved drying process increases quality and adds control.
	Yarn shipped on beams instead of cones, saving users a process step.
Continuous spinning	Improved thread-advancing reel developed, and continuous spinning implemented by Industrial Rayon Corp. One machine takes over nine process stages.

Sources: Drawn from Daniel Hollander, *The Sources of Increased Efficiency: A Study of DuPont Rayon Plants* (Cambridge, Mass.: MIT Press, 1965), pp. 59–177; and H.J. Hegan, "The Historical Development of and Outlook for Viscose Fibers," *Journal of the Textile Institute,* Proceedings, vol. 42 (1951), p. 399.

of cones for shipment was requested by the converters (rayon users) and developed by DuPont (rayon manufacturer). Motors for increased spinning speed and equipment for continuous solution preparation were developed by DuPont with help from equipment suppliers. Some development in solution preparation equipment was done by equipment manufacturers working on their own.

The appearance of nylon cut short the development of the rayon industry in the 1950s. However, the new nylon industry may be thought of as a product discontinuity in the human-made fiber industry, since the basic spinning method and many of the process steps for nylon production were similar to the rayon production process.

Once the spinneret innovation was in place, process improvements were incremental in nature. For example, DuPont's work tended to be in minor cost- and volume-oriented change. Some of these changes, although incremental, were nevertheless quite capital intensive—examples are the automatic equipment used in solution preparation and the increase in spinning speed. These changes solidified the existing production process, a clear sign of a mature industry in the specific state.

FLUID, TRANSITIONAL, AND SPECIFIC PHASE PATTERNS

The model first presented in Chapter 4 discussed product and process innovation in terms of *fluid, transitional,* and *specific* phase patterns, and these are seen to apply also to nonassembled products. In the glassmaking example, the pre-1880 period was typically fluid with respect to the dimensions of competitive emphasis, product change, product process, materials, organization, and the rest. Both assembled and nonassembled product industries at this phase are characterized by competition along unique product lines, where functional performance is key, and product changes are easily accommodated without a heavy cost penalty; production methods are flexible but inefficient, relying on general-purpose equipment with a heavy input of skilled labor; organizational control is likewise informal and entrepreneurial.

At the other end of the continuum, the specific phase, patterns are also similar to those experienced in assembled product industries. Competition focuses on the cost-to-value relationship, and most innovations are aimed at favorably enhancing that relationship. Product and process innovations in this phase become incremental because of the high cost associated with fundamental changes, and they become more tightly bound to one another.

It is in the transitional phase, the broad middle area between the fluid and specific phases, where the differences between assembled and nonassembled products appear greatest with respect to our model. In a word, the greater extent to which nonassembled products become process driven is the important difference. Figure

FIGURE 6–7. **Comparison of the Transitional Phase for Assembled and Nonassembled Products**

	Assembled	Nonassembled
Innovation	Emphasis on incremental product improvement and product variation	Emphasis on process changes required by rising demand
Source of innovation	Users; manufacturers	Manufacturers; equipment makers
Products	Many features unique to individual producers	Increasingly undifferentiated
Production processes	Some subprocess automated, creating islands of automation	Becoming more rigid, more continuous, more capital intensive
Equipment	Special-purpose equipment being introduced	Special-purpose equipment
Plant	General purpose with specialized sections	Single purpose, but small
Cost of process change	Moderate	High
Competitors	Many, but declining in numbers after emergence of the dominant design	Many, but declining in numbers after emergence of the enabling *process*
Vulnerabilities of industry leaders	To both improved products and more efficient producers of current products	To more efficient and higher quality producers

6-7 compares important characteristics of the transitional phase for both assembled and nonassembled products.

In the transitional phase, production processes become automated first through the creation of islands of automation, and later through their linkage via materials transfer and other mechanisms. This phenomenon occurs sooner and much more dramatically in the production of nonassembled products, where the ultimate outcome is most often a continuous process. The creation of an island of automation in this phase from a manual production process may involve a different type of technology and greater skill requirements, particularly when several islands of automation are linked into a new process step. A consequence of major jumps in process technology and productivity is that fewer and larger productive units are required to meet forecasted demand.

While market entry and changes in competitive position in assembled product markets occur with new generations of product technology and technological competition, the same phenomenon in nonassembled product lines appears to be linked not to product change but to major equipment innovations, often those that combine in one step operations that were previously done in two or three separate steps. Also, steps that may have been done in separate productive units can be combined within a new process.

THE MOVEMENT OF PROCESSES
TOWARD CONTINUITY

An earlier paragraph hinted at the idea that some assembled products have become more like nonassembled products; that is, in terms of the means of producing them, they have become more continuous in their manufacture. Integrated circuits were used as an example. The complexity of the integrated circuit is moving more into up-front development, making the actual manufacturing process more continuous (though exceedingly demanding). The same can be said with respect to electronic calculators. The first models contained about 2,300 parts, but over the years the function of these parts has been simplified to the point that many simple four-function calculators contain only five separate parts. This makes simple calculators more similar in this respect to glass, rayon, and ice—each of which has only one part—than to steam irons (50 to 90 parts), automobiles (5,000 to 7,000 parts), and 747s (1 million parts). It also suggests that manufacturers who hope to achieve the cost-saving effects of major process innovations and continuous-flow production might think about ways to reduce the number of parts and the complexity of their assemblies.

Significant part reductions have already taken place in a number of product categories. The IBM Selectric typewriter is one obvious and successful example. Originally a device of over 1,000 components, the current model has less than 200, and its reliability is said to have increased by a factor of 10.[15] Writing in the *Harvard Business Review,* former IBM executive Ralph Gomory relates the success of another of the firm's office products, the Proprinter dot-matrix printer, which had been developed for use with the IBM PC in the early 1980s. Personal computer printers then on the market were observed to have about 150 parts. By the time IBM's development team finished its work, it was able to introduce a printer of only 62 parts that outperformed its competitors.[16] Besides the usual benefits of simpler manufacturability, fewer parts meant that the Proprinter proved unusually reliable in the field. Fewer parts meant fewer assembly errors, fewer adjustments, and fewer opportunities for things to go wrong.[17] The Ford Taurus is another successful example: the first production model of the the Taurus contained 28 percent fewer parts than the Ford LTD (4,000 versus 5,700), the vehicle it was designed to replace.

Similar major parts reductions have been reported by Alvin Lehnerd in an article on Black & Decker and Sunbeam. Sunbeam engineers discovered wide variations in the number of parts contained in competing steam/dry irons sold in major markets around the world. Part counts varied from 147 to 74; fasteners from 30 to 16; and the number of fastener types from 15 to 9. Sunbeam's own products fell in the middle to the lower end of these ranges. In redesigning its line of steam/dry irons, Sunbeam gave careful attention to both the number of parts and the labor cost of assembly. The company's new product line, launched in 1986, was based on a design with only 51 parts and 3 fasteners in just 2 configurations. Manufacturing costs to Sunbeam fell substantially, giving it a tangible competitive advantage.[18]

Black & Decker redesigned its entire line of power tools in the early 1970s. The object was to make them double insulated, with fewer parts and with lower labor content. Perhaps as important, the process of manufacture was redesigned at the same time. The result of highly coordinated product and process change led to remarkable increases in productivity. At 2,400 units of production per hour, the new system required one-seventh the labor input and 39 percent less in terms of materials and overhead costs.[19] Electric motors for these tools were reconfigured so that all types—from 60 watts to 650 watts—could be produced on the same machines, the only differences being the stack length and the amount of copper and steel used. As Lehnerd described it, the manufacture of these motors seemed a far cry from the normal assembled product process, resembling instead the kind of continuous process more often associated with nonassembled products: "Motors are now manufactured automatically, untouched by human hands. The laminations, placed at the head of the mechanized line, are stacked, welded, insulated, wound, varnished, terminated, and tested automatically."[20] Moreover, the motor-making machines are run 24 hours per day, seven days per week just as in a petrochemical or glass production process, and for similar reasons of capital use and process stability.

This leads us to speculate that instead of dividing the world of products into assembled and nonassembled, future research might consider a single spectrum graded by number of parts and process operations, with homogeneous products like glass on one extreme, and jet aircraft on the other. And in the center might be found products of few individual parts with manufacturing processes that resemble those of glass, steel, and other homogeneous materials.

Notes

1. Robert Stobaugh, *Innovation and Competition: The Global Management of Petrochemical Products* (Boston: Harvard Business School Press, 1988).
2. Ibid., pp. 25–27.
3. William D. Bygrave and Jeffry A. Timmons, *Venture Capital at the Crossroads* (Boston: Harvard Business School Press, 1992), p. 104.
4. J.A. Allen, *Studies in Innovation in the Steel and Chemical Industries* (New York: Augustus M. Kelley, 1968), pp. 7–51.
5. Eric von Hippel, *The Sources of Innovation* (New York: Oxford University Press, 1989).
6. John Enos, *Petroleum Process and Profits: A History of Process Innovation* (Cambridge, Mass.: MIT Press, 1962).
7. This point is also emphasized by Chandler. See Alfred D. Chandler, Jr., *Scale and Scope: Dynamics of Industrial Capitalism* (Cambridge, Mass.: Harvard University Press, 1990).
8. John Enos, "Invention and Innovation in the Petroleum Refinery Industry," in *The Rate and Direction of Inventive Activity: Economic and Social Factors,* a conference report of the National Bureau of Economic Research (Princeton, N.J.: Princeton University Press, 1962), p. 300.

9. Enos, "Invention and Innovation," p. 304.

10. Philip Anderson and Michael L. Tushman, "Technological Discontinuities and Dominant Designs: A Cyclical Model of Technological Change," *Administrative Sciences Quarterly,* 35 (December 1990), p. 607.

11. Johan E. Gullichsen, "Innovations Through Exploration of Fibre-Water Interactions," *Innovations For Survival* (Falun, Sweden: The Marcus Wallenberg Foundation, 1986), pp. 44–68.

12. I am grateful to Teresa C. Nolet for her work in researching the rayon case presented here. See James M. Utterback and Teresa C. Nolet, "Product and Process Change in Non-Assembled Product Industries" (Cambridge, Mass.: MIT Center for Policy Alternatives working paper 78-12, September 18, 1978).

13. J. Leeming, *Rayon: The First Man-Made Fiber* (New York: John Wiley, 1950), pp. 10–11.

14. Ibid., pp. 20–34.

15. "For Better Products, Use Fewer Parts," *New York Times,* June 26, 1988.

16. Ralph Gomory, "From the 'Ladder of Science' to the Product Development Cycle," *Harvard Business Review,* November–December 1989, pp. 99–105.

17. Hewlett-Packard had the same experience with three generations of its printers. The first, a pen-matrix machine, had slightly over 300 parts; the second generation, the Paint Jet, contained approximately 120 individual parts; the third, the Paint Jet 500, had only 60 parts.

18. Alvin P. Lehnerd, "Revitalizing the Manufacture and Design of Mature Global Products, in Bruce R. Guile and Harvey Brooks, eds., *Technology and Global Industries* (Washington, D.C.: National Academy Press, 1987), pp. 63–64.

19. Ibid., p. 55.

20. Ibid., p. 54.

CHAPTER **7**

Invasion of a Stable Business by Radical Innovation

Whenever technological discontinuities occur, companies'
fortunes change drastically.
Richard N. Foster, from *Innovation: The Attacker's Advantage*

O N A RECENT STAY IN LONDON my family and I were foiled in our attempt to find a carton of fresh milk in a small grocery store near our quarters. The refrigerated cabinets contained other perishables, but no milk. Observing our confusion, the storekeeper directed us to a section of ordinary unrefrigerated shelves where, to our surprise, the milk was stored in normal abundance along with a variety of nonperishable products. What made this possible was asceptic packaging, an innovation of Tetrapak, a Swedish firm, which developed the process of "flash sterilization" to eliminate the costly necessity of refrigeration and special handling for milk and fruit juices. This method of dealing with food preservation has been a success with the food industry and with consumers where refrigeration is limited. Asceptic packaging has been slow to enter the large U.S. market with its abundant refrigerated distribution and home refrigerators, but has grown rapidly in areas where refrigeration is less plentiful. Indeed, U.S. packagers of milk have adopted extra sterilization to preserve its shelf life in partial adoption of Tetrapak's idea. To date the U.S. market has seen only speciality and convenience items such as coffee cream and small cartons of fruit juice in asceptic form.

Earlier chapters mentioned how waves of innovation—or discontinuities—have swept through typing, lighting, and plate glassmaking. This chapter examines that process in detail, focusing on the early history of an industry for which aseptic packaging may very well represent the next wave of transforming innovation.

AMERICA'S ICE INDUSTRY

Contemporaries called him the "Ice King," and in 1833 Frederic Tudor of Boston was ready to take his greatest gamble ever. In the spring of that year he had 200 tons of ice cut from a local pond and hauled to the wharf in neighboring Charlestown. There the cold cargo was carefully packed aboard the ship *Tuscany,* with generous amounts of sawdust between each layer and all around, for a 180-day voyage to India. The long months under sail were almost entirely through tropical waters: down past the West Indies, then across the equator off the west coast of Africa, around the Cape of Good Hope into the Indian Ocean, and across the equator once again en route to Calcutta. At the end of the journey, *Tuscany* still had 100 tons of ice to sell. This venture lost money but opened a new market that would soon contribute profits to Tudor's farflung ice empire.

Tudor could well afford this initial loss. Since his first shipment of ice from Charlestown, Massachusetts to Martinique in the West Indies in 1806, he had built the harvested ice business into a major industry, and the best days were yet to come (see Figure 7-1). By 1856, his company was shipping 146,000 tons per year in 363 separate cargos to such U.S. ports as Philadelphia, Charleston, Savannah, New Orleans, and San Francisco, and to the Caribbean islands, Havana, Rio de Janeiro, Madras, Bombay, and Hong Kong. A comparable amount of ice was marketed locally, where it was now an indispensable commodity for the brewing and fishing industries as well as for meat processors, dairyfarmers, restaurants, and hospitals. The ice business was a young enterprise on which many economic activities had come to depend and through which great fortunes were made. Most remarkable was the fact that Tudor and those like him succeeded in turning something once considered totally worthless into a financial bonanza.

It was the resourcefulness of Tudor, and other Bostonians who became his competitors, that prompted historian Daniel Boor-

FIGURE 7–1.   **Tudor Ice Company, Quantity of Ice Shipments, 1806–1856**

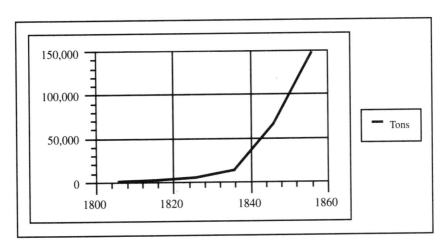

Source: Based on data in Henry Hall, *The Ice Industry of the United States with a Brief Sketch of Its History and Estimates of Production,* U.S. Department of the Interior, Census Division, Tenth Census, 1880, v. 22 (Washington, D.C.: U.S. Government Printing Office, 1888, reprinted by the Early American Industries Association), p. 3.

stin's remark that "Using the sea, New England versatility made the very menaces of the landscape [granite and ice] into articles of commerce."[1]

This chapter and the next continue our exploration of the relationships between innovation and its impact on competitive success. Here we investigate the case of the American ice-harvesting industry and its subsequent decline in the face of machine-made ice. Far from being an arcane historical curiosity, this case provides a look at a familiar process technology over its full life cycle. This long-term perspective helps us to see how a competing technology emerged, from what source, and how the dominant technology responded when challenged.

We also observe here how one generation of technology applied to a commonplace requirement (cooling) gave way to others. Thus refrigeration using harvested ice was rendered obsolete by machine-made ice—an innovation based on a radically different technology—which in turn was superseded by electromechanical refrigeration.

THE SECOND ICE AGE IN NEW ENGLAND

Farmers had for years cut and chopped ice for storage in their own underground ice wells. No less a progressive agrarian than George Washington built a "dry well" ice house at Mount Vernon in the fall of 1784, using a design described to him by Robert Morris, then U.S. Superintendent of Finance. Washington's original underground facility, which provided no drainage, had been a failure, but Morris's design worked very well, and thereafter Washington spent many days each January supervising the cutting and hauling of ice from the Potomac to his new, improved ice house. Farmers in northern states made a community event of ice harvesting; as in barn raising, the men and boys cut, loaded, and transported ice to each farmer's ice house in turn, while the women and girls cooked up a big communal meal and provided warm clothing for any who fell into the frigid water. It was heavy work—cutting and chopping chunks of ice, hauling them out by hand, and loading and unloading them from farm wagons and sleighs. It remained for Frederic Tudor to turn this winter ritual into a commercial venture, to create a uniform and marketable "product" in place of assorted chunks of ice, and to support innovation of the processes that would make it highly profitable.

Successful innovators often have able collaborators. George Eastman had chemist Henry Reichenbach; Edison had mechanic Charles Batchelor; Henry Ford relied on the engineering management know-how of Charles Sorenson. Frederic Tudor was no exception. Tudor benefited greatly in knowing a young Harvard graduate named Nathaniel Jarvis Wyeth, who had taken over the management of his family's hotel on the shores of Fresh Pond in Cambridge, Massachusetts in the early 1820s. Like other establishments serving food during the summer, Wyeth's hotel put in a load of ice each winter. But unlike other operators, Wyeth developed methods and equipment to make ice harvesting more efficient and the final product more uniform for ease of storing.

In 1825, Wyeth designed and applied for a patent on an "ice plow"—a cutting device that harnessed the muscle power of horses to the task of etching uniformly shaped blocks that could then be cut from the pond and more efficiently transported and stacked in barn-like ice houses. That same year, he became exclusive supplier to Frederic Tudor, and before long ice from Fresh Pond was finding its way down the Atlantic seaboard and around the world in Tudor

Company ships with names like *Ice King, Iceland,* and *Iceberg*. Wyeth's invention of the ice plow was followed by more than 50 specially designed saws, snow scrappers, and other assorted tools, each of which enhanced and systematized the process of ice harvesting.[2] These process innovations are said to have cut the price of delivered ice by one-third.

Crews using Wyeth's methods foraged broadly among Boston area ponds and even invaded the solitude of Concord's Walden Pond, where the reclusive Henry David Thoreau observed the harvest and offered this description in the pages of *Walden*:

> . . . a hundred Irishmen, with Yankee overseers, came from Cambridge every day to get out the ice. They divided it into cakes by methods too well known to require description, and these, being sledded to the shore, were rapidly hauled off on to an ice platform, and raised by grappling irons and block and tackle, worked by horses, on to a stack, as surely as so many barrels of flour, and there placed evenly side by side, and row upon row, as if they formed the solid base of an obelisk designed to pierce the clouds. They told me that in a good day they could get out a thousand tons, which was the yield of about one acre.

By the time *Tuscany* returned from India in 1834, the Tudor Ice Company enjoyed a virtual monopoly in the Boston area; it had exclusive arrangements with both the British and Dutch governments for supplying the West Indies and had a similar understanding with Spanish colonial authorities in Cuba. Storage facilities were sited in Charleston, South Carolina and Savannah, Georgia as well as at Kingston, Jamaica, and Havana, Cuba. Preventing ice from becoming an instant puddle in the scorching climates of these cities was no simple task, and Tudor himself supervised construction and experiments with dockside ice houses, the first being set up in Havana in 1816. This facility was a square, double-shell building prefabricated in Boston and sent down to Havana by ship. The sides measured 25 feet on the outside, and 19 feet on the inside, and the structure was designed to hold 150 tons.[3] We must assume that the space between the two sets of walls was filled with wood shavings or some other form of insulating material. Tudor conducted a number of empirical studies on the "decay" rate of ice at this facility, measuring the amount of run-off using different forms and methods of insulation. His best recorded decay rate for the

Havana ice house was 56 pounds of water per hour. His own ice elevator on Fresh Pond boasted of being able to store ice for upward of three years. Improved methods permitted Tudor to bring down the price of his product and expand its distribution. In Charleston, South Carolina, for example, per-ton prices dropped from $166 in 1817 to $25 in 1834.

Tudor's growing success was not lost on his Boston neighbors, and several entered the business. One of these rivals, a Mr. Hittinger of Gage, Hittinger and Company, sought to develop a British market with a cargo of Fresh Pond ice sent in 1842. Hittinger knew that the tradition-bound British would not use ice unless they were shown how, so he hired a number of Boston bartenders and took them to London on a ship scheduled to arrive before the ice. When the cargo of "cold comfort" arrived, Hittinger and his bartenders were already set up in an opulent and brightly illuminated hall and there "initated the English into the mysteries of juleps, cocktails" and "Boston notions" of various types.[4] Before long, fashionable Britons were hooked on New England ice.

Once the British trade was in full swing, a pecking order in the snob appeal of American ices emerged—just as we witness today with various bottled waters. The product of the Wenham Lake Ice Company (near Beverly, Massachusetts) came to be cherished above all others for its clarity and supposed purity. According to claims of the time, a newspaper could be read through a block of Wenham ice two feet thick. (The British lords and ladies most likely did not realize the extent to which teams of horses strained on the surface of pristine Wenham Lake, doing what horses do in abundance. Ice companies, in fact, had a job category for young boys whose sole duty was to pick up after these horses. How thorough they were is anyone's guess.) No London dinner party was thought to be complete without Wenham Lake ice. This British bonanza ended within just four or five years when Norwegians invaded the market with much lower-priced ice, most of it drawn from Lake Oppengaard, which the Norwegians spuriously renamed "Wenham Lake" and sold under that name.

By the late 1870s, a decade before the high-water mark of the natural ice business, there were no fewer than 14 firms in the Boston area cutting almost 700,000 tons of ice each year. Maine and New Hampshire also had thriving ice companies. It was the perfect occupation for New England in that it drew on a number of abundant local resources: cold winters; many freshwater ponds; farmers, immigrants, fishermen, and mariners in search of winter occupation; mountains of sawdust (for insulation) that was otherwise a nuisance to the logging industry; and a maritime infrastructure for shipping. Process innovation continued to make the product more uniform and lowered the cost of production. For example, many winters were not sufficiently cold in New England to produce thick ice. So, once a few inches of ice were formed, icemen would pump a thin layer of water onto it; this would freeze easily overnight. This process would be repeated each day, building the thickness inch by inch, until the entire sheet was thick enough for harvesting.

Northern-tier states from New York to Wisconsin also developed regional ice industries during this period to serve the growing meat-processing and dairy industries and to accommodate the growing urban populations of the heartland. And while these landlocked ice producers lacked the means to reach overseas markets, they did have access to good railroads, which made long-distance transportation to cities like Chicago, St. Louis, and hundreds of others—large and small—efficient and inexpensive. Railcars were loaded directly at lakeside during the harvest season and from ice elevators during the remainder of the year.

The ice business was a large and important part of the U.S. economy of the 1870s and expanded as householders became regular consumers of harvested ice. City dwellers had begun purchasing "ice boxes" in growing numbers after 1850, and these soon became a modern necessity. By the turn of the century, household consumers accounted for half of the total domestic ice market. The future looked rosy. As the Ice King himself had told the Boston Board of Trade back in 1857, "The ice trade was born here in Boston, and has been growing and extending itself with no successful competitor for more than half a century, and there is reason to think it is yet in its infancy."[5]

Though no one recognized it at the time, the 1880s were to be the zenith of the harvested ice industry. The market for refrigeration was to continue expanding with the growing nation, but a radical innovation based on a totally different technology had already invaded the periphery of the industry. Though generally unnoticed at the time, the new technology was destined to eventually dominate the market for ice and refrigeration.

THE INVASION OF MACHINE-MADE ICE

As industry and households became more dependent on ice for food preservation, iced drinks, confectioneries, and medical applications, its cost and supply reliability became more serious issues.

Because of the industry's seasonal nature and dependence on the weather, the price of harvested ice fluctuated greatly, especially during the summer, according to one's distance from the sources of production. Summer prices in the north were typically in the range of $6–$8/ton delivered. Even in years when warm winters resulted in poor harvests, supplies of ice were not seriously disrupted because of the producers' efficient ice houses, which could carry ice through several years. In southern port cities, however, transportation costs and losses due to melting pushed summer prices to the $20–$30/ton range. When yellow fever epidemics created abnormally high demand, or when poor northern harvests reduced supply, the price of ice soared to $60–$75/ton.[6] Inland southern cities had to pay even more, often as much as $125/ton. As a result, southern markets offered the greatest receptivity to innovations affecting the supply and price of ice.

This situation bears a striking resemblance to the experience of the United States with regard to petroleum during the 1970s. In both cases the resource was found in abundance where it was needed least. The oil producers of the Middle East had most of the oil and very little domestic need for it; New Englanders lived in a natural ice box for half the year and enjoyed temperate weather for most of the remainder. At the same time, the users of the resource who needed it the most were far away and had to pay premium prices for it. It is no surprise that all the innovations in creating substitutes and efficiencies for petroleum (synfuels, solar power, and conservation) are occurring in countries faced with uncertain supplies and high prices. Likewise, the radical innovations to challenge the ice industry of New England, and the first large-scale adoptions of them, occurred in the steamy regions of the South. Brewers and meat packers in the rural South were among the earliest experimenters with mechanical methods of producing ice. They represented the market niches where high prices for substitutes could be tolerated.

Attempts to produce ice by mechanical or chemical means were made as early as the mid-1700s, but only out of scientific curiosity. Evaporation of water in a vacuum was used successfully to make ice in a laboratory in 1755. The use of sulfuric acid to absorb water vapor and enhance this process was attempted in 1810 and improved in 1824. In 1834, a New Englander named Jacob Perkins, then living in London, received a British patent for a mechanism that produced ice by vaporizing a volatile liquid and then condensing that vapor in a continuous and closed cycle. Perkins's was the first practical ice-making innovation, and its principles form the basis for refrigeration to this day, incorporating as it does a compressor, a condenser, an expansion valve, and an evaporator.[7]

In hot, humid Apalachicola, Florida Dr. John Gorrie began experimenting in 1838 with the use of ice to cool hospital rooms where he treated victims of malaria. The price and unreliable supply of northern ice led Gorrie to design and build an ice-making machine based, apparently without foreknowledge, on the same general principles followed earlier by Perkins. Gorrie received a U.S. patent in 1851. Gorrie attempted to form a commercial venture in New Orleans to develop and exploit his patent, but this initiative ended with Gorrie's death in 1855.

A number of French, German, English, and American inventors experimented with new designs, using either ammonia, ether, naptha, or some other vapor. Historical sources differ as to just when the first successful commercial applications of ice-making machinery were made, and as to their capacity. Jones mentions 1862 as the year in which a machine of French design was brought into San Antonio through Mexico—thus skirting the Union blockage of shipping to and from the Confederate states. In 1868, New Orleans got its first ice-making plant, which began selling manufactured ice for around $35 per ton, substantially less than the price of natural ice. Another commercial-scale operation began in Waco, Texas in 1869.[8] In an 1886 industry study sponsored by the U.S. government, Henry Hall described the rocky road faced by the innovators:

> There are now about forty different styles of ice machines in operation in different parts of the world. Nearly a hundred have been patented at Washington. Not over half a dozen, however, are in this country considered of much practical value at the present time. . . . In order to carry on a successful business in artificial ice-making the product must be manufactured at a cost of not to exceed $2 or $3 a ton. The chief cause of the numerous disastrous

failures so far has been that the product costs anywhere from $20 to $250 a ton. One aim of inventors in this country is to make ice at from 75 cents to $1 per ton. Many times during the last ten years the announcement has been made that the result has been accomplished. It is doubtful if, in practice, any ice-maker in America has yet been able to produce ice so cheaply; but the cost has, nevertheless, been reduced at length to a point where the making of ice is commercially practicable, and it is now carried on as a regular industry in a large number of southern cities in competition with the importation of natural ice from the north.[9]

From less than a handful of plants in the 1860s, the number had grown to 30 in the southern states and 5 in California by 1879. The largest of these, the Louisiana Ice Company in New Orleans, had a daily capacity of 118 tons.[10] A decade later, in 1889, 222 ice-manufacturing plants were in operation, still mostly in the south, but now also in middle states like Ohio, Illinois, and Indiana. In the decades that followed, the number of ice plants skyrocketed (see Figure 7-2). Improvements to compressors and other aspects of ice-making equipment increased rapidly, and a number of firms,

Figure 7–2. **Ice Making Plants in the United States, 1869–1920**

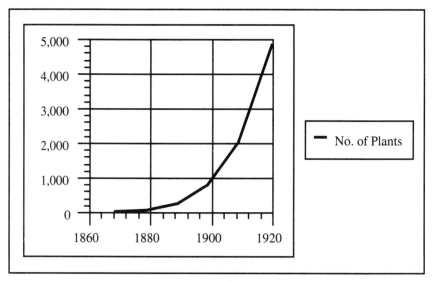

Source: U.S. Bureau of the Census, cited in Cummings, *The American Ice Harvests*, p. 11, and Jones, *America's Ice Men*, p. 159.

including several makers of steam engines, entered the field. New England ice was finding itself effectively driven out of southern markets.

Even as the new technology bit off larger chunks of the industry, the ice merchants of the north pushed ahead with their own improvements and still greater production. Steam-powered circular saws were applied to the job of cutting blocks from rivers and ponds; mechanical conveyors were installed to provide continuous hauling of ice cakes from ponds to ice houses, or directly onto specially designed railroad cars. On the Hudson River, 100 specially designed barges were introduced to transport ice more efficiently from their source to inland river ports farther south. The Knickerbocker Ice Company—the leading manufacturer of ice-harvesting equipment and one-ton "ice wagons" for urban distribution—introduced steam-powered conveyors to lift ice from boats and barges and move it efficiently into the many ice elevators the company owned and operated.[11] Many producers milled their ice blocks into more uniform sizes with incised edges to keep them from freezing together and to make storage more efficient. Thus, even as the door was closing on their industry, the northern ice men continued to make incremental improvements to both their product and the processes by which it was harvested, stored, and delivered. These improvements resulted in greater volume and lower unit costs.

The ice harvesters had developed an entire "system" for production, storage, and distribution that was remarkably efficient. Despite the rapid spread of machine-made ice throughout the south, the 1886 ice harvest was the biggest ever—25 million tons, suggesting how the demise of a technology can be obscured by a growing market.

It was, as we now know, a losing battle, because the technology for manufacturing ice was improving by orders of magnitude while incremental improvements to ice harvesting yielded smaller and smaller gains. Experimentation with vapor compression machines was continuing, and a number of refrigerants were tried, including methyl, ether, oil, and ammonia. The use of ammonia as a refrigerant was an important step forward for, in addition to its thermodynamic advantage over other refrigerants, the pressures it required were easy to produce and the machines that used it could thus be made smaller. David Boyle patented the first ammonia compression machine in 1872 and many improved versions quickly followed. The ammonia compression machine represented an enabling technology, one that opened the door to other important advances.

One problem with early machine-made ice was its cloudiness owing to included air. This gave natural ice a distinct quality advantage insofar as certain users were concerned. It was soon discovered that distilled water, when frozen, was nearly transparent, and this led to a variety of designs using condensed steam from the vaporization stage of ice-making equipment as the water to be frozen in the final product. Other operators found ways to cut down on the amount of refrigerant leakage from pumps and joints—a common problem when using high-pressure gases.

From the workshops of inventors and individual mechanics, companies were formed to produce ice-making equipment, and some became large enterprises. A number of major improvements to the equipment were introduced by users, such as a New York City brewery that developed a system of oil sealing for its compressors to prevent ammonia leakage. After 1890, electricity began to be substituted for steam as a source of power. The first trade journal, *Ice and Refrigeration,* made its appearance in 1891. Improved efficiency, automation, and ease of use characterized the process of producing ice.

THE END OF THE HARVESTED ICE ERA

Despite efforts to lower costs and improve their product, the ice harvesters steadily lost markets to plant-made ice. A few gave in and acquired ice-making equipment of their own; most went down with the ship. As industrial historian Richard Cummings described it, "Some ice distributors found it cheaper to abandon natural ponds and set up plants. Others sought to cut harvesting cost by time saving devices. . . . But, since plant ice processes were being constantly improved, natural ice harvesters were in a losing fight."[12] Massachusetts, the last bastion of the ice empire, itself had seven mechanical ice plants by 1909.

As the mechanical ice-making technology spread abroad, the export market for ice plummeted (Figure 7-3). The *coup de grace* came after World War I, when old-fashioned ice boxes, the local—and last—sizable market for harvested ice, began to give way to electric refrigerators.

FIGURE 7–3.   **U.S. Ice Exports, 1850–1910**

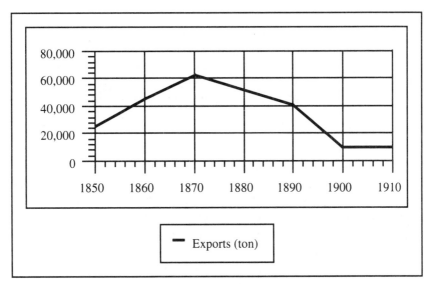

Source: U.S. Census Bureau, cited in Cummings, *The American Ice Harvests.*

By the mid-1920s, the natural ice industry was gone for good, except in a few outlying areas. Ice elevators stood vacant and over the years fell into ruins. Today, along the shores of Fresh Pond and Wenham Lake no visible signs remain of the great ice houses of the nineteenth century or of the vast and prosperous industry they represented.

In later years, even the new ice-making plants would become outmoded, replaced by a new wave of innovation: electromechanical refrigeration. Blocks of ice—from any source—became less important as refrigerated rail cars, ships, storage lockers, and electric home refrigerators satisfied the basic requirement for cooling more conveniently and at lower cost.

As a footnote we might consider the emergence of several small companies with a high-price, unique product: glacial ice. In the 1980s, several Alaskan entrepreneurs began bagging ice from glaciers and selling it as a premium product for use in mixed drinks in the lower 48 states. As with Wenham Lake ice in England over a century before, it wasn't a party without the perfect ice, in this case ice with its own prehistoric effervescence!

PATTERNS IN THE EMERGENCE OF
RADICAL INNOVATIONS

This long tale about the ice industry is not told here merely as a quaint story, but as an example of how a radical technological innovation can emerge and successfully invade—and eventually overwhelm—the established technology in almost any circumstance. It is a recurring phenomenon in industries past and present, and the same struggle between new and old can be seen today in duels between plywood and strandboard, copper wire and optical fiber, supercomputers and massively parallel computers.

There is a general pattern to the invasion process of this story, other industries previously discussed, and still others encountered beyond the covers of this book. One could generalize that in any product market there are periods of continuity, when the rate of innovation is incremental and infrequent, and periods of discontinuity when major product or process changes occur. Radical changes create new businesses and transform or destroy existing ones, just as mechanical ice-making destroyed the New England ice-harvesting industry.

An invading technology has the potential for delivering dramatically better product performance or lower production costs, or both. Figure 7-4 shows that the performance of a particular product improves rapidly during the period when many alternative design approaches are being tried. With the appearance of a dominant design, however, product performance accelerates. After major advances have been made, a period of more incremental and infrequent change sets in, as indicated by a leveling off of the product performance curve.

At the time an invading technology first appears (t_1), the established technology generally offers better performance or cost than does the challenger, which is still unperfected. The typewriter case provided an excellent example of this in its latest wave of innovation, when the first word processors appeared. These were crude devices by contemporary standards and difficult to master. And Apple Computer's first personal computer, like Mark Twain's Remington, produced only uppercase letters. No self-respecting typist would have given up an IBM Selectric for one of those toys! The new technology may be viewed objectively as crude, leading to the belief that it will find only limited application. The performance superiority of the established technology may prevail for

FIGURE 7–4.   **Performance of an Established and an Invading
Product Contrasted along One Performance
Dimension**

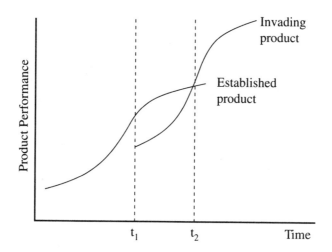

quite some time, as was the case for harvested ice relative to
machine-made ice in most locations for the last quarter of the nineteenth century, but if the new technology has real merit, it typically
enters a period of rapid improvement—just as the established technology enters a stage of slow innovative improvements. Eventually, the newcomer improves its performance characteristics to the
point where they match those of the established technology (t_2) and
rockets past it, still in the midst of a period of rapid improvement.

Of course, the established players do not always sit back and
watch their markets disappear. Most fight back. The gas companies
came back against the Edison lamp, as we saw in Chapter 3, with
the Welsbach mantle, which increased the efficiency of gas lighting
by five times. There was nothing incremental about that. Purveyors
of established technologies often respond to an invasion of their
product market with redoubled creative effort that may lead to substantial product improvement based on the same product architecture. Figure 7-5 describes this behavior. Here, the established
product enjoys a brief period of performance improvement (the
dotted line), but by time t_3 the relentless pace of improvement in
the new product technology allows the challenger to equal, and
then surpass, the established product. Continued investment in

FIGURE 7–5. **Performance of an Established and an Invading Product. Burst of Improvement in Established Product.**

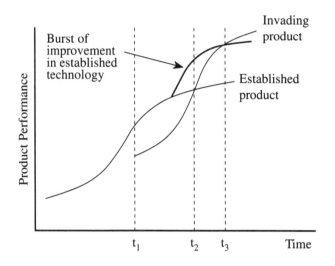

older technologies invariably leads to performance improvement, but this generally becomes marginal over time. The new technology, on the other hand, often has so much more potential for better performance that it is usually just a matter of time before that potential is realized and the new surpasses the old.

In cases where cost was the dimension of performance that determined the outcome, Figures 7-4 and 7-5 could easily be inverted to describe declining cost curves for the established technology and its challenger.

Innovations from Outsiders

In the cases we have examined thus far, innovations have not come from the industry leaders as much as from outsiders. Thinking back to our typewriter story, Christopher Sholes was a civil servant working in the obscurity of a Milwaukee office; he had no standing in the printing or document-processing establishment of his day. Yet his innovation set the pattern for processing documents for several generations. When the next wave of innovation hit that industry—electrics—it was not one of the giants of the typewriter business that pioneered its development or growth. It was the outsider, IBM. Still later, when computer technology moved into the document-processing business, the innovating came from unknown hardware companies such as Wang, Apple, Tandy, and dozens of software firms. IBM would eventually acquire its share of the hardware business, but as a follower, not as a technical leader.

In the lighting industry we observed how the great leap forward into incandescent electric lamps was not led by anyone with standing in that business but by Thomas Edison, whose accomplishments to date had been in totally unrelated fields: telegraphy and recorded sound. Those with the biggest stake in home and commercial lighting at the time, the gas illumination companies, were totally out of the picture. Years later it would be a market bit player—Sylvania—that would make the greatest innovations in the next wave of lighting technology: fluorescent lamps.

The case of mechanical manufacturing of ice again conforms with our pattern of innovation by outsiders. The great fortunes in ice had all been made by northerners, primarily in the Boston area. They created the product and controlled distribution; the Knickerbocker Company, not a producer itself, was nevertheless a major player in process equipment, distribution equipment, and ice elevators. Despite the great stakes of Knickerbocker and the ice barons in this business, the radical innovation came from outsiders. (One is tempted to say that *because* of their great investments in the established forms of the business, they were impeded from making the industry-altering innovations.) We have already discussed the economic logic of this phenomenon, and we can speculate that if the merchants of Calcutta and Hong Kong—the farthest borders of the ice empire—had been handier with Western science and technology, it might have been they who created the first important innovations in ice manufacturing.

Industry outsiders have little to lose in pursuing radical innovations. They have no infrastructure of existing technology to defend or maintain and, as is made clear through the case of ice innovators in the southern United States, they have every economic incentive to overturn the existing order.

Industry insiders, on the other hand, have abundant reasons to be slow to mobilize in developing radical innovations. Economically, they have huge investments in the current technology; emotionally, they and their fortunes are heavily bound up in the status quo; and from a practical point of view, their managerial attention is encumbered by the system they have—just maintaining and marginally improving their existing systems is a full-time occupation. Owners and managers of dominant firms who are deliberate in their pursuit of radical innovation are remarkable and few.

Reluctance to Adopt the New Technology

A critical pattern in the dynamics of technological innovation—and one that should give every business strategist a great deal of discomfort—is the disturbing regularity with which industrial leaders follow their core technologies into obsolescence and obscurity. Firms that ride an innovation to the heights of industrial leadership more often than not fail to shift to newer technologies. Few attempt the leap from the fading technology to the rising challenger; even fewer do it successfully. No one has addressed this gloomy phenomenon or articulated its dimensions more fully than Richard Foster. Foster cites a long list of products in the container and packaging business with market positions that have been overturned by innovative competitors: glass bottles by steel cans; steel cans by aluminum cans; glass bottles by plastic bottles; plastic-coated milk cartons by plastic jugs; and so forth. In each case, he notes that market leadership passed from one set of firms to another. Today's leaders, in these cases, were never leaders in the next product generation:

> I don't know of any comprehensive statistics that would stand up to academic scrutiny, but my feeling is that leadership changes hands in about seven out of ten cases when discontinuities strike. A change in technology may not be the number-one corporate killer, but it certainly is among the leading causes of corporate ill-health.[13]

It is easy to understand how established firms can ignore a radical innovation when it first appears. For one thing, in the early stages it is far from clear that the radical innovation will have much impact. Like biological mutations, radical innovations crop up sporadically, but very few have the qualities that lead to long-term survival. The problems that plagued the early mechanical ice-making technology were sufficiently large that industry analyst Henry Hall, writing in the early 1880s, just when the technology was about to take off, failed to see any major role for manufactured ice outside the South. In the nineteenth-century lighting industry, the "gas men," as Edison called them, certainly recognized trouble when the first incandescent lighting systems were being introduced. But one wonders if this would have been the case if an unknown technologist—and not the acclaimed Edison—were its guiding spirit. In the early days of the photographic industry, as the next chapter will make clear, the low quality of the celluloid roll film innovated by Eastman failed to convince many that it could be perfected to the standards of first-rate photography—even to the standards of that time.

Established firms also carry the burden of large investments in people, equipment, plant, materials, and knowledge, all of which are closely linked to the established technology. It takes a rare kind of leadership to shift resources away from areas where one currently enjoys success to an area that is new and unproven.

Finally, there is the very human problem of managers resting on their laurels—or in this case, on the technologies that have made them successful. Few, if any of us, are blameless in this. These managers bind up their thinking and planning too closely with their own technology and not closely enough with customer needs. When this happens, managers can satisfy changing customer needs only by making improvements or enhancements to their own technology, even though a different technology may address the customer's needs much more successfully. In the case of the ice industry, the northern producers responded to the technological threat by increasing the efficiency of their existing processes of production and distribution; there is no indication that any northern ice producers adopted plant-ice technology, at least until the end of the harvested ice era. None built ice plants in the South to serve their existing customers. None experimented with what today seems like a reasonable adaptation: sending harvested ice south in refrigerated ships (to reduce melting), and returning to the populous, urban northeast with southern agricultural produce in those same refrigerated holds (though this was suggested at the time).

More recently, when rising fuel prices in the 1970s created customer demand for smaller, more efficient automobiles, U.S. automakers responded (with minor exceptions) by offering slightly smaller versions of their existing, inefficient line of cars. Only after many years of market failure did the notion of developing small cars from the bottom up result in managerial action.

MEETING THE CHALLENGE OF
DISCONTINUOUS CHANGE

Established leaders face two hurdles in their contest with invading innovation. First, they need to develop an awareness of their own vulnerability—a slow and difficult process for any firm that has experienced substantial success. In 1980–1981, General Motors experienced horrific problems with its newly introduced "J" platform cars. The J cars were overweight and underpowered; they resisted starting in cold weather and caused tremendous problems on the assembly line because of poor body-panel alignments. The causes of these quality-related problems were investigated by a special focus group and presented to top management, which refused to believe what it heard. In 1982, another study was commissioned and pursued by the firm's newly established corporate quality and assurance department, this time to assess the quality methods of a number of highly respected American industrial firms. When presented with the results of the study, top management again refused, at least initially, to accept the notion that GM quality practices were not in a class with those firms. Full recognition of its quality problems would only take hold among GM leadership over time. Meanwhile, it was losing pieces of its market to foreign and domestic competitors.[14] Recognition of an external threat is the first requirement for effective action.

The second hurdle is to make the organizational adjustments that facilitate successful competition with an invading technology. The organizational problem for most established firms is that they and their technology are often stuck in the specific phase of development, while the challenger and its innovations are still in the fluid phase. The challenger brings a new and perfectable product with better performance (or performance potential), organizational flexibility, and entrepreneurial spirit; the challenger is unencumbered by human and physical assets geared to highly specific production. The established firm, on the other hand, is more bureaucratic, enjoys economies of scale (but in the wrong product), has tremendous investments in inflexible systems, and is managed by nonentrepreneurs. Thus we agree with Foster's estimate: the contest between the slow, muscle-bound champion and the nimble challenger will go to the challenger 70 percent of the time.

Foster believes that "the attacking and defending ought to be done by separate organizations."[15] This contention has intuitive appeal and can be supported by evidence from a number of industries. When IBM determined that it should take the personal computer market seriously, it did not attempt to develop its product offering from within the sprawling camp of IBM. It set up a separate unit in Boca Raton, Florida—far from its Armonk, New York, headquarters—to tackle the job. Ford Motor Company followed a similar path in its creation of "Team Taurus," a multidisciplinary development team headed by the late Lewis Veraldi and vested with extraordinary decision-making powers.[16] Team Taurus launched the most successful new American automobile model in the past ten years. General Motors went even further in setting up the Saturn company to be its champion in the contest with the best of Japan's small car makers; Saturn would design, build, and market its own products, free of GM doctrine on sourcing parts and labor. Saturn would have many of the earmarks of what our model describes as a "fluid phase" organization.

Meeting the challenge of technological discontinuities is one part of the broader issue of corporate renewal, which is addressed in Chapter 10.

Notes

1. Daniel J. Boorstin, *The Americans: The National Experience* (New York: Random House, 1965), p. 10.
2. Joseph C. Jones, Jr., *America's Ice Men: An Illustrative History of the United States Natural Ice Industry, 1665–1925* (Humble, Tex.: Jobeco Books, 1984), p. 20.
3. Philip Chadwich Foster Smith, *Crystal Blocks of Yankee Coldness: Development of the Massachusetts Ice Trade from Frederic Tudor to Wenham Lake* (Salem, Mass.: Essex Institute Historical Collections, vol. XCVII, 1961), p. 203.
4. A.P. Putnam, "Wenham Lake and the Ice Trade," in John C. Phillips, ed., *Wenham Great Pond* (Salem, Mass.: Peabody Museum, 1938), p. 36.
5. Henry Hall, *The Ice Industry of the United States with a Brief Sketch of Its History and Estimates of Production*, U.S. Department of the Interior, Census Division, Tenth Census, 1880, v. 22 (Washington, D.C.: U.S. Government Printing Office, 1888, reprinted by the Early American Industries Association), p. 3.
6. Oscar Edward Anderson, Jr., *Refrigeration in America: A History of a New Technology and Its Impact* (Princeton: Princeton University Press, 1953), p. 43.
7. Jones, *America's Ice Men*, p. 150.
8. Ibid., pp. 151–152.
9. Hall, *The Ice Industry*, p. 20.

10. Anderson, *Ice and Refrigeration,* pp. 86–87.
11. Hall, *The Ice Industry,* p. 17.
12. Richard O. Cummings, *The American Ice Harvests: A Historical Study in Technology, 1800–1918* (Berkeley, Calif.: University of California Press, 1949), p. 48.
13. Richard N. Foster, *Innovation: The Attacker's Advantage* (New York: Summit Books, 1986), p. 116.
14. See Gregory Watson, *Strategic Benchmarking* (New York: John Wiley, 1993), pp. 129–148.
15. Foster, *Innovation,* p. 210.
16. Presentation by Lewis Veraldi to Management of Technology students at MIT in 1987.

CHAPTER **8**

The Creative Power
of Technology in
Process Innovation

You press the button and we do the rest.
Eastman Kodak advertisement

THIS CHAPTER CONTINUES THE discussion of
innovation as a creative force, but focuses
on a new industry in which innovation in both product and process
technology were key factors in eventual success. It presents the
case of chemical-based photography from its inception in the early
nineteenth century through George Eastman's innovation in the
use of long strips of light-sensitized celluloid, which quite inadver-
tently created a huge market in amateur photography and later cinematography.

Anyone who watched the PBS series, "The Civil War," first
aired in 1990, must surely have been struck by the hundreds of
photographs used by producer Rick Burns to acquaint us with the
the history of that dramatic conflict. The images of generals, private soldiers, battlefields, and the war's hapless victims played
across the screen as a background to interviews with historians and
readings from letters and diaries of the period. Most of these pictures were remarkably vivid and lifelike, despite the fact that they
were taken with equipment based on mid-nineteenth-century technology.

Indeed, by the time of the American Civil War, the technology
for producing photographic images was two decades old, widely
disseminated, and had already entered its second wave of technical

167

innovation. The first wave of this technology had originated in France in 1839 with the development of daguerreotype, a method of producing images on sensitized silver-coated copper plates. This technology was an instant hit in the United States and very quickly produced a small industry of practitioners, suppliers, and manufacturers. Samuel Morse, who would later invent the telegraph, was America's first daguerreotypist. Having obtained Daguerre's instruction manual along with some equipment, Morse took an image of Boston City Hall in October of 1839, no doubt the first photographic picture taken in the Western hemisphere. Later, Morse took on a number of pupils, among them Matthew Brady, who went on to establish a fashionable studio where the socially elite came to have their portraits made in the years that preceeded the Civil War.[1] By the mid-1840s, Boston's John Plumbe had established a chain of 14 portrait studios in major cities as far west as Dubuque, Iowa.

FROM COPPER PLATES TO WET AND DRY GLASS

By the mid-1850s daguerreotype imaging technology had given way to the use of glass plates, the technology that produced the remarkable photography of the Civil War years. This innovation used a transparent and sticky substance called collodion to coat a glass plate. Just before shooting a picture, the photographer would photosensitize the collodion-coated plate with silver nitrate. When the glass was exposed to light, a photonegative image could be developed on it, "fixed" in a dark-room, and then printed on photosensitive paper by exposing the glass plate and paper to bright sunlight. This technology is referred to as wet collodion plate photography.[2]

The use of wet collodion plates greatly improved the photographic arts, and with the exception of its slowness and lack of color, provided images of a quality that rivals that which can be produced today. One major drawback, of course, had to do with the fact that the plates had to be sensitized and developed immediately before and after exposure. This required an abundance of equipment, a darkroom, and a fair knowledge of the underlying chemistry. One of Matthew Brady's breakthroughs was taking this laborious process out of the studio and into the field. With a handful of assistants, Brady roamed the encampments of the Union Army and its grim battlefields, taking thousands of photographs and developing the plates on the spot in his "What's It Wagon"—the name curious soldiers gave to Brady's horsedrawn darkroom. Hundreds of other itinerant photographers with portable studios tagged along with Union and Confederate armies, and for a dollar per picture, did a booming business providing portraits for boy soldiers to send home. Another drawback to the wet collodion technology was the sheer weight and size of the dozens—if not hundreds—of glass plates that a photographer might deal with in a short time.

Taken together, the requisite chemical processes and cumbersome methods of processing photographs limited its market to a cadre of professionals and dedicated amateurs. The huge industry in equipment and supplies that was to develop in our century was thus forestalled. Historian Reese V. Jenkins, who has provided the most complete history of the photographic industry, remarked:

> The barrier to expansion of photographic supply production was not the lack of a market but two internal technological restraints: (1) the rapid perishability of photosensitive materials; and (2) the complexity of photography for the average person. Thus, initially, the broad boundaries within which occurred the development of photography and the photographic industry were technological. Once these restraints had been removed, the forces of the national market could come into play.[3]

But the technological developments that were to allow the photographic industry to grow to its full potential required a few intermediate steps. One of these was the introduction of glass plates coated with a dry gelatin emulsion. This emulsion, introduced in the late 1870s, made it possible to produce nonperishable photosensitized glass plates in factories, thus making photography less complicated, more convenient, and lowering cost through large-scale production of one of its key components. They were also "faster" than the wet plates.

One of the many entrepreneurs to jump onto the dry plate innovation was a young amateur photographer from Rochester, New York named George Eastman. With a practical understanding of photo chemistry, a little business experience, and the financial backing of a successful Rochester businessman named Henry A. Strong, Eastman started a dry plate supply company in 1878. Like his competitors, Eastman's Dry Plate Company developed manufacturing processes to produce plates for a national market, and

Eastman would be the first to develop the processes and equipment (stamping machines, ventilation systems, glass cleaning and coating machines) to achieve large-scale production.[4] But unlike his many competitors, Eastman was among a handful to develop process improvements and production capabilities in a range of other photographic products: cameras, enlargers, printing paper, and assorted supplies.

Before long, the dry plate business took on all the hallmarks of a commodity business. The product was fairly undifferentiated to begin with, and as process improvements diffused rapidly within the United States, prices headed dramatically downward. The recession of 1854–1855 helped drive many small plate manufacturers out of the business, leaving an oligarchy of producers, none of whom were making substantial money on dry gelatin plates.

The Diffusion of Technology

Readers are surely familiar with the way that today's technological innovations travel from firm to firm and to startup companies with the migration of scientists and engineers. During the 1950–1990 period in American industrial history, a good number of the companies that emerged with computer, biotech, software, and genetic engineering technologies sprang from the scientific and technical knowledge developed in either government-sponsored laboratory research projects, or within large, established firms. Scientists and engineers were routinely recruited from competitors or were motivated to start their own firms to develop and commercialize new technologies. A recent book by Edward Roberts, *Entrepreneurs in High Technology,* documents the movement of scientific talent from MIT's many laboratories to literally hundreds of startup technology-based firms, Digital Equipment being the most prominent.[1]

Technological diffusion has traveled in the minds of its practitioners since the beginning of the industrial revolution, and their movements are difficult to control. One very early example is provided by Samuel Slater, an English mechanic from Derbyshire who memorized the design of his employer's newly invented cotton spinning machinery. In 1789, Slater emigrated to Providence, Rhode Island, where he took over the management of a local textile mill and proceeded to duplicate the entire set of machines owned by his former employer.[2] British laws passed to impede the emigration of mechanics and artisans to foreign rivals were largely unsuccessful, as trained workers disguised themselves or stowed away in barrels to reach promising opportunities on America's shores.

A similar phenomenon was responsible for the diffusion of photographic innovations in the nineteenth century. Reese Jenkins points out that Frank M. Cossitt carried the photographic paper production technology of the Eastman company to the Anthony company—a new competitor—in the late 1880s. Early in the next decade Cossitt left Anthony to use what he had learned at both Eastman and Anthony to start his own firm—New York Aristotype Company.[3] Several years later, in December 1891, Eastman learned that several of his most important and trusted employees, including his head chemist, Henry Reichenbach, were planning to leave and form a competing firm using their knowledge of Eastman products and processes.[4]

As we observed in previous chapters, this phenomenon was operative in the typewriter industry, where Yost, the original sales agent for the Remington Company, jumped ship to form a competing company. His Yost Caligraph was designed by another former Remington hand, Franz X. Wagner. Wagner and his brother in turn developed the important innovation of visible type, which they sold to John T. Underwood. The Underwood No. 1 that resulted from the Wagners' design quickly outsold both the Caligraph and Remington machines.

Notes

1. See Edward B. Roberts, *Entrepreneurs in High Technology* (New York: Oxford University Press, 1991).
2. James A. Henretta, W. Elliot Brownlee, David Brody, and Susan Ware, *America's History* (Homewood, Ill.: The Dorsey Press, 1987), pp. 310–311.
3. Reese V. Jenkins, *Images and Enterprise: Technology and the American Photographic Industry, 1839–1925* (Baltimore and London: Johns Hopkins University Press, 1975), p. 89.
4. Ibid., pp. 152–153.

The availability of dry plates most certainly simplifed the job of professional photographers and serious amateurs but appears to have done little to broaden the market beyond those limits. Cameras remained large, bulky contraptions, the dry plates were just as heavy and breakable as the old wet ones, and a photographer still needed the wherewithal to develop and print photo negatives. Eastman seems to have recognized this very early and, like Edison with incandescent lighting, had resolved to develop an entire *system* to change the picture-taking business. Also like Edison, he would not start with a clean slate but would draw on the technological currents of his time. And the coated dry plate technology provided the stepping stone to what he was looking for.

FILM PHOTOGRAPHY

As early as the late 1870s, Leon Warnerke, a Russian emigrant living in England, devised a camera system that operated in a manner similar to that common today. A collodion tissue coated with a gelatin emulsion underlaid with rubber was rolled up in the back of a camera. The tissue/rubber "film" was stretched across the area where the glass plate would normally go, and advanced as each picture was taken. The exposed emulsion was then laboriously separated from the rubber backing and affixed to a glass plate for processing.

Warnerke's system was clumsy, costly, and went nowhere. But its essential architecture was known to Eastman and his camera-designing associate, William Walker, and by 1885 the two developed a special camera back with a roll film system, using a coated paper material that presaged the one that would eventually dominate the field. Their holder could be fitted to the back of the standard plate camera and held up to 48 exposures on a roll.[5] This represented a tremendous weight advantage over the glass plate system. But the paper roll film was a failure for Eastman, as it did not meet the standards of the professional market in speed, resolution, and contrast. So Eastman and associates went back to their lab.

Another technology of interest to the photography industry at the time was celluloid. Invented in Europe during the 1860s, this plastic-like material had excited the imaginations of several people in the photography industry in the 1870s and 1880s, and the process innovations of two Albany, New York brothers—John and Isaiah

Hyatt—eventually served their interests. One of these was a Hyatt mechanism capable of slicing sheets of celluloid as thin as 1/100 inch; another was the development of a solution of nitrocellulose in amyl acetate that could be poured and dried into extremely thin sheets.[6] The first suggested the substitution of celluloid plates for glass plates; the second suggested a still thinner film.

In his search for a material to replace glass plates, Eastman eventually turned to celluloid. It had the properties that suited the purpose of providing a base for the photosensitive emulsion: it was lightweight, flexible, transparent, durable, and would not combine with the chemicals used in photo processing. What would be a more logical progression than to move from coating glass plates with a photosensitive emulsion than doing the same with a thin strip of clear celluloid? Working with his chief chemist, Henry Reichenbach, Eastman succeeded by the spring of 1889 in developing a photosensitive celluloid film and the production processes to manufacture it commercially. In a letter to his associate, William H. Walker, Eastman described celluloid film as "the 'slickest' product we have ever tried to make. . . . The field for it is immense."[7]

At about the same time, he and his associates developed a simple and inexpensive camera called the Kodak, especially for using the new roll film. With film, camera, and production processes in place and coordinated, Eastman now had all the elements to break through the traditional boundaries of the photographic market.

PROCESS INNOVATION AND THE SUCCESS OF THE EASTMAN SYSTEM

Having failed in his earlier attempt to sell roll film to professional photographers, Eastman now went after a market that so far had not responded to any of the evolutions in photographic products: amateurs. The picture-taking system he offered them was simplicity itself. The Kodak camera came loaded with a 100-picture roll of film at a price of $25. Once these were shot, the customer mailed the entire camera back to the Eastman Company in Rochester, New York, where the film was taken out, developed and printed, and the camera reloaded with film. The customer paid $10 for the processing and the return of his reloaded camera.[8] Taking photographs with the Kodak system was absolute simplicity when compared to existing alternatives, and Eastman played up this fact in advertising in Europe and America. The novice photographer had only to perform three simple tasks: "pull the cord" (to cock the shutter), "turn the key" (to advance the film), and "press the button."

The new system was offered to the public in the summer of 1888 (using paper roll film, soon to be replaced by celluloid) and was an immediate success. The national photographers convention named the Kodak the "photographic invention of the year."

Deja Vu All Over Again

Interestingly, almost a century after it first simplified the business of picture taking with its system of selling pre-loaded cameras that were returned to the factory for development, Kodak in the late 1980s began selling a returnable camera operating under the same system. With little more than a plastic box to contain the film, and an inexpensive plastic lens, the recyclable Kodak was offered to the public for about $10. It contained film for 24 pictures. The camera could be taken to any processor for development, and the body of the spent camera could be returned by the processor to Kodak, where it was reloaded and resold. The "disposable camera" today has become one of the fastest growing products in Kodak's repertoire and has led many novices into photography in just the same manner as did the original Kodak!

With the development of this system, the two internal technological restraints cited earlier by Jenkins—the perishability of photographic material and the complexity of picture taking for the average person—were effectively overcome. Photography could now make a quantum leap beyond the limitations of the professional market. Demand for Kodak cameras and film took off, and the company struggled desperately to keep up with it during the next decade. Figure 8-1 indicates total domestic sales of Eastman Kodak during its formative years. The slow rate of total company sales growth during the half-decade following introduction of the Kodak roll-film system was caused in part by the decline of other segments of its business (dry plates and photographic paper).

FIGURE 8–1.   **Sales Growth of Eastman Kodak Company, 1889–1909**

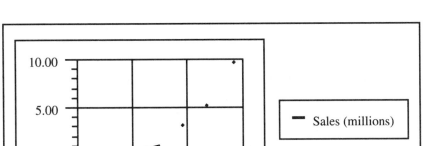

Note: Data for many years not available.

Source: From Eastman Kodak reports as cited by Jenkins, *Images and Enterprise,* p. 157; and Edwin Frickey, *Production in the United States, 1860–1914* (Cambridge, Mass.: Harvard University Press, 1947), series P13, as cited by Jenkins, p. 178.

Developing production process improvements to manufacture the new celluloid film in large quantities became a major concern. George Eastman had earlier shown himself to be quite astute in matters of process innovation. In fact, his first principle of business was to achieve production in large quantities through the use of machinery. From his early invention of a mechanized system of cleaning, coating, and drying glass plates he had also developed (with Walker) an ingenious system for coating and drying very long strips of photographic paper. These later were run over a roller that was partially submerged in a trough of gelatin emulsion and coated the paper. The very long strips of paper were suspended from the ceiling in long, serpentine loops (to save room) until the emulsion dried, then cut into individual sheets. Eastman was scrupulous in patenting every step of his manufacturing processes, as he understood their importance to the success of his business far into the future.

Like photographic paper, roll film was a matter of coating, drying, and cutting; but those steps had to be preceeded by the major step of creating celluloid from liquid ingredients. Initial production was done by the batch method on 12 glass tables, each $3\frac{1}{2}$ feet wide by 50 feet long.[9] A solution of nitrocellulose and solvents was spread evenly over these tables by a hopper and allowed to dry overnight. The next day, the resultant celluloid was coated with emulsion in darkness, stripped off the glass tables, and cut into long ribbons of film ready to be rolled. Demand induced Eastman to build a new research and film production facility outside Rochester in 1890–1891. Here again, the same process was employed, but the 12 tables were extended from 50 to 200 feet. Within a year, this capacity needed to be doubled.

Strangely, Eastman remained with this batch method of film making and coating until the mid-1890s, five years after methods of continuous casting of celluloid had been achieved by the Hyatt brothers, and several years after a photographic film competitor, the Blair-Waterman Company, had developed the technology to coat and dry the Hyatts' film in a continuous process. It was Eastman's replacement for the departed Reichenbach, a young MIT graduate named Darragh de Lancey, who was instrumental in buying the patents and creating the designs that would allow Eastman in 1899 to successfully operate the first machine to both cast and photosensitize continuous ribbons of celluloid film.[10] Others were soon brought on line.

By 1902, Eastman Kodak was producing 80–90 percent of the world's celluloid film.[11] By the 1930s, the company operated dozens of huge, specially designed film-making machines at its Kodak Park plant. The raw material for these was film "dope"—a solution with the viscosity of honey that was produced from cotton treated with nitric and sulfuric acids and dissolved in solvents (chiefly wood alcohol). The film dope was spread over the polished surfaces of gigantic circulating wheels. Heat speeded the evaporation of the solvents, leaving a thin film of clear celluloid. These machines were designed to run night and day, turning out continuous ribbons of film.[12]

THE OLD TECHNOLOGY REACTS

While sales of roll film and roll film cameras exploded with the introduction of the Kodak system, neither glass plate photography nor the companies that supported it were condemned to rapid decline. Sales of dry gelatin plates held fairly steady for the next 15 to 20 years[13] as professional studio photographers continued to favor the traditional system. Nevertheless, firms that confined themselves to this market missed all of the growth that the industry was to enjoy and eventually succumbed to obsolesence.

Some equipment makers made their peace with roll film, producing cameras under their own patents that would accommodate the Eastman product. Others sought to imitate directly, but had a plague of lawsuits for their trouble, as Eastman had built up a thicket of protective patents on products and processes that few could penetrate—and these he defended vigorously.

One of the most interesting reactions of the establishment producers was the introduction of products that hoped to improve the existing technology of dry plate photography. As we witnessed with gas lighting in Chapter 3, and ice harvesting in Chapter 7, the old technology often finds ways of improving itself when faced with a serious challenger. In this case, Jenkins points out that a number of improvements came to the market: self-setting shutters, cameras that used sheets of celluloid in place of glass, small plate cameras. One producer, actually anticipating the multiexposure capabilities of Edison roll film by a few years, introduced a plate camera featuring an internal "magazine" of some 20 plates.[14] As one photo was taken, the exposed plate would be mechanically moved out of the focal plane and stacked at the bottom of the camera chamber while a fresh plate was brought into place. This camera must necessarily have been large and extremely heavy. Later versions of these magazine cameras could accommodate either glass plates or celluloid sheets.

The Family Tree of Nineteenth-Century Photography

1839   Daguerreotype invented in France. Image produced on a silvered copper sheet.

1855   Wet collodion on glass plate.

1855   Ambryotype and tintype. Inexpensive variants on wet collodian technology enjoy some popularity.

1880   Dry gelatin emulsion on glass plate.

1885   Roll film, first paper backed, then celluloid.

LESSONS FROM THE EVOLUTION OF PHOTOGRAPHY

The evolution of photography provides many good examples of how technological innovation plays a role in industries producing nonassembled products—in this case, photosensitive plates and film. In many respects, the patterns we find here are often shared with assembled products, and from them managers can draw quite a few important lessons. Similarly, many lessons learned earlier are confirmed by this extended case, and it may be useful to review them here.

Waves of Innovation and Change

The family tree of photography illustrates how the underlying technology of an industry can experience waves of change in just four decades. We observed the same in typewriting, plate glassmaking, refrigeration, and lighting; and these are summarized in Figure 8-2.

Within and between each of these waves, the following phenomena are regularly observed.

Parallels to Existing Forms

Innovations are often suggested by existing forms. This is easily found in the technological progression from daguerreotype to wet collodian to dry gelatin plate to celluloid film, which carried along many artifacts from the old to the new in terms of the underlying photochemical processes. The same is observable in the typewriter case; some important elements were carried forward in each wave of technological change. The QWERTY keyboard is the prime example, having been a common element of manual, electric, and now computer-based typing systems. When mechanical icemakers went head to head with the New England ice harvesters, they did so by producing blocks of the same dimensions, even though their technology gave them the freedom to create ice in other sizes. Edison sold his electric lighting system by deliberately aping as many of the forms of the gas lighting system as possible.

The Emergence of a Dominant Design.   Except for special applications, the roll-film format pioneered by Eastman rapidly emerged as the dominant design in photographic film. Today, 35mm film in light-tight canisters is the accepted product form from Baltimore to Bangkok; even Kodak's own attempt to introduce disk film has

FIGURE 8–2.   **Waves of Innovation and Change**

Industry	Waves of Innovation
Typewriters	• manual • electric • word processors • personal computers with word-processing software
Ice and refrigeration	• harvested ice • machine-made ice • electromechanical refrigeration • asceptic packaging
Lighting	• candles and oil lamps • distilled gas • incandescent electric lamps • fluorescent lamps
Plate glassmaking	• crown glass • cast glass • float glass
Photography	• daguerrotype • tin type • glass plates • dry plates • celluloid roll film • electronic imaging

failed to make inroads. This phenomenon is as much a result of the need for technical standards as anything else. Certainly a strong case could be made for 30mm or 45mm film, but the need to match the film to a set of camera standards is much more powerful. In this sense 35mm film is to modern photography as QWERTY keyboards are to typewriters and personal computers.

Outsiders as Innovators.   Particularly in assembled product industries, major innovations come from outsiders. Edison is a wonderful example of this. He had no experience in the lighting industry prior to his first experiments with incandescent lamps. Similarly, the innovations that killed harvested ice came from outsiders. In the case of typing, IBM was an outsider when it began to trade in electric typewriters; none of the firms that made word processors and personal computers had any standing in the typewriter industry. The photography case offers the weakest evidence for this generalization, as Eastman was an important member of the photography industry at the time he innovated celluloid roll film. However, the latest innovation in imaging now comes from the electronics industry, which is unrelated to chemical-based photography. In process-oriented industries such as glass, innovation very often comes from the suppliers of process equipment, and not from the processors themselves.

A Reluctance by Established Firms to Adopt Radical Technology. In almost all cases analyzed here, established firms were slow to adopt radical technologies as they appeared. Some, like gas lighting and harvested ice companies, simply abandoned or were driven out of their markets. Others made an attempt; some of the camera companies, for example, adapted their camera bodies to accommodate celluloid roll film; among those manual typewriter firms that survived the 1930s and 1940s, most made some effort to branch into electric machines, but none have successfully caught the next wave of word processors or personal computers.

The result of this reluctance to adopt successful new technologies has been a change of leadership at breakpoints in technology. The torch is passed to new leaders as established firms fail to leap across technological discontinuities. Royal was eclipsed by IBM in the transition from manual to electric typewriters; the gas companies faded from the lighting business as the likes of Edison Electric and Westinghouse emerged; the leading dry plate makers faded away as Eastman's roll film gained market dominance.

With respect to the modern photographic industry, leadership may be poised to change once again. In 1989, Sony Chairman Akio Morita called a press conference to unveil a new product of the giant consumer electronics firm. The product was not a new portable TV, not an improved microwave oven, but—of all things—a new camera. The remarkable thing about this camera was that it reproduced an image using electronic digital technology, a radical departure from the chemical imaging tradition that began in France in 1839 and has dominated the industry ever since. With Sony's new system, the image could be viewed immediately on any television screen without development processes.

As of 1993, the future of Sony's new image-producing technology is not clear. It may be a technology with only a few special applications; but then, it may become the way people take pictures in the future—which raises the question of how the massive industry based on photosensitive film will respond. The multibillion dollar industry of Kodak, Fuji Film, dozens of camera makers, and tens of thousands of independent film processors around the world may be in the same situation as the nineteenth-century harvested ice industry. If electronic imaging becomes the wave of the future, which of these current producers has the competencies to make the leap to the new and unrelated technology?

Linkage of Product and Process Innovation

The linkages between product and process innovation have been demonstrated throughout this book. These linkages are fundamental to the development of industries and are expressed in a number of important ways.

A Shift From Product to Process Innovation. As product features are agreed to by producers and customers, and as markets expand, a shift takes place in the rate at which product and process innovations occur. Although the Eastman Company never stopped innovating with respect to its products, moving on to faster, sharper, and then color films of great intricacy, there was a major shift early on from product to process innovation, just as we observed in other industries—ice and incandescent lamps in particular. In general, this shift takes place sooner in nonassembled product industries. Photographic film as a product certainly had all the hallmarks of a nonassembled product, however, as it entered the age of color, its complexity increased from that of a simple strip of coated celluloid. In this sense, photographic film is something of a hybrid between the simplest of nonassembled products and those of more complexity.

Dual Focus on Cost and Quality. It was ever an Eastman strategy to consider cost, both in the design of the product and the process that would manufacture it. We know, for instance, that he quickly replaced his original Kodak camera with his model No. 1 because the design of the Kodak's shutter system was inherently costly to make. Today, many believe that about 70 percent of manufacturing costs are dictated by product design; Eastman understood this intuitively. His No. 1 camera featured a much simplified and more easily manufactured shutterworks. Speculating why Eastman, operating out of provincial Rochester, became the global market leader instead of the Germans, who were the technical leaders in the sciences of optics, fine chemicals, and camera design, Jenkins observes that "German products usually were very expensive and, therefore, produced in relatively small quantities. In contrast, George Eastman struck an enviable balance between quality and cost, focusing his financial and human resources on an international mass market and large-scale production."[15] In this some may see parallels to the mass-production/good-quality American auto industry that prevailed from Henry Ford's day until the 1970s versus the low-volume/high-quality European auto industry of the same period.

High Cost of Introducing Process Innovation. As an industry becomes more "specific," greater reliance is placed on the use of specialized and expensive equipment. Innovations that require alteration of the production system are very expensive. This is a cruel irony for decision makers: process innovations hold out the promise (and not the guarantee) of truly major productivity gains, but at staggering costs. Pilkington's glass company faced this difficult situation, as did Eastman when Kodak moved from the use of relatively inexpensive glass tables to manufacture photographic film by the batch method, to the tremendous outlays necessary to implement continuous film production. In these cases, costs were certain to be high, but there was no certainty as to outcomes.

The Importance of Systems

We also note the importance of systems in achieving large-scale success in an emerging industry. Edison's system of incandescent lighting required the simultaneous development of lamps, wiring, sockets, generators, and so forth; the ice harvesters similarly created a system for cutting, storing, and distributing ice both locally and to distant ports; photography for *everyone* required a system of a simple camera and no-fuss processing, both at low costs. In the modern personal computer field, network system externalities—linkages with phone and fax machines, and even touch-typing skills—have proven to be extremely important. The development of systems by industry pioneers undoubtly created barriers to aspiring competitors.

The Importance of Competence

One way to appreciate the dimensions of the challenge that traditional firms may face—be they typewriter makers, ice harvesters, gas companies, or automakers—is to consider innovations in terms of their relationship to existing business and technical capabilities. To a great or lesser degree, innovations either enhance or destroy competencies that a firm already possesses. In photography, the innovation of roll film by Eastman involved some elements that were competence enhancing to established firms of that time (coating a transparent material with a photochemical emulsion) and some that were truly new and competence destroying (casting and cutting strips of celluloid that were uniformly thin and free from dust and air bubbles). Eastman's talent for developing and improving automated processes for coating dry plates and photographic paper served him well in developing the competencies he needed to make a success of mass production of roll film. His competitors in the dry gelatin plate business were equally girded with coating capabilities, but the business of casting celluloid film was entirely outside their experience and may have been the reason that so few of them bridged the discontinuity to roll film. Similarly, General Electric moved easily from manufacturing incandescent lamps to vacuum tubes for radios and televisions, but did not so easily bridge the gap from tubes to transistors; Kodak successful navigated from photographic movie film to videotape; Sylvania moved from incandescent lamps to fluorescents. In each case, the innovations were competence enhancing. The sway of existing skills and attitudes is so great that J. Herbert Hollomon once commented that it was only when he built a new factory in a new place with entirely new people that General Electric finally managed to produce transistors.[16]

Eastman's competence in film production served him well as applications presented themselves. When Thomas Edison asked Eastman to produce a special film for use in the newly invented motion picture camera, Eastman already had the competencies needed to develop that product: he merely had to strengthen and lengthen his strips of film and add holes to engage the movie camera's sprocket.

The importance of competence is equally well illustrated in the transition that took place between mechanical typewriters (manual and electric) and word processors. Nothing in the skills bank of Royal, Remington, Underwood, and the other established typewriter firms prepared them for the innovation of word processing, which operated without carriages, type bars, ink ribbons, and the other paraphernalia of the traditional industry. Competence in those areas served the established firms not at all in making the transition to word processing. The gas-illuminating companies were similarly done in by their lack of competences with respect to electricity and electric lampmaking when that technology challenged their hold on the market.

As a general rule, competence-enhancing innovations come equally from established firms and from outsiders. Competence-destroying innovations nearly always come from outsiders. (This subject will be developed more fully in the next chapter).

The need to build new competences in anticipation of future developments is an important element of long-term business success. George Eastman appears to have been one of the successful innovators who recognized this requirement. His firm had no competence in color film when its early precursors began to appear in European laboratories, but he recognized the importance of developing them. The advent of color photography in the first decade of the twentieth century was, like most radical innovations, pioneered by a firm outside the circle of leadership: Lumiere Brothers. Eastman was acutely aware of the threat that their Autochrome process (1904) posed to his firm, even though it did not enjoy commercial success when marketed in 1907. He encouraged a number of independent efforts to develop the technology and had a trusted associate monitor the pace of progress by competing firms, mostly German. All of Eastman's early attempts at color photography failed, and these failures spurred him to institutionalize R&D in the Eastman Kodak Research Laboratory.[17] As he entered his twilight years, Eastman was concerned that his company develop the capability to produce color film, which it did in the late 1920s. Very likely the aging founder, whose long experience had taught him the necessity of bridging the discontinuities of technological change, saw color film as critical to his company's continued leadership in the industry.

This idea of competences is critical to the survival of all firms as they encounter incremental and discontinuous technological change, and it will be developed more fully in the following chapters.

PREPARING FOR TECHNOLOGICAL DISCONTINUITIES

Slightly more than 20 years ago, James W. Brown and I published an article entitled "Monitoring for Technological Opportunities"[18] that evaluated methods used by firms to scan the horizon for indications of imminent technological change. The method was directed, as an example, to traditional film photography. We used evidence of a growing gap between increasing commercial use of silver (an important ingredient in photo film making) and anemic growth in silver production as a "signal" that some form of technological change in the business of taking pictures seemed probable. We saw the implications of this gap as leading possibly toward 1) development of more efficient silver based films; 2) development of films based on substrates other than silver; and 3) development of competing media—electronics, for example. Today, the last two developments are in evidence. First, the use of videotape—a film base coated with magnetized powder—has largely eliminated traditional film in nearly all motion-picture taking applications (the exception being professional film-making, the niche in which the technology started). Second, the development of electronic imaging continues to make progress, though it, like all radical innovations in their early stages, is unperfected, expensive, and has no assurances of success.

The challenge for the company George Eastman built will be to retain leadership when and if these or other innovations render the traditional industry obsolete. If electronic imaging represents the future, Kodak will have to leap from its century-old expertise in fine chemicals and the production of coated films and papers to a field in which expertise in electronics and digital technology is critical. Eastman has stated its strategic intent to dominate the market in both chemical and electronic imaging. To date its products have been hybrids of the new technology and the old. These include inexpensive cameras stuffed with electronics to make them simple for the user to operate while getting splendid results. They include an Instaprint® system, which transforms a negative into an electronic image that the user can then manipulate, changing composition, color balance, and shading. When the image composed on a television screen pleases the user, he or she just "pushes the button" and in four minutes a finished print of up to 10 × 14 inches appears—digitally transferred back to sensitized printing paper! A further step in this direction is Kodak's Photo-CD® system. Here color negatives taken on an ordinary 35mm camera are transferred via a digital scanning system similar to that in the Instaprint machine to a special compact disc or CD, which can then be put in an inexpensive CD player attached to the customer's television set for viewing. The same player can be attached to the customer's home computer and provided with software that will allow him or her to compose and adjust the photographic images.

One is tempted to compare such hybrid systems to Gilfillan's steaming sailship—a use of new technology in a futile attempt to extend the life of and defend the old.[19] But the photo CD system does have the great advantage of compatibility with an enormous inventory of existing negatives and slides. While yet to be proven a commercial success, it plays to Kodak's well-established competences in color imaging.

Finally, an advantage of the hybrid system is that photography can still capture an astonishingly richer and finer range of color and detail than any electronic video or photographic system. Will a generation raised on relatively crude television images appreciate or pay for this degree of sophistication? Will customers warm to the idea that the image captured on their photo CD is close to that of real life even though the version played back on their television or perhaps a color printer is not?[20]

Polaroid is also poised to enter the electronic imaging business and has announced a new system called Helios® for the medical imaging market. Helios incorporates a laser scanner and a new carbon-based instant film system. The Helios machine will take digital inputs from an ultrasound diagnostic machine and convert them in one step into the extremely sharp black and white image customary for this application.

Striking in all of the examples is the fact that the road to profit is still based on the production and one-time consumption of film even though that is facilitated with electronic means. Images are still to be captured on a negative with a camera and stored to be viewed using a print (except for Kodak's Photo-CD system). Neither Polaroid nor Kodak has yet grasped the nettle of a fully electronic system in which images are captured, stored, and played back using electronics. Video cameras have captured nearly all of the home movie and television news photography markets. Will amateur and professional still photography be next? The jury is still out.

Notes

1. Reese V. Jenkins, *Images and Enterprise: Technology and the American Photographic Industry, 1839–1925* (Baltimore and London: Johns Hopkins University Press, 1975), p. 19.
2. Ibid., pp. 37–38.
3. Ibid., p. 67.
4. Ibid., pp. 72–73.
5. Brian Coe, "The Roll Film Revolution," in Colin Ford, ed., *The Story of Photography* (London: Century, 1989), p. 60.
6. Jenkins, *Images and Enterprise,* p. 123.
7. George Eastman to William H. Walker, cited in Douglas Collins, *The Story of Kodak* (New York: Harry N. Abrams, 1990).
8. The need for this system was largely eliminated with the 1891 introduction of light-tight film cartridges, which allowed the amateur photographer to load and unload the camera in subdued light instead of a darkroom. Thenceforth, only the cartridge, and not the whole camera, needed to be sent in for processing.
9. Jenkins, *Images and Enterprise,* pp. 131–132.
10. Ibid., pp. 179–183.
11. Helmut Gernsheim, *A Concise History of Photography* (New York: Grosset & Dunlop, 1965), p. 36.
12. Eastman Kodak employees' pamphlet, 1934.
13. See Table 9.9., "Net Sales of Leading American Dry Plate Manufacturers, 1902–10, in Jenkins, *Images and Enterprise,* p. 228.
14. Jenkins, *Images and Enterprise,* p. 167.
15. Reese V. Jenkins, "Science, Technology, and the Evolution of Photography, 1790–1925," in Eugene Ostroff, ed., *Pioneers of Photography* (Springfield, Va.: Society of Imaging Science and Technology, 1987), p. 21.
16. Discussion with the author.
17. Jenkins, *Images and Enterprise,* pp. 304–305.
18. James M. Utterback and James W. Brown, *Business Horizons,* vol. 15 (October 1972), pp. 5–15.
19. S.C. Gilfillan, *The Sociology of Invention* (Cambridge, Mass.: MIT Press, 1935) (2d ed., 1963).
20. After finishing this chapter I decided to train a jeweler's loupe on the 8 × 10-inch enlargement I recently made to try the Instaprint system. The dots of color from the negative to electronic to film transfer were clearly visible! Indeed, some photography buffs have begun to complain that the inexpensive enlargements provided by many photofinishers are similarly produced, not created by the "true" light and chemical process that (much more expensively and laboriously) preserves their negatives' fine detail.

CHAPTER 9

Innovation as a Game
of Chutes and Ladders

There are rare moments in technology when the next 5, 10 or 15 years begin to crystallize; this is one of those moments.
Glen Zorpette, "Supercomputers," *IEEE Spectrum,* September 1992

IN THE CHILDREN'S GAME of Chutes and Ladders one moves ahead in painstaking steps, turn after turn, in much the way that incremental improvement inches technology forward. Ralph Gomory and Roland Schmitt make the point that most products sold today were here in slightly inferior form last year, and most competition is between variants of the same product. Occasionally a player is lucky enough to land at the bottom of a ladder, which allows him to climb quickly up to a higher level of the game's twisting path. Gomory and Schmitt liken this to the creation of a new idea leading to the potential for rapid development. The unlucky player can also land at the top of a slide or chute that whisks her to a lower level, as is the case for the firm that chooses to coast in the face of rapidly changing technology. The generality of technological competition is that most time is spent on the tortuous, gradually inclined path, and firms that can run only a little faster than others will pull far ahead given time. Gomory and Schmitt contend the following:

> It is this process of incremental improvement that, after the initial ladder style invention of the transistor has given us better computer memories every year. In the last 20 years the number of memory bits per chip has gone from one to one million. Incremen-

tal improvement also has given us jet engines with double the thrust per unit weight of two decades ago, plastics that can be used at temperatures twice as high as a decade ago, and incandescent light bulbs that are fifteen times as efficient as Edison's.[1]

Indeed, a considerable part of this book has been devoted to detailing the process of continuous innovation and improvement in a number of industries. But what of the chutes and ladders? Despite their rarity, the player who encounters a break in the path will have his or her fortunes either rudely reversed or happily improved. What happens when the evolutionary trajectory is disrupted by new technologies or other forces?

One arena in which we can see this clash of technologies now is in the field of supercomputing, where there is a discontinuity in the making. Cray in the United States and NEC in Japan hold the lead in speed and in market shares in what are today the fastest computers produced, the so-called supercomputers based on four, eight, or sixteen blindingly fast processors made from exotic materials often running at extremely cold temperatures. The development of such processors has been methodical and constitutes the tortuous path for Cray and NEC. Other companies, however, led by Thinking Machines and by Intel Scientific Computers, are rapidly climbing a ladder that threatens the traditional makers of supercomputers by interconnecting hundreds or thousands of microprocessor-based nodes to form what have been described as "massively parallel supercomputers," whose processing powers may reach levels 100 times those of today's best machines.[2] Massively parallel supercomputers have the great advantage that they can be created from standard processor technologies and run at normal temperatures.

The market for massively parallel supercomputers came from nowhere to $538 million in revenues in 1993 and is expected to leap to the $1.6–$2.7 billion range by 1997.[3] In so doing, massively parallel supercomputers are expected to peel away business that would otherwise go to the old line supercomputer makers, as well as the traditional mainframe makers, like IBM. As one would expect, given earlier cases, the leading firms in this new market are all new entrants.

Naturally, the computing establishment is not totally oblivious to this threat. IBM, whose mainframe business has been under attack on the high end by supercomputers and on the low end by personal computers and workstations, is developing its own capabilities through its Power Parallel Systems unit. "This is the future—and IBM will ride it," is how the leader of that unit, Irving Wladawsky-Berger, described parallel machines to the *New York Times* in the fall of 1993.

Identifying the path to the future is one important requirement for survival and success when discontinuities surface. For established firms, getting off the path they are currently on is another, more difficult challenge. The impulse for firms to continue on the path of cash-generating technologies is powerful. IBM, for example, has to deal with the reality that an estimated $1 trillion worth of mainframe software is up and running in the customer universe and that thousands of its employees and thousands of shareholders benefit mightily from its current mainframe business, however diminished.[4] The extent to which resources are diverted into parallel machine development—indeed, the very success of the new technology—threatens many of these interests.

As we will see shortly in the case of Digital Equipment Corporation, established firms are apt to approach discontinuities and conflicting corporate interests with compromises. In the case of IBM, the same article that quoted its parallel computing executive also described a forthcoming machine—the 390 Parallel—as a traditional mainframe computer with a parallel processing turbocharger. Bridging a technological discontinuity by having one foot in the past and the other in the future may be a viable solution in the short run, but the potential success of hybrid strategies is diluted from the outset compared to rivals with a single focus.

THE TORTOISE AND THE HARE

Gomory and Schmitt contend that if a firm moves only slightly faster than its rivals in incremental improvement, it will appear to have newer products with newer technologies, even though all the firms are drawing from the same level of technical knowledge. This is surely true when all are pursuing improvement of the same basic design or production process. However, Fernando Suárez and the author have shown that the advent of a new technological ensemble, or ladder, is marked by a wave of new competitors entering the industry. To sustain success requires mastery of the infrequent discontinuities as well as mastery of the constant competitive and customer demands for rapid incremental improvement. How can companies sustain success when they know that the technologies underlying their products and markets will change periodically?[5]

Even the largest and strongest firms find this to be a struggle. IBM for example, according to David Kirkpatrick, has been from three to eleven years behind the curve in each case of revolutionary change.[6] Digital led IBM by eleven years in introducing the minicomputer; Apple led by four years in introducing the personal computer; Apollo was five years ahead in introducing the engineering workstation; Toshiba led by five years with the PC-compatible laptop; and Sun Microsystems led by three years with its Sun 4 RISC workstation. IBM's late introduction of RISC is particularly troubling in that it was clearly years ahead of others in originating and advancing RISC technology in its corporate laboratory. And though IBM is now seriously moving to enter the market for massively parallel supercomputers, its newer rivals have again stolen the march by five or more years. Evidently it is the very success and dominance of large firms that leaves them vulnerable to new entrants to their business. Indeed, former chairman John Akers proposed that splitting IBM up into more manageable pieces may be the right course to reduce complacency and to increase the market responsiveness of each part.

EVIDENCE AND ADVICE

We contended earlier that new technologies have made industrial giants out of once-small upstart firms, invigorated older firms that were receptive to change, and swept away those that were not. This chapter draws the threads of both examples and observations more tightly together to reexamine the question raised at the outset: Can we better understand which firms will be able to ride the crest of a wave of change while others are left gasping in the undertow? Are there managerial principles for staying on top, or is long-term success and survival a matter of pure luck?

At the outset of this book we noted that Schumpeter considered innovation both the creator and destroyer of corporations and entire industries. Cristiano Antonelli, Pascal Petit, and Gabriel Tahar note that

> in his early works Schumpeter (1912) insisted on the role of entrepreneurs in seizing discontinuous opportunities to innovate. Inno-

vations were taken in a broad sense of new "combinations" of producers and means of production, which includes new products, new methods of production, opening up of new markets, utilization of new raw materials, or even the reorganization of a sector of the economy. . . . This initial approach stressed the discontinuities of the innovation process.[7]

In later years (1942) Schumpeter began to place greater stress on the role of larger enterprises in innovation, seeming to believe that as scientific knowledge accumulated there was a threshold investment in R&D below which a firm could not be an effective player. I have always been troubled by this conflict in Schumpeter's views. The present analysis suggests that the former hypothesis is true for areas of emerging product technology and firms involved in product innovation, especially for assembled products (that is for discontinuous and fluid phases), while the latter hypothesis might well hold for process innovation, for many nonassembled products, and for firms producing standard products and large systems (the specific phase).

Following Schumpeter's pathbreaking, work researchers in the main focused on the concepts he laid out, and studied invention (ideas or concepts for new products and processes), innovation (reduction of an idea to first use or sale) and diffusion of technologies (their widespread use in the market). Indeed, this was the framework used by Myers and Marquis in their influential study,[8] by me,[9] and by Project Sappho,[10] the first extensive study of matched successful and unsuccessful innovations. Cooper and Schendel were the first to turn the lens in the opposite direction in a provocative analysis of major technological innovations from the viewpoint of firms in established industries threatened by innovation. They note that

> a typical sequence of events involving the traditional firm's responses to a technological threat begins with the origination of a technological innovation *outside the industry,* often pioneered by a new firm. Initially crude and expensive, it expands through successive sub-markets, with overall growth following an S-shaped curve. Sales of the old technology may continue to expand for a few years, but then usually decline, the new technology passing the old in sales within five to fourteen years of its introduction. [Emphasis added.][11]

Not only do the sales of the established technology decline, but the traditional leaders in the industry also lose position. Why is this so? Clearly the traditional firms are financially strong, and they have sophisticated market knowledge and distribution channels as well. Richard Foster and I were inspired by the questions posed by Cooper and Schendel's work and by cases and observations posed by James R. Bright, and we began to work independently to examine them. Foster has based his analysis on the theory of technological limits, while Linsu Kim and I were more concerned with firms' behavior and competitive responses. We came up with remarkably similar results. The most obvious explanation for the demise of established leaders in an industry would be that they have skills in the old product or process technology, while the entrepreneurial firms have a base in the new. Perhaps the most surprising observation from examining many cases of discontinuous change is that differences in technological resources do not much discriminate between invading and traditional firms in an industry. Most threatened firms do participate in the new technology and often have preeminent positions in it. The basic problem seems to be that they continue to make their heaviest commitments to the old, which reaches the zenith of its development only after it is mortally threatened. Cooper and Schendel put it as follows:

> The traditional firms fight back in two ways. The old technology is improved and major commitments are made to develop products using the new technology. Although competitive positions are usually maintained in the old technology, the new field proves to be difficult. In addition to the major traditional competitors (who are also fighting for market share in the new field), a host of new competitors must be confronted. Despite substantial commitments, the traditional firm is usually not successful in building a long-run competitive position in the new technology. Unless other divisions or successful diversifications take up the slack, the firm may never again enjoy its former success.[12]

Cooper and Schendel conclude that a dual strategy is simply not a viable way to gain a leading position in the new. Threatened firms continue to make added commitments to developing old products even after their sales have begun to decline rapidly. Their explanation for this difficulty is that "decisions about allocating resources to old and new technologies within the organization are loaded with implications for the decision makers; not only are old product lines threatened, but also old skills and positions of influence."[13]

If one were to bet purely on the basis of technological resources that a firm would master a discontinuity, then one would probably bet on an entrepreneurial firm with a sophisticated technology base and a high degree of development spending (as a proportion of sales) in an industry characterized by rapid generational changes, each of which represents a relatively small step from the past. Surely such a firm would find it difficult to become entrenched. Henderson and Clark have recently studied just such an extreme case. They conducted a comprehensive review of the semiconductor photolithographic alignment equipment industry. Every firm in the industry was studied through five generations of architecturally different product technologies, meaning that components were integrated into a system in different ways. Astonishingly, no firm that led in one generation of product figured prominently in the next! Henderson and Clark conclude that even relatively minor shifts that lead to changes in systems relationships can have disastrous effects on industry incumbents. Their explanation is that such innovations "destroy the usefulness of the architectural knowledge of established firms, and since architectural knowledge tends to become embedded in the structure and information-processing procedures of established organizations, this destruction is difficult for firms to recognize and hard to correct."[14]

The Survival of Some Threatened Firms

Once the old technology begins to modernize itself in response to the invasion by the new, the emphasis in competition shifts to product change and away from cost and quality, while at the same time prices may drop with extraordinary rapidity, and many new options and performance dimensions may become available to users. The total market may even expand as a direct consequence of the invading innovation. However, this only postpones the inevitable abrupt decline of the established technology and lends false strength to arguments against withdrawal from the old and rapid investment in the new.

In some product lines, the last few firms in the established technology can be highly successful and profitable and even highly innovative. There will probably always be a demand for fine mechanical watches for example, and perhaps the few firms that survive the present shake-out in the industry will be highly profitable and stable companies. And the few firms which remain manufacturing vacuum tubes probably supply a highly specialized and profitable market for high performance designs, research and other specialized applications.[1]

Note

1. James Utterback and Linsu Kim, "Invasion of a Stable Business by Radical Innovation," in Paul Kleindorfer, ed., *The Management of Productivity and Technology in Manufacturing* (New York: Plenum, 1986), pp. 129–130.

While each of the studies reviewed, as well as my own work with Kim, describe the dynamics of discontinuous change, the advice given to management is disappointing. Cooper and Schendel believe that their work illustrates some of the approaches and pitfalls in discontinuous change that management should consider. Their message accurately portrays the low probability of success in either defending the old position or successfully entering the new and seems to recommend diversification as a singularly viable option. Foster speaks to the entrepreneurial attacker with excellent advice on ways to take advantage of established firms that tenaciously want to believe that the looming threat of an innovation either is unimportant or will go away. Anderson and Tushman argue that "the closing of an industry standard is an inherently political and organizational phenomenon constrained by technical possibilities," and that "the passage of an industry from ferment to order is not an engineering issue as much as a sociological one."[15] Henderson and Clark conclude that their work underscores the need to deepen our understanding of the distinction between innovation that enhances and innovation that destroys competence within the firm, and they point out that systems changes can subtly do both, sometimes misleading the firm to believe that because it understands the components, it must therefore understand the system they form as well. They suggest that an organization that can learn quickly and effectively about components may not be able to fathom systems relationships at all. Christensen counsels firms not to be so attentive to large and familiar customers. The demands of these customers can lead a firm down the garden path to spending royally on marginal improvements for older concepts, all the while ignoring newer customers in small but growing markets that support new concepts. This advice is especially valuable in view of the current doctrine to "listen to the customer." But which customer should firms listen to? Linsu Kim and I concluded that discontinuities that break market *and* manufacturing process linkages will be more threatening to the firm than those that break either one or the other. We suggested that discontinuous process changes will more likely be introduced by established firms producing homogeneous products like glass than assembled products like televisions. Finally, we suggested, as did Cooper and Schendel, that discontinuities that expand the market are seemingly less threatening to established firms than are those that simply create substitute products.

None of these studies, unfortunately, successfully addresses the key problem: how established firms can renew their core technologies when they become obsolete, thereby avoiding retrenchment and failure. (This question is the more compelling in a year when retrenchment for firms like IBM, DEC, Kodak, and General Motors means quarterly reductions of tens of thousands of employees.) Each analysis is limited in much the way that the views of the fabled eight blind men and the elephant were limited. Each has a part of the truth, but that part alone is misleading. To more fully develop our understanding, I will combine the data from the earlier studies mentioned plus those from a number of single but intensive case studies of discontinuous change and use these combined data to construct a three-factor model. I will show that under some circumstances leaders of well-established firms should certainly plunge forward to invest in a radically different technology, while in other circumstances they clearly should not, and certainly not with a dual strategy.

A CASE OF FOCUSED VERSUS DUAL STRATEGY

As earlier chapters have made clear, discontinuities caused by innovation more often than not create chasms that few firms can bridge. A few find their ways across, but most fall into the abyss. Susan Walsh Sanderson of Rensselaer Polytechnic Institute has provided a vivid contemporary example of two leading firms in the same industry that ran up against a technological discontinuity, describing how one firm effectively bridged to a new product architecture, while the other continued to struggle. In "Managing Generational Change: Product Families Approach to Design,"[16] Sanderson used the shift from CISC (complex instruction set) to RISC (reduced instruction set) architectures in computer workstations to show how Sun Microsystems made a clean break from its established system to launch a new and successful generation of workstations. (RISC architectures are simpler and faster than the now-common CISC architecture.) Digital Equipment Corporation, burdened by the success of its popular VAX system, "dragged its heals in making an investment in RISC and then did so in a halfhearted way."

Figure 9-1 represents the product family strategies of the two firms. In the case of Sun, continued extension of its CISC-based products effectively ends at the point where RISC technology creates a discontinuity. In 1989, the firm developed a new family of workstations with the RISC architecture, based on a microprocessor of its own design: the "Sparc" chip. By 1991, Sun had made a clean break with its older-generation workstations, devoting all of its energies to the family of products that emerged from the new architecture.

DEC, with its wide range of minicomputers and workstations, according to Sanderson, had a long-standing strategy of supporting compatibility among its own products and those of major competitors. Its large established base of customers and installed equipment presented an obstacle to DEC's making the transition to the RISC architecture, where continuity and compatibility would be threatened. It waded into the RISC technology slowly, all the while maintaining its commitment to its existing family of VAX-station products. A new generation of workstation based on a proprietary Alpha chip was planned for the future.

The bottom of Figure 9-1 describes DEC's workstation family and development strategy. Here, the CISC-era VAX family is shown being carried through into the RISC era, while its own RISC-based machines (using MIPS Corporation chips) provide a smaller part of its workstation effort. The new Alpha machines are shown proceeding from development to market to product family somewhat later in the game. As Sanderson relates, "DEC had built its empire on the VAX architecture and could not find a painless migration either for itself or its customer. It waited too long to

FIGURE 9–1.   **Sun and DEC: Generational Product Strategies**

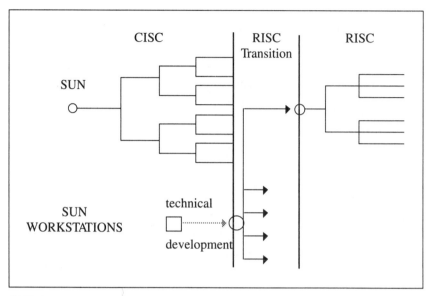

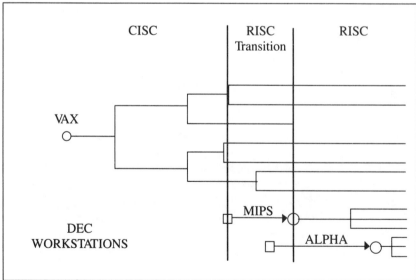

Source: Sanderson, see note 17, reprinted with permission.

make the necessary transition and *almost lost the company* [my emphasis]."

While it may be that DEC's Alpha chip will lay the groundwork for future success and growth, many observers believe that the company will bear greater-than-necessary dislocations in moving forward because of its continuing commitment to multiple but parallel product architectures. The extent to which Sun Microsystems "bet the company" in this episode, or the extent to which its strategy of abandoning the older generation of workstations burdened future cash flows, is not made clear in Sanderson's discussion. We can surmise, however, that the stakes were considerable. By 1991, the year in which the firm made its break with its CISC-based architecture, Sun was already a multibillion company with 38 percent of the workstation market. Workstations were, in fact, its only real business. Thus Sun's decision to move entirely to RISC-based architecture was more survival threatening than was DEC's decision to move with all deliberate caution. DEC was a much smaller player in the total workstation market and had plenty of other business to sustain it. The CISC to RISC transition going on in computers seems a compelling example of the reasons not to play a dual strategy of sustaining both the new and the retiring product at a time of radical change.

CONTINUITIES AND DISCONTINUITIES

The evolutionary model outlined in Chapter 4 described continuous change in products and processes as a transition from an earlier fluid state to one that is highly specific and rigid. As continuous change proceeds, technological diversity gives way to standardization. These evolutionary periods do not continue indefinitely, but are often interrupted by a new cycle of creativity and discontinuous change. By discontinuous change or radical innovation, I mean change that sweeps away much of a firm's existing investment in technical skills and knowledge, designs, production technique, plant, and equipment.

Earlier chapters of this book have provided abundant examples of powerful discontinuities in which either a change in product or the process architecture caused important dislocation at the level of the firm and throughout entire industries. Figure 9-2 presents a summary of these discontinuities.

FIGURE 9–2. **Product and Process Discontinuities**

Industry	Discontinuities
Typewriters	Manual to electric; to dedicated word processors; to personal computers
Lighting	Oil lamps to gas; to incandescent lamps; to fluorescent lamps
Plate glassmaking	Crown glass to cast glass through many changes in process architecture; to float process glass
Ice and refrigeration	Harvested natural ice to mechanically made ice; to refrigeration; to asceptic packaging
Imaging	Daguerreotype to tintype; to wet plate photography; to dry plate; to roll film; to electronic imaging; to digital electronic imaging

The Typewriter

Discontinuities were observed between the periods of the manual typewriter, electrics, dedicated word processors, and personal computers. Of the large manual typewriter firms of the early twentieth century, none were successful in jumping onto the bandwagon of electric typewriters; it was IBM, an outsider, that developed both the product and its market. Subsequently, the move to word processors and then personal computers caused equal dislocation, virtually none of the original typewriter companies, excluding IBM, having made the leap. Indeed, virtually none survive in their past forms.

Lighting

The change from lighting with candles to the modern system of electrical illumination has all taken place (in most of the Western world) within a period of 150 years. Oil lamps displaced candles and were in turn displaced by gas in most urban areas. Electric lamps of the Edison design displaced gas, and fluorescent lamps have displaced these in many instances. Each wave of change has brought a different champion to the fore; and,.with the exception of the nonleadership position of Edison's successor firm (GE) in fluorescents, no firms have successfully bridged the discontinuities.

Plate Glass

The generations of discontinuous and incremental change in this industry have virtually eliminated all but a handful of highly capitalized, high-volume producers. There would be even fewer firms in this important industry today had Pilkington Brothers decided to protect its patents on the float glass process and simply run over its competition. Instead, it chose to license that breakthrough technology to other glass firms, which allowed them to survive. With almost all the glass in the developed world being made under this process, those that did not switch to it were largely eliminated.

Ice and Refrigeration

No doubt a few local holdouts in places like Maine and northern Minnesota continue to harvest ice for commercial sale, but the other firms are gone. So too are most of the firms that displaced the ice barons with mechanically manufactured ice. They in turn fell prey to the innovation of electro-mechanical refrigeration; the broad market for ice produced by nature or by machines disappeared almost 40 years ago. Here again, the agents of change were not the leaders of the established technology.

Imaging

The transition from daguerreotype to modern film photography and the emerging technology of electronic imaging was punctuated by many discontinuities: tintype to wet and then dry coated glass plates, and then sheet celluoid and roll film. Each transition was inspired by a different party, rarely the market leader, and each transition led to the period in which old producers were replaced by new ones.

In addition to these cases we will cover those analyzed by Cooper and Schendel: steam to diesel locomotives, vacuum tubes to transistors, fountain to ballpoint pens, safety razors to electric razors, fossil-fuel boilers to nuclear boilers, propellers to jet engines, and natural to synthetic leather. We will cover cases from the cement industry and minicomputer industry contained in Anderson and Tushman and cases from Utterback and Kim;

mechanical to electronic calculators, woven to tufted carpet, transistor to integrated circuit, open- to closed-body cars, rayon to nylon tire cord, air-cooled to hydrogen-cooled generators, open hearth to basic oxygen furnaces, and other examples from steelmaking, continuous drawing of copper wire, synthetic gems, and small-scale production of industrial gases. To add to the case so completely analyzed by Henderson and Clark we include a number of other intensive single-product cases: radial for bias ply tires, oriented strand board for plywood, optical fibers for copper wire, and massively parallel for von Neumann supercomputers.

FRAMEWORK

The combined sample just described consists of 46 discontinuous innovations, of which 26 are product discontinuities and 20 are process discontinuities. Nearly one-quarter of the 46 innovations come from within firms that are established competitors (12 of 46), while the remainder—a large majority (27 of 46)—come from firms entering the industry. (The sources of the other 7 are undefined for the most part because no industry existed prior to the innovation in question.) The entire sample is shown in detail in Figures 9-2, 9-3, and 9-4.

The purpose here is simply to attempt to put the differing blind men's views of the elephant together in order to get a more comprehensive and accurate picture of the whole. Doing so will provide a remarkably accurate discrimination between the cases that were mastered by traditional firms and those that came from beyond their circle of known competitors. To put this mosaic together, we will first look at each of three factors highlighted in the prior studies separately and then endeavor to examine them jointly. Stated as questions, these are the factors:

- Does the discontinuity pertain to an assembled or a nonassembled product?
- Is it simply a substitution or does it create a broadened market?
- Is it competence enhancing or competence destroying for the established firms in the industry?

Our hypothesis is that each factor is important and that they will operate more powerfully jointly than separately.

ASSEMBLED VERSUS NONASSEMBLED OR HOMOGENEOUS PRODUCTS

Linsu Kim and I argued in 1986 that discontinuous changes in process pertain primarily to industries producing homogeneous products. In fact this is true for the entire 20 process discontinuities in the combined sample. We claimed that such discontinuities would usually be introduced by established firms in sharp distinction to the general arguments posed here, often by marginal firms seeking to expand market share or by dominant firms under severe cost, supply, or regulatory pressure. We further concluded that occasionally such changes might be introduced by equipment suppliers, who may also enter production in their own right. We reasoned in part, based on von Hippel's work and earlier findings from Project Sappho, that the most demanding users of process equipment and those with the most subtle information about demands would be the users of the manufacturing equipment themselves. It was our contention that discontinuous changes in processes will primarily emphasize real or potential cost reduction, improved product quality, and wider availability, and require movement toward more highly integrated and continuous production processes.

Figures 9-2 and 9-3 show that discontinuous innovations in assembled products almost always come from outside the industry (15 of 21 cases, with 3 from internal sources and 3 inconclusive). Discontinuous innovations in nonassembled products often come from inside the industry (9 of 25 cases, with 12 from external sources and 4 inconclusive), but more often from outside. Fully three-quarters of all the cases coming from within the established industry fell into the homogeneous product category.[17]

IS A DISCONTINUITY A SUBSTITUTE OR DOES IT CREATE A BROADENED MARKET?

A discontinuous change may drastically increase the aggregate demand for the products of an industry. The replacement of the vacuum tube by the transistor and later by the integrated circuit has increased the sales of the electronics industry from several billions of dollars to hundreds of billions. The replacement of piston aircraft engines by turbojets has correspondingly dramatically reduced the costs and increased the seat miles flown by commercial aircraft. The advent of the electronic calculator has made such equipment commonplace rather than something rarely encountered. The advent of Eastman's Kodak camera and roll film system transformed photography from a small professional market to the large and now familiar amateur market. Replacement of carbon filament incandescent lamps by those based on metal filaments multiplied the demand for incandescent lamps from twenty million to hundreds of millions per year in the United States alone. The invasion of machine made ice tripled the demand for harvested ice from five million tons per year to fifteen million tons per year. Each revolution in glassmaking led to a corresponding sharp increase in aggregate demand for flat glass, and the advent of on-site production of oxygen led to more than a doubling in the demand for oxygen.

FIGURE 9–3.   **Competence-Destroying Product and Process Discontinuities**

Assembled/ Substitutes Photolithographic aligners (A) Radial tires (A) Diesel locomotive (A) Ballpoint pen (A) Jet aircraft engine (A) Refrigerators (A) Incandescent lamps (A) All-steel automobile (A)	**Assembled/ Market Broadening** Solid-state minicomputers (N) Integrated circuits minis (A) Transistor (A) Electronic calculator (A) Tufted carpet (A) Massively parallel supercomputers (A)
Nonassembled/ Substitutes Suspended preheating (D) Glass drawing (D) Continuous forming (D) Float glass process (D) Basic oxygen steel (A) Direct reduction of iron (A) Optical fibers (A)	**Nonassembled/ Broadening** Rotary kiln (A) Container machine (N) Owens process (A) Vinyl (E) Celluloid film (A) Manufactured ice (A) Synthetic gems (A) Small liquid oxygen plants (A)

(A) denotes an innovation originated predominantly from a new entrant or attacker; (D) denotes an innovation originated predominantly from an established firm or defender; (N) denotes that the origin of the innovation has not been classified, mainly cases in which no prior industry existed.

Reasoning from the general arguments given in Chapter 2, one would expect that innovations that broaden the market would create room for new firms to start, and that innovation-inspired substitutions would cause established firms to hang on all the more tenaciously, making it extremely difficult for an outsider to gain a foothold and the cash flow needed to expand and become a player in the industry. Figures 9-3 and 9-4 show that discontinuous innovations that expand markets will almost always come from outside the industry (15 of 18 cases, with 1 from inside and 2 inconclusive). Discontinuous innovations that substitute for established products and processes often come from inside the industry (11 of 28 cases, with 12 from outside and 5 inconclusive). This is in line with our explanation. Of the 12 internally created discontinuities, 11 were substitutions, but 12 of the discontinuities that were substitutes also come from outside sources for this combined sample.[18]

In summary, some discontinuities broaden a market, allowing new firms to enter and survive. Established firms are more likely

FIGURE 9–4. **Competence-Enhancing Product and Process Discontinuities**

Assembled/ Substitutes Nuclear steam supply (A) Air-cooled engines (D) Nylon tire cord (N) Hydrogen-cooled generator (D) Fluorescent lamps (N)	Assembled/ Market Broadening Semiconductor memory (D) Electric typewriter (A)
Nonassembled/ Substitutes Computerized kiln (D) Edison long kiln (D) Machine cylinder glass (D) Gob-fed bottle machine (D) Double gob machine (D) Continuous casting (D) Continuous drawn copper (D) Oriented strand board (D)	Nonassembled/ Broadening Integrated circuits (A) Continuous vertical kiln (A)

(A) denotes an innovation originated predominantly from a new entrant or attacker;
(D) denotes an innovation originated predominantly from an established firm or defender;
(N) denotes that the origin of the innovation has not been classified, mainly cases in which no prior industry existed.

to fail than succeed, but many do succeed. New and established firms have roughly equal chances. Examples include the transistor, personal computer, and massively parallel supercomputer cases discussed earlier. Some discontinuities do not broaden a market or create a new niche. In such a situation new firms experience tough sledding. Fewer and larger firms may survive. Established firms are likely to enter successfully. Established firms also have greater survival chances in these instances than do new firms. Examples include the electric typewriter and metal filament lamp cases discussed in earlier chapters.

Some discontinuities create a wholly new market niche, encouraging the many new entrants. Here, established firms are unlikely to enter successfully, and new firms have better survival odds. Examples include the typewriter, automobile, television, and television tube cases discussed in earlier chapters. Recall that "new" has a specific meaning: Corning in optical fibers, Remington in typewriters, General Motors in locomotives, as well as new entrants such as Genentec in biotechnology, Digital Equipment in minicomputers, and so forth.

IS A DISCONTINUITY COMPETENCE ENHANCING OR COMPETENCE DESTROYING?

Tushman and Anderson have characterized technological discontinuities as either competence enhancing or competence destroying. A competence-destroying discontinuity renders obsolete the expertise required to master the technology that it replaces. For example, the skills of mechanical watch manufacturers or vacuum-tube producers were rendered irrelevant by quartz watches and integrated circuits, respectively. Similarly, the skills of the glassmaking artisan were made obsolete by the Lubbers machine, which allowed unskilled operators to make glass cylinders. But knowing how to make and flatten cylinders contributed little to knowing how to draw a continuous ribbon of glass from a tank. Drawing-machine know-how in turn did not translate to the float glass process, which critically depends on understanding properties of the alloy bath.

According to Tushman and Anderson,

> A competence-enhancing discontinuity "builds on know-how embodied in the technology that it replaces. For example, the turbofan advance in jet engines built on prior jet competence, and the

series of breakthrough advancements in mechanical watch escape-
ments built on prior mechanical competence. Similarly, the Edison
cement kiln allowed cement makers to employ their existing rotary
kiln knowledge to make much greater quantities of cement. Later
retrofitting of process controls to cement kilns again allowed manufacturers to build on accumulated know-how while dramatically
accelerating production through minute control of the process.[19]

Figures 9-3 and 9-4 show that discontinuous innovations that
destroy established core competencies (in technology) almost
always come from outside the industry (23 of 29 cases, with 4 from
inside and 2 inconclusive). Discontinuous innovations that enhance
established core competences (in technology) often come from
inside the industry (10 of 17 cases, with 4 from inside and 3 inconclusive).[20,21]

ALL THREE FACTORS TAKEN TOGETHER

Discontinuous innovations that would be most disruptive
based on the preceding arguments, those in assembled products
that expand established markets and that destroy established core
competences virtually always come from outside the industry (5 of
6 cases, with 1 inconclusive). These cases have been given a score
of 3 in Table 9-1.[22] Discontinuous innovations that would be least
disruptive based on the preceding arguments, those in nonassembled products that substitute for established products and that
enhance established core competences (in technology) virtually
always come from inside the industry (7 of 8 cases, with 1 inconclusive). These cases have been given a score of 0 in Table 9-1.
Intermediate cases—for example, ones that expand established

TABLE 9–1. **Number of Cases for Three Variables
Considered Together**

Score	Inside Source	Outside Source
Three factors positive	0	5
Two factors positive	1	16
One factor positive	6	6
All factors negative	7	0

markets and/or that destroy established core competences—will virtually always come from outside the industry (16 of 18 cases, with 1 from inside and 1 inconclusive). Cases in which just one of the three factors discussed is present in its most disruptive form have been scored 1. Such cases come about equally from inside and outside the industry (6 of 14 cases from new entrants, with 6 from inside and 2 inconclusive).

Using the eight categories formed by the three dimensions, it is striking to see that the cases contained in the extreme cells are classified perfectly. It would be hard to imagine this happening with a larger and more representative sample.

SUMMARY

Earlier work on technological discontinuities has concluded if not that practically all established firms fail to master radical innovation, then at least that it is a highly random and unpredictable process. However, extracting the three factors highlighted in earlier work that attempted to discriminate between situations in which new entrants were advantaged and those in which established firms hold the cards may allow us to tell a slightly different story. While it is true that a large fraction of radical innovations are indeed introduced and taken up by competitors new to an industry, in about one-quarter of the cases studied existing competitors either introduced radical innovations or were able to initiate them quickly and survive as major players in their markets. Thus established firms need not always fail in this arena. More important, we may be able to see even in the preceding rough analysis the conditions favorable to their success, so that they can analyze and act accordingly.

Clearly, technology is not the key in and of itself. Market conditions are an equally powerful influence. And while technology and markets are important, their importance must be understood in conjunction with the human factors determining organizational competence or core capabilities. When core capabilities are aligned (as in the case of the replacement of plywood by oriented strand board), management can attempt to make a discontinuous change internally. When they are not, either an alliance or outside venture is called for, or great effort must be invested to create appropriate human resources and cultural change before attempting the innovation.

Clay Christensen's work shows that established firms were the real leaders in introducing thin film disk drives, which displaced their own magnetic technologies. Most of the new entrants failed in this essentially evolutionary change.[23] Similarly, IBM spent $300 million to develop the thin film head for its hard disk drives, while DEC spent $200 million. However, new entrants were the leaders in introducing new architectures (in Henderson and Clark's terms the same technological idea, but having components related in different ways). Established firms led the difficult but incremental improvement of components. New firms led with new architectures using established components. The leaders in incremental innovation were not able to keep that proprietary. Incremental innovation did not affect industry structure despite its high cost. New entrants with architectural change, despite its being fast and cheap, dethroned the leading companies in the Winchester disk drive industry.

Why were firms willing to pay hundreds of millions of dollars for incremental changes and not a few million dollars for a new frame size? Because the new frame size did not address the *needs of their established customers*. (Another kind of persistence of competence.) Smaller drives at first were much slower and more expensive, but they did enable a hard drive on the desktop. A good analogy is the car companies discouraging Goodyear, Firestone, and others from introducing radial tires because they did not want to change the design of the suspensions on their cars.[24] Similarly, IBM's problem is not that it fails to listen to its customers carefully, but may be that it attends to a powerful set of customers dragging it along the wrong technical trajectory. Virtually all mainframe computers are sold to customers who already use mainframe computers and who have large switching costs because of investments in software, procedures, and so on. Perhaps this is one of the critical clues to the failure of established firms. Clay Christensen finds very uniformly that the competitors firms monitor are the ones that are in the same technology and architecture. But the competitors that are most threatening will be those coming from the unexpected direction with a new architectural concept such as massive parallelism in computation.

Ironically, then, following advice to be market driven in pursuing innovation, delighting one's customers through continuous improvement of products, and seeking out lead users may be powerful concepts for success or may pave the road to failure, depending on circumstances. These are good ways for a new entrant to identify and specify a valuable direction for change. They are good lessons to follow in promoting evolutionary change in well-understood product lines. But when applied to a discontinuity, they may lead a strong firm into a dangerous trap. Similarly, ideas such as lean manufacturing (with regard to product and manufacturing competences) and mass customization (with regard to marketing and distribution competences) may be thought of as a way to build core competence and to be highly successful in differentiating well-known products. But these concepts may lead to a dead end when radical change is in the wind.

The destructiveness of a change such as machine-made ice is rather surprising. Product, market, and distribution linkages were left entirely intact. Only the ice harvesters' manufacturing competences were severed, but this seemed like a total revolution to them. By the same reasoning the electric refrigerator should have been, and was, much more competence destroying, laying waste to product, marketing, and distribution competences as well as manufacturing. Now the customers could make their own ice for drinks on demand! The key question is not just whether an innovation is competence enhancing or destroying, but for whom? Goodyear and Firestone saw radial tires as cutting into the market for bias-ply tires, while Michelin saw them as expanding the market both in size and geography. Kodak may see electronic imaging as cutting into its market for chemical imaging and eroding high profit margins, while Canon and Sony may see the same innovation as expansive and raising relatively lower margins.

Being able to answer this question may give us a sharper understanding of firms' potential vulnerabilities and strategies. We will turn to the question of core capabilities and the renewal of corporate vitality in the final chapter.

Notes

1. Ralph Gomory and Roland W. Schmitt, "Science and Product," *Science*, vol. 240 (May 27, 1988), p. 1131.
2. Glenn Zorpette, Issue Editor, "Teraflops Galore," *Special Report: Supercomputers, IEEE Spectrum,* September 1992, p. 27.
3. Steven Lohr, "Well, Somebody's Got to Reinvent the I.B.M. Mainframe," *New York Times,* September 12, 1993, p. 8.
4. Ibid.

5. I have shown that the frequency of these sorts of changes depends on the type of industry and the intensity of competition.

6. David Kirkpatrick, "Breaking Up IBM," *Fortune,* July 27, 1992, p. 47.

7. Cristiano Antonelli, Pascal Petit, and Gabriel Tahar, *The Economics of Industrial Modernization* (London: Academic Press, Harcourt Brace Jovanovich, 1992).

8. Sumner Myers and Donald Marquis, *Successful Industrial Innovations* (Washington, D.C.: The National Science Foundation, NSF 69–17, 1969).

9. James M. Utterback, "The Process of Innovation: A Study of the Origination and Development of Ideas for New Scientific Instruments," *IEEE Transactions on Engineering Management,* vol. EM-18, no. 4 (November 1971), pp. 124–131.

10. Roy Rothwell, C. Freeman, A. Horsley, V.T.P. Jervis, A.B. Robertson, and J. Townsend, "SAPPHO Updated—Project SAPPHO Phase II," *Research Policy,* vol. 3, no. 4 (1974), pp. 258–291.

11. Arnold Cooper and Daniel Schendel, "Strategic Responses to Technological Threats," *Business Horizons,* vol. 19, no. 1 (February 1976), pp. 61–69.

12. Ibid., p. 61.

13. Ibid., pp. 68–69.

14. Rebecca Henderson and Kim Clark, "Architectural Innovation: The Reconfiguration of Existing Product Technologies and the Failure of Established Firms," *Administrative Science Quarterly,* vol. 35, no. 1 (1990), p. 9.

15. Philip Anderson and Michael Tushman, "Technological Discontinuities and Dominant Designs: A Cyclical Model of Technological Change," *Administrative Science Quarterly,* vol. 34, no. 4 (December 1990), p. 627.

16. Susan Walsh Sanderson, "Managing Generational Change: Product Families Approach to Design," Proceedings of the Design and Manufacturing Systems Conference (Washington D.C.: National Science Foundation, January 19, 1993).

17. The probability that this strong a relationship would be found by chance alone is less than one in one hundred. (Chi-square test, $p < .01$.)

18. Ibid.

19. Anderson and Tushman, "Technological Discontinuities and Dominant Designs," p. 609.

20. The probability that this strong a relationship would be found by chance alone is less than one in one hundred. (Chi-square test, $p < .01$.)

21. The massively parallel and von Neumann supercomputers case is taken from Allan Afuah and James Utterback, "The Emergence of a New Supercomputer Architecture," *Technological Forecasting and Social Science,* vol. 40, no. 4 (December 1991), pp. 315–328; cases from the cement industry and minicomputer industry, the Owens process and other machinery for glass bottle making, and the direct reduction of iron are contained in Anderson and Tushman, "Technological Discontinuities and Dominant Designs," pp. 604–633; transitions from steam to diesel locomotives, vacuum tubes to transistors, fountain to ballpoint pens, safety razors to electric razors, fossil-fuel boilers to nuclear boilers, propellers to jet engines, and natural to synthetic leather are taken from Cooper and Schendel, "Strategic Responses to Technological Threats," pp. 61–69; the radial for bias-ply tire case is from Daniel-Guy Denoual, *The*

Diffusion of Innovations: An Institutional Approach, DBA diss. (Boston: Harvard Business School, 1980); the case of photolithographic alignment equipment is from Henderson and Clark. "Architectural Innovation," pp. 9–30; the case of oriented strand board and plywood is from Henry Montrey and James Utterback, "Current Status and Future of Structural Panels in the Wood Products Industry," *Technological Forecasting and Social Change*, vol. 39, no. 4 (December 1990), pp. 15–35; transitions from woven to tufted carpet, open- to closed-body cars, rayon to nylon tire cord, air-cooled to hydrogen-cooled generators, open-hearth to basic oxygen furnaces, and other examples from steelmaking, continuous drawing of copper wire, synthetic gems and small-scale production of industrial gases are from Utterback and Kim, "Invasion of a Stable Business by Radical Innovation," pp. 113–151; and the case of optical fiber substituting for copper wire is from John McCormack and James Utterback, "Technological Discontinuities: the Emergence of Fiber Optics," in Philip Birnbaum, ed., *Competitive Strategies in the Telecommunications Industry* (Greenwich, Conn.: JAI Press (forthcoming). All other cases are from the previous chapters and the sources cited there.

22. The probability that this strong a relationship would be found by chance alone is less than one in one thousand. (Chi-square test 3,2 vs. 1,0, $p < .001$.)
23. This dovetails nicely with McCormack and Utterback's forthcoming fiber optics data as well, ibid.
24. This point is disputed by Donald Frey, formerly at Ford, who says that Ford persistently sought radial tires from its reluctant suppliers.

CHAPTER 10

Innovation and Corporate Renewal

E VEN THE CASUAL OBSERVER of industrial enterprise must be struck by the cycle of development, growth, maturity, and decline through which many individual firms pass. Growth companies eventually run out of steam, or are eclipsed by new competitors. Solid blue chip companies that once seemed permanent fixtures of the economic scene suddenly fall under a weight of problems. Their descents from market leadership are often public and painful, marked by massive financial losses and employment dislocations. Some blame widening global competition for the difficulties of beleaguered firms, while others see them as victims of macroeconomic and structural shifts beyond the clear control of government and corporate managers. Overshadowed by the troubles of these firms are the many, small victories won by new firms, and by individual divisions of the troubled giants.

The examples and arguments in the preceding chapters should have convinced the reader that a strong technological base is as critical to the prosperous survival of a firm as a good understanding of markets and a strong financial position. They should also have sown doubts about the permanence of a competitive position, no matter how strong it may seem on a national or an international scale to contemporary observers. Indeed, one of the advantages of choosing examples spread over so great a span of time is that the vulnerabilities of prominent current industries can easily be recognized by an analogy. At the same time, it is clear that there are few or no general answers to the challenges that technological changes pose to a leading large firm. Solutions will depend on the circumstances of both the firm and its industry, the types of products produced, and the sources of added value, and even the path by which the firm reached its current status. I believe that the illustrations and patterns discussed in this book will be helpful, even provocative, for managers dealing with the opportunities and crises produced by technological change and innovation.

Firms owe it to themselves to improve and extend the lives of profitable product lines. These represent important cash flows to the firm and links to existing customers. They provide the funds that will finance future products. At the same time, managers must not neglect pleas that advocate major commitments to new initiatives. Typically top management is pulled by two opposing, responsible forces: those that demand commitment to the old, and those that advocate for the future. Unfortunately, advocacy tends to overstate the market potential of new product lines and understate their costs. Management, then, must find the right balance between support for incremental improvements and commitments to new and unproven innovations. Understanding and managing this tension perceptively may well separate the ultimate winners from the losers.

Clearly, there are important lessons in this book for the entrepreneurial founders of new firms. Starting a firm with a new product in a new industry involves much borrowing of diverse elements from others and synthesizing them creatively. We have seen that the winners are often the ones that are the most experimental and flexible in matching the early forms of the product with unexpected demands and opportunities and that think through the development of their innovation in the most thorough and systematic way. As we have seen, firms that stay the course must be prepared to shift their strategic and competitive postures at several points along the way. That entrepreneurs must prepare themselves to address global markets and prepare to meet competitors from many fronts is also a truism, evident even in the earliest cases discussed. However, it seems that the larger and more well-established firms face the more difficult problems. They must constantly renew, even regenerate, their businesses, and it is to them that this chapter is primarily addressed. First I will address the need for the constant improvement and renewal of established products, and the issues of how to encourage ceaseless incremental innovation. In the second section of the chapter I will conclude the discussion, begun in Chapter 9, of the issues facing the firm beset by the challenges of radical innovation.

CONTINUOUS RENEWAL OF ESTABLISHED PRODUCTS

Incremental innovation is clearly of critical economic and competitive importance. We have seen that the firms that perfected the typewriter and invested in large-scale plants to become low-cost producers stayed at the top of their industry for half a century. Incremental product improvements raised the efficiency of the incandescent electric light, while process improvements reduced the cost of production one-hundredfold. Similarly, dramatic efficiencies in production were accomplished in the first thirty years of the harvested ice industry. These cumulative changes moved typewriters, electric lighting, and ice refrigeration from being luxury items for the few to being commonplace in businesses and homes. The same can be said about plate glass, photographic film, rayon, and countless other products.

Success in continuous incremental improvement requires equal emphasis on product and process design, which must be closely integrated. This was a novel idea when William Abernathy and I first proposed it, but it has become widespread today as simultaneous engineering and design for manufacturing. Moreover, process advances often enable further improvements in products, particularly in reliability and cost. Leadership in incremental improvement requires persistence in measuring product and process performance, and in seeking improvement from any source. Savings may come from better use of materials, energy, and labor, but are often the result of reductions in the number of parts, product complexity, and process steps as well. Value may also be added by finding simple ways to do complex jobs (as in the use of "getters" to remove the last bit of oxygen from light bulbs) and making product use simple (as in Eastman's pre-loaded camera).

The challenge of renewing the vitality of an established firm should not be thought of as limited to technical choices or effective research and development. Innovation entails much more for the firms that adopt it. As Lewis Branscomb has pointed out,

> . . . technologies must be mastered, reduced to practice, supported by cost effective production processes, and introduced to the mar-

ket. Then that market position must be sustained by appropriate complementary assets, by effective channels of distribution, and by responsive customer service. Even that, however, is not enough, for many innovating products have found strong initial markets, only to see other firms—sometimes other nations—capture the lion's share of the market growth through incremental functional improvements, cost reductions, quality superiority, and better marketing and service.[1]

Over the past decade business leaders have adopted a number of panaceas for extending their period of leadership. By right sizing and refocusing, by removing layers of management and building teams, by installing total quality management and lean manufacturing, and by striving toward time-based competition, today's corporations are attempting to bolster lagging sales, productivity growth, and profitability. More recently, managers have been urged to listen to the voice of the customer, to mass customize their products, and to reengineer their corporations. Although each of these approaches to corporate maintenance have merit, and many have demonstrated remarkable effects, they are, nevertheless, limited solutions. They help companies be more effective in their current lines of business for a time, but they do little to help them if the changes prescribed are made in isolation or if, as is often the case, they have little staying power.

Charles Baden-Fuller and John Stopford have recommended that managers view each action they take for change as a step on a strategic staircase. Although an organization can seldom attend to more than one campaign for change at a time, it is equally important to be sure that the just-completed and dearly won campaign not be reversed by the next one. Thus, Baden-Fuller and Stopford suggest that managers consider ways to mount the entire staircase of changes with cumulative effect, rather than simply bumping along the floor.[2] Branscomb, Baden-Fuller and Stopford, and this book argue against any one suggestion or solution as *the* key to sustained corporate success in the face of technological change. Clearly, the key is the thoughtful and persistent development of the firm's capabilities and resources, and, even more important, the balance among them. As we have seen in the cases and examples described, the balance required is dynamic and constantly shifting; achieving it is somewhat akin to riding a bicycle.

A fundamental approach to renewal then is the development of core capabilities. C.K. Prahalad and Gary Hamel have suggested that a firm's ability to identify, nurture, and exploit its basic strengths as "core products" is both directly related to competitiveness and provides a new perspective on organizational form and process.[3] They have suggested that instead of examining their firms as portfolios of businesses, executives should view them as portfolios of core competencies that transcend specific strategic business unit boundaries. These competencies are defined as "the collective learning in the organization," especially as they coordinate diverse production skills and integrate multiple streams of technologies. Such competencies, according to Prahalad and Hamel, become the basis for multiple market applications, are difficult to imitate, and provide a substantial part of the design in final products that solve customers' perceived problems and needs. The core products needed for the firm's thrust toward new markets flow from organizational strengths. Prahalad and Hamel provide neither methods to measure the concept of core competencies nor data, but their argument is nonetheless compelling.

CHOOSING THE RIGHT CAPABILITIES

The idea of fortifying the core competences of a firm as a means of increasing its survivability is not in itself a solution; it merely provokes two further questions. First, which competences should the firm develop? The ones it already has? The ones it expects to need in the future? Or some of both? The harvested ice industry of New England invested heavily in its core competences. Over time it learned better ways to score and cut cakes of ice; it became expert at storing ice over several years; it developed its capabilities to transport a heavy, perishable product efficiently over great distances. It reduced costs from 10 or 20 *dollars* per ton to 10 or 20 *cents* per ton and owned world markets. It was the most competent ice harvesting industry ever. These efforts were essential. But none of those competences assured its survival when technology changed. With the rise of mechanical ice making, competence in cutting blocks of ice became irrelevant. With electric refrigeration, what was the value of competence in storing and transporting blocks of ice? What was the value of a house-to-house ice delivery system once most people had acquired electric refrigerators?

The failure to keep up with innovation is really the failure to develop and focus core competences in the direction of change and progress. And that direction is often unclear except in hindsight. The U.S. tire industry represents another case in which firms increased their core competence, but not in a direction that had a promising future. Tire producers continued to develop their ability to manufacture bias-ply tires when they should have been learning to design and manufacture the new radials being produced in Europe. The bias-ply producers had every reason to continue in their old direction: they had tremendous investments in fixed assets, distribution arrangements, and specialized knowledge. Just as important, their best customers, the Big Three U.S. automakers, manufacturers of vehicle suspensions that would not run smoothly on radial tires, discouraged them from pursuing the new technology through their requirements for traditional bias-ply tires.[4]

Unfortunately, there is no easy answer as to how firms should choose the core competences that will assure their progress and survival. Certainly it is essential to anticipate discontinuities and to try to act in advance of their full impact. Doing so requires constant monitoring of the firm's external environment to notice forerunners of significant change. We have seen that most firms look in exactly the wrong places for vital signs of technological change: namely, their universe of traditional rivals. Large and similar competitors are the focus today of vigorous benchmarking efforts by many firms. Benchmarking is an excellent source of information to guide evolutionary change and continuous improvement, but probably a poor source for signals of discontinuities. Looking toward more obscure new entrants and unconventional sources of competition is more fruitful, although these sources are more diffuse and difficult to monitor.[5] Technological and market uncertainty, however, implies that no one can act with clear anticipation or forecasts. Among equally capable generals the one with the best contingency plans will usually win the battle. Unexpected departures from the anticipated plan are almost certain to arise, and in the best of cases they will open the way to greater opportunities than at first imagined. This is crucial in the choice of capabilities to foster.

THE QUESTION OF FOCUS

The second important question to answer is: How narrowly or how broadly should a firm construe its core competences? Here again, there is no simple answer. Each firm must make that determination in light of the trade-off between the virtues of having broad competences and those of having a more concentrated set of technical and market skills.[6] A broad set of related and unrelated competences hedges the future of the firm against many possible technological changes, but leaves it with no strong suit. A highly focused set of competences concentrates a firm's powers of knowledge, but in a narrow range, making it vulnerable to radical innovation. Like other living organisms, the firm that becomes too highly specialized—too keenly adapted to the peculiarities of its environment of technologies, production processes, and markets—is in danger of extinction if that environment changes even slightly.

One possible way to finesse this problem is to build core capabilities into diverse product lines. Consider, briefly, the case of the incandescent light bulb, the low-cost manufacture of which required a very specific set of competences: the ability to draw thin-walled glass bulbs by mass production, to insert a fragile wire filament, to create a vacuum and seal the bulb, and so on. For bulb producers, the development of the vacuum tube for use in radio and electronic equipment provided a test of their abilities to diversify into an area where many of their core competences could be directly transferred. This resulted in an entirely new market for bulb makers. For those that went into vacuum tubes, the innovation of the transistor represented a true technological discontinuity. Transistors were a substitute product for vacuum tubes and eventually nearly drove them from the marketplace. The transistor was a radical innovation, and few of the tube makers' competences helped them cross over to it. A similar chasm confronted transistor makers with the appearance of integrated circuits, which represented a synthesis of old competences and new ones.

Renewal of well-established products does not create new industries, however, nor will it save established firms from decline when their markets are invaded by radical innovations. This is the lesson of the typewriter industry, oil, and then gas illumination, photography, and harvested ice. Simply becoming better and better with current technology will not, in the long run, keep new firms with new technology from absorbing markets and relegating unresponsive established firms to the scrap heap of industrial history. It is this second type of innovation radical innovation, that is so necessary for the regeneration of a corporation's business, yet it is the most painfully difficult to master.

Although sustained leadership in innovation and business clearly requires persistence and continuous improvement, examination of radical change suggests that most firms persist in defending well-established products and ways of making them too ardently, even when the seeds of far more effective new alternatives are clearly in evidence.

RADICAL INNOVATION AND CORPORATE REGENERATION

As individuals, each of us are keenly aware of our own mortality. We know we will die some day, but when and how are almost never certain. Corporate managers know that their products, like people, are mortal. And like people, the future for those products is seldom knowable, except in retrospect. A product's life could end quite suddenly with the appearance of a radical new competing product that invades and quickly conquers the market. Or the end might come gradually, allowing time to prepare and launch new products. Whatever the case, managers are faced with tough decisions for which there are no pre-determined or universal answers.

Not many firms have the dexterity to retool their capabilities in order to survive successive waves of innovation. A striking fact drawn from earlier chapters is that over the life of a product, few of the firms that enter the market to produce it survive. Ironically, just as a firm seems most successful in its chosen product and market, that product generation is often challenged by a newer generation. In the resulting contest even fewer of the firms that produce the older version survive in the market to produce the new generation.[7] Firms holding the largest market share in one product generation seldom appear in the vanguard of competition in the next.

These are grim facts, yet examples exist of firms that have successfully defied the odds and leaped from one generation of product or process technology to the next, making it clear that no morbid natural law of predetermined failure is in force. Motorola is an example of one of these survivors, having successfully made the transition from the age of vacuum-tube car radios to the new era of cellular communications and computer chips. Hewlett-Packard, whose beginnings go back to the late 1930s as a maker of video oscillators and electrical testing equipment, is now a world leader in precision plotters, laser printers, computer workstations, professional calculators, and medical analytic devices—all products based upon technologies unimagined just two decades ago.

Looking back over the descriptions of industry evolution and of individual firms that have successfully mastered several generations of technological change, we can see that the idea of developing and balancing core competences as the key to success seems more credible than any number of current management philosophies and fashions. Ford and Kodak started early in developing their competence in distribution with early market entry in Europe and Japan. Kodak and General Electric were among the first firms in the world to set up central laboratories to advance their understanding of the principles of their products' operation—both clear examples of the deliberate enhancement of core competences. Black & Decker and Canon have been pioneers in modular design. Thomas Edison and Sony's Akio Morita, though generations apart, both set overarching goals for their enterprises and painstakingly and persistently pursued them for decades. Thomas Watson, Jr., transformed IBM when he announced that all new developments would be based on solid-state electronics, abandoning a generation of expertise and accepted product designs and leading the way to the System 360, one of the most successful products of all times. Many of the characteristics that these firms exhibit seem timeless, rooted in a respect for the value of human resources and skills and their continuing development.

In summary, the most important change of all would seem to lie in top managements' renewed appreciation of the people who build and sustain their firms and in their ability to learn and to adapt to changing and challenging circumstances.

ORGANIZATIONAL IMPEDIMENTS TO RADICAL INNOVATION IN ESTABLISHED FIRMS

To understand why established firms find radical innovation so difficult, we need to look at their organizational behavior and at the priorities of their leaders. Established firms with massively profitable businesses are almost invariably more conservative and risk averse than are fledgling competitors with none. Staffs of planners and analysts, and review committees and controllers all serve as bulwarks protecting the known, identifying and quantifying the risks associated with proposed changes. As firms grow larger, their top managers necessarily function more as conservators than as creators; they have income-producing products that must be nurtured and preserved to continue the benefits of shareholders and fellow employees. They see themselves as conscientious servants, implementing wise choices, and in many respects they are. Many attempts by newcomers to break into an industry and unseat the leading competitors will fail. Therefore in this regard conservatism usually has a positive survival value.

We have seen how Thomas Edison, whose reputation is synonymous with change and new ideas, could become a change resister—as he was in the cases of alternating current and metal filament bulbs—once he had deep commitments to earlier technologies. Similarly, Henry Ford, whose innovations of the Model T, and in production of the paced assembly line made him the richest man in America, stubbornly resisted changes to the Model A, believing that he had perfected the automobile. In fact defense of the one idea was correct, while defense of the other was not. Ford's process innovations rewarded the firms that extended it for decades. Trying to defend the product failed, while Ford's process ideas succeeded brilliantly. In this regard Ford exemplifies both sides of the story.

These very human and organizationally induced flaws turn the one-time creator into a change resister. In a stable and effective but conservative organizational environment the reward for improving existing technology, products, and processes is greater than the incentive to turn the world on its head. Thus ground breaking changes are viewed as difficult, disruptive, unpredictable, and risky, while incremental innovations are seen as reliably producing more predictable results more quickly. It is a great irony that wisdom for many firms that derive current good fortune from radical innovations of the past lies in erecting barriers to these same types of innovations today. Indeed, for some, the development projects that made them wealthy would be rejected if presented to current corporate staffers. "Too risky," they would say. "The projected stream of cash flows is too small to meet our internal rate-of-return hurdle." "The market is too small." Taken by itself, the decision not to abandon well-worn products in a timely manner is transitory. It leaves much greater risks for the business down the line and increases chances of failure. Doing only incremental innovation leaves the firm closer to the inevitable end of its business, but with no preparation for the future.

Incremental innovation, then, is a wise path of least resistance for the established firm, but sustained success in this form of innovation forms a trap for management. When radical innovation is plausible, according to Donald Frey, constant incremental innovation can create myopia in the ranks of top management. Frey contends that after decades of success, chief executives tend to become bureaucratic and process oriented, viewing their core businesses and competences as givens; board members who share similar backgrounds reinforce this tendency. "Successful chief executives," according to Frey, "are products of a bureaucratic selection process run with the wrong paradigms. When companies get into trouble late in their principal business life cycle, they cannot cope with the ambiguity of a new future, and their analytical tools can't predict an uncertain future."[8] To survive, firms must prepare to cope with an emerging new future, even though when action is needed, the form of the future will be far from clear.

Arnold Cooper and Clayton Smith recently examined 27 firms in 8 industries that were threatened by radical innovations. They found that the strengths of these firms did not necessarily provide an advantage in the new technology, and that in every case some new skills were required to enter. More important, the established firms tended to closely tie their entry into the new to the old (for example, transistors being placed under the vacuum tube division). This often led to a situation of divided loyalties, meaning that the effort to enter the new was often undertaken half-heartedly, even when the established firm was among the early entrants. Usually the new product was essentially folded into the existing strategy, which, however appropriate for the old product was seldom suited for the new one.[9] The result is not surprising, given these findings and those of Chapter 9. Only seven of the 27 threatened firms were successful. But the irony is that these firms all made the right decisions to enter with the threatening innovation. They were simply blocked by organizational impediments and the constraints of established patterns of thought and action.

INVESTMENT IN RADICAL INNOVATION IS DIFFICULT TO JUSTIFY

The medical dictum to "never take a well patient into surgery" finds its parallel in modern business: "When you have a good thing going, don't change it." Similarly, money spent on development of technologies that could potentially undermine existing profitable product lines is generally seen as counterproductive, "shooting oneself in the foot," or otherwise misdirecting funds from incremental improvement of the existing business. Obviously, this is a problem that the bias-ply tire producers must have confronted when the European technology for radial tires appeared likely to emerge in the United States.

Another important barrier is the mathematical logic of discounted cash-flow analysis, a useful method for evaluating and ranking competing projects, but a method that favors modest near-term rewards of high probability to extravagant long-term possibilities of high uncertainty. Discounted cash flow tends to favor investments in incremental change, where cost dimensions and payoffs are more reliably forecasted, than investments in radical innovation, which are by nature long term, unfamiliar, and questionable. Discounted cash-flow analysis provides no room for the unexpected surprises that destroy existing businesses. The earlier testimony of Alastair Pilkington with respect to his company's tremendous investments in the float process of making plate glass reminds us how public companies, which must report earnings that please analysts and shareholders on a quarterly basis, are constrained in their abilities to invest heavily, or otherwise "bet the company" on unproven technology.

Investments in incremental change may produce measurable benefits in the short term, but they cannot save established firms when their markets are demolished. These firms will not find their long-term vitality renewed, but will follow the lead of the gas lighting industry, the ice harvesters of New England, and others who have failed to make the bold leap across chasms of technological discontinuity.

THE FAILURE OF PIECEMEAL APPROACHES
TO THE FUTURE

The analogy of technological discontinuity as a chasm between the present and the future is useful. On one side of the chasm stands the established technology and the firms that embrace it; on the other side we find the radical new technology, its adherents, and a budding market. Often the former represents the present and the latter represents the future for the industry. Once they recognize their peril, firms on the established side of the chasm must find a way across if they hope to stay in the game. But what forms the bridge across the chasm?

Established businesses have adopted any one of several piece-meal approaches for managing their way to the future:

- Diversified portfolios of R&D projects and technology
- Mergers, acquisitions, alliances, and joint ventures
- Dual strategies

A portfolio approach to managing innovation ranks prospects in terms of predictable returns. The result is too often a grab bag of minor process and product improvements considered one by one, each judged on its own financial merits without sufficient consideration given to the long-run strength and competence of the firm in the face of change.

Mergers and acquisitions very often have unsatisfactory outcomes. When a large firm acquires a small entrepreneurial company to get its technology, it often finds that it has bought an empty box. The real assets were the brains of the entrepreneurs, who find the culture of the new company stifling and quickly leave. The current fashion of alliances and joint ventures among firms having complementary skills is also less than adequate as a solution for corporate revitalization. The motivation for this solution, particularly for both small technology-based firms and large established firms, is obvious; each has something the other desperately needs. New firms in technology product industries are often closer to the frontiers of progress than are established firms, while established firms have the financial, manufacturing, and distribution clout that the new firms lack almost entirely. The flaw in the seemingly idyllic marriage of these parties is the substantial cultural differences that set them apart. The new firms are entrepreneurial and unburdened by organizational controls; the established firms are just the opposite. And these differences tend to undermine the benefits of the relationship. Alliances will not correct the flaws in management posture that Frey describes. Moreover, they are often used by larger companies to justify reductions in research staffs and costs. Alliances may be of value, but they are no panacea for the problems of flagging corporate vitality. Only commitment by top management to renewing the business of the firm—and patience and persistence in that commitment—will have a chance to succeed.

Dual strategies have already been mentioned in Chapter 9, in the case of Sun and DEC. DEC's dual strategy of addressing the needs of current customers while simultaneously moving to a more modern computer architecture did not prove satisfactory. Dual strategies also carry the danger of creating destructive turf battles within the firm, as partisans of different strategies compete for power and scarce resources. A dual strategy essentially is an attempt to stand with one foot on each side of the chasm—a seemingly untenable position in the best of circumstances.

ORGANIZING SEPARATE DIVISIONS AND ALLIANCES TO BRIDGE TECHNOLOGICAL DISCONTINUITIES

As preceding chapters have made clear, the struggle for corporate survival in industry is unceasing. Further, the challenge of survival appears to take place in a series of successive tests: first at the level of the fluid phase of a product or process technology— just as the 80 or so manual typewriter firms in North America battled for position and survival; and, again, at the breakpoints between waves of technologies—as when the surviving manual typewriter companies had to make the leap to electrics, and again to computer-based word processing. Each of these tests eliminates industry participants and opens the door to others, and each has a bias against long-term survival. These tests may appear in many forms over time.

Preceding chapters indicate the necessity for businesses to rejuvenate themselves as changes in markets and technological discontinuities come their way. Although many firms fail this test, some have passed it successfully. They seem able to introduce dynamic, distinctive new products time and time again, while many others quickly exhaust their ability to keep generating new products that are competitive and the basis of sustained success. The main difficulty for established firms seems to be their reluctance to abandon old positions and embrace new ones when radical innovations invade their markets and undermine them. Some firms may be strong in product development yet fail to gain commercial rewards from their technical efforts, while their more successful counterparts exhibit the right mix of skills and capabilities not only in product design and implementation, but also in understanding user needs, in manufacturing, and in distribution. Thus a viable strategy for corporate renewal may be to build on established competences in marketing and distribution to renew a firm's line of business in its chosen market. Another might be to build on its strengths in product development and manufacturing to address new markets.

Organizing especially to meet the challenge may also be part of the solution. There are a number of cases in which established firms gained a foothold in markets generated by radical technology by reorganizing their efforts. In dealing with discontinuities, where the fluid-phase attributes of organizational flexibility and entrepreneurial spirit are required, managers of large established firms can either set up autonomous, independent units or forge alliances with the small firms that typically appear in the vanguard of an invading new technology. If they choose the latter course, they should do so with the knowledge that these arrangements are not always successful.

Cooper and Smith found that even in the rare instances in which a large firm did decide to organize separately to pursue a radical idea, other problems sometimes emerged. These included intense conflicts between organizational units and tacit attempts to derail the new initiative by withholding critical support and experience when needed.[10] William Hamilton and Harbir Singh have shown in their study of corporate capabilities and emerging technologies that neither established firms nor upstart competitors have all the competences needed to make a success of revolutionary technology, at least in its early stages. Both attempt to develop these over time.[11] Ironically, the competences of these rivals in the early stage are, according to Hamilton and Singh, highly complementary: the established firms have financial, marketing, and manufacturing resources in abundance and the emerging firms generally possess greater technical know-how. The result is that alliances often benefit both firms. The problems of these alliances, however, have been noted above, and need to be recognized and dealt with.

Chapter 1 described how IBM successfully entered the personal computer market through a separate dedicated unit set up far from the firm's headquarters; later in the book we saw an independent Team Taurus put Ford Motor Company back on the map and how General Motors entered the small-car market through the Saturn Motor Company. In each instance, the task of creating the competences needed to successfully bridge into chosen markets hinged on creating organizations with clear mandates and a great deal of independence from the staffs, committees, and other encumbrances of their parent companies.

Organizational separation, however, does not always lead to success. Xerox's attempt to revitalize itself through its Xerox Palo Alto Research (PARC) facility is a notable example. Xerox PARC was a paragon of inventive genius, creating the technology for a truly superior personal computer, the facsimile machine, Ethernet™, and the laser printer. Few of these ideas accrued to Xerox's benefit, however. Most found their way to the marketplace via new firms.[12]

SUMMARY

Innovation is not just the job of corporate technologists, but of all major functional areas of the firm. And the support of radical innovation by these areas must be managed with boldness and persistence from the top. Here the responsibility of management is nothing less than corporate regeneration in the face of radical innovation.

Little success will result from any program of innovation, of course, unless the people of the firm are properly deployed, given sufficient resources, and provided with a climate that encourages and rewards new thinking and risk taking. For radical innovation to occur, traditional organizational controls must loosen. Capital-budgeting procedures that push projects with long-term horizons and uncertain payoffs to the back of the line must be reevaluated. Committee systems and organizational requirements that diffuse responsibility too broadly need to be recalibrated. Investors must be educated to the new direction of the firm, and reminded that greater rewards are only associated with greater risks. Otherwise new initiatives will almost inevitably be starved for resources, allowing competitors to establish formidable positions at the expense of the once-preeminent industry leaders. Attending mainly to the needs of the established business will ensure that entering the new area will be done with strategies well honed for the old but compromised or flawed for the new. For success certainly these efforts should at least be equally balanced and emphasized.

The importance of leadership should never be underestimated. Historian Arnold Toynbee concluded in his famous *Study of History* that the decline of a civilization can be arrested or reversed when strong leaders come forward to meet the challenges of their times—be the challenges from outside invaders or from internal decay. "Challenge and response" was for Toynbee the dynamic process through which the fortunes of great past civilizations were sorted out. Similarly, managers of established industrial firms eventually find themselves faced with threats to their continued prosperity and survival, either from the invasion of radical innovations or from the gradual deterioration of the potency of their own core businesses. In either case the effect is the same: firms lose their ability to satisfy their traditional market. To stem the eventual tide of decline, they must either find new markets for existing products or regenerate themselves.

From the viewpoint of a new firm radical change gives it its only chance to enter a business and grow at the expense of powerful existing rivals. We have seen that the first versions of a new product are crude and expensive. This often catches stronger firms unaware because the nascent threat seems objectively so absurd. Entrepreneurial firms, though, can be more nimble and experimental and find a niche market for the new technology from which to grow, often rapidly. From the viewpoint of the established firm it is patently foolish to give up the development and production of the old product and technology. The new will arguably be a long time growing to be of any importance, if ever, and this conservative position is probably more often right than wrong. Only the prospective and imminent loss of the established business can justify a shift by a major firm, but this often seems impossible or incredible to them, even when it is clearly beginning. The problem is that we cannot judge or predict which of many threats will have such potency, but the cases and examples developed in this work show that even the strongest product and business strategy will eventually be overturned by technological change. The central issue is not when or how this will happen, but that it will happen for sure. In the final analysis only that understanding will allow a firm to bridge a discontinuity, because only a total commitment will win the day.

NOTES

1. Lewis M. Branscomb (ed.), *Empowering Technology: Implementing a U.S. Strategy* (Cambridge, Mass.: MIT Press, 1993), p. 269.
2. Charles Baden-Fuller and John M. Stopford, *Rejuvenating the Mature Business: The Competitive Challenge* (Boston: Harvard Business School Press, 1994).

3. C. K. Prahalad and Gary Hamel, "The Core Competence of the Corporation," *Harvard Business Review,* May–June, 1990, pp. 79–91.
4. As mentioned in the previous chapter, this point is disputed by Donald Frey, formerly at Ford, who says that Ford persistently sought radial tires from its reluctant suppliers.
5. James M. Utterback and James W. Brown, "Monitoring for Technological Opportunities," *Business Horizons,* October 1972, pp. 5–15; and James M. Utterback and Elmer H. Burack, "Identification of Technological Threats and Opportunities by Firms," *Technological Forecasting and Social Change,* vol. 8 (1975), pp. 7–21.
6. One is reminded here of the complaint that our society has developed two classes of people: generalists and specialists. The generalists spend their time learning less and less about more and more; the specialists are committed to learning more and more about less and less. Ultimately, we will have one group that knows nothing about everything, and another that knows everything about nothing.
7. Arnold Cooper and Dan Schendel, "Strategic Responses to Technological Threats," *Business Horizons,* vol. 19, no. 1 (February 1976), pp. 61–69.
8. Donald Frey, correspondence with the author.
9. Arnold C. Cooper and Clayton G. Smith, "How Established Firms Respond to Threatening Technologies," *Academy of Management Executive,* vol. 6, no. 2 (May 1992), pp. 55–70.
10. Ibid., p. 64.
11. William Hamilton and Harbir Singh, "The Evolution of Corporate Capabilities in Emerging Technologies," *Interfaces,* vol. 22, no. 4 (July–August 1992), pp. 13–23.
12. Douglas K. Smith and Robert C. Alexander, *Fumbling the Future* (New York: William Morrow, 1988).

Bibliography

Abernathy, William. *The Productivity Dilemma: Roadblock to Innovation in the Automobile Industry.* Baltimore, Md.: Johns Hopkins University Press, 1978.

Abernathy, William, and Kim B. Clark. "Innovation: Mapping the Winds of Creative Destruction." *Research Policy,* vol. 14, no. 1 (January 1985).

Abernathy, William J., and James M. Utterback. "Patterns of Industrial Innovation." *Technology Review,* vol. 80, no. 7 (June/July 1978), 40–47.

Abernathy, William, Kim B. Clark, and Alan Kantrow. *Industrial Renaissance: Producing a Competitive Future for America.* New York: Basic Books, 1983.

Adler, Paul, Henry Riggs, and Steven Wheelwright. "Product Know-How: Trading Tactics for Strategy." *Sloan Management Review,* Fall 1989, 7–17.

Afuah, Allen, and James M. Utterback. "The Emergence of a New Supercomputer Architecture." *Technological Forecasting and Social Change,* vol 40, no. 4 (December 1991) 315–328.

Allen, J.A. *Studies in Innovation in the Steel and Chemical Industries.* New York: Augustus M. Kelley, 1968.

Anderson, Oscar. *Refrigeration in America: A History of a New Technology and Its Impact.* Princeton, N.J.: Princeton University Press, 1953.

Anderson, Philip, and Michael L. Tushman. "Technological Discontinuities and Dominant Designs: A Cyclical Model of Technological Change." *Administrative Science Quarterly,* vol. 35, no. 4 (December 1990), 604–633.

Antonelli, Cristiano, Pascal Petit, and Gabriel Tahar. *The Economics of Industrial Modernization.* London: Academic Press, Harcourt Brace Jovanovich, 1992.

Augarten, Stan. *Bit By Bit: An Illustrated History of Computers.* New York: Ticknor & Fields, 1984.

Baden-Fuller, Charles, and John M. Stopford. *Rejuvenating the Mature Business: The Competitive Challenge.* Boston: Harvard Business School Press, 1994.

Basalla, George. *The Evolution of Technology.* Cambridge, England: Cambridge University Press, 1988.

Bliven, Bruce. *The Wonderful Writing Machine.* New York: Random House, 1954.

Boorstin, Daniel J. *The Americans: The National Experience.* New York: Random House, 1965.

———. *Hidden History.* New York: Harper & Row, 1987.

Branscomb, Lewis M. (ed.). *Empowering Technology: Implementing a U.S. Strategy.* Cambridge, Mass.: MIT Press, 1993.

Braun, E., and S. MacDonald. *Revolution in Miniature: The History and Impact of Semiconductor Electronics.* Cambridge, England: Cambridge University Press, 1978.

Bright, Arthur A. *The Electric Lamp Industry: Technological Change and Economic Development from 1800 to 1947.* New York: Macmillan, 1949.

Bright, James R. *Automation and Management.* Boston: Division of Research, Harvard Business School, 1958.

Burgelman, Robert A., and Richard S. Rosenbloom. "Technology Strategy: An Evolutionary Process Perspective." In Robert A. Burgelman and Richard S. Rosenbloom, eds. *Research on Technological Innovation, Management and Policy,* vol. 4. Greenwich, Conn.: JAI Press, 1989.

Burns, T., and G.M. Stalker. *The Management of Innovation.* London: Tavistock, 1961.

Bygrave, William D., and Jeffry A. Timmons. *Venture Capital at the Crossroads.* Boston: Harvard Business School Press, 1992.

Chandler, Alfred D., Jr. *Scale and Scope: Dynamics of Industrial Capitalism* Cambridge, Mass.: Harvard University Press, 1990.

———. "The Enduring Logic of Industrial Success." *Harvard Business Review,* vol. 90, no. 2 (March–April 1990), 130–140.

Christensen, Clayton. *The Innovator's Challenge: Understanding the Influence of Market Environment on Processes of Technology Development in the Rigid Disk Drive Industry.* DBA diss., Harvard Business School, 1992.

Clark, Kim B., "The Interaction of Design Hierarchies and Market Concepts in Technological Evolution," *Research Policy,* vol. 14, no. 5 (October 1985), 235–251.

Coe, Brian. "The Roll Film Revolution." In *The Story of Photography,* Colin Ford, ed. London: Century, 1989.

Collins, Douglas. *The Story of Kodak.* New York: Harry N. Abrams, 1990.

Cooper, Arnold, and Daniel Schendel. "Strategic Responses to Technological Threats." *Business Horizons,* vol. 19, no. 1 (February 1976), 61–69.

Cooper, Arnold C., and Clayton G. Smith. "How Established Firms Respond to Threatening Technologies." *Academy of Management Journal,* vol. 6, no. 2 (May 1992), 55–70.

Cummings, Richard O. *The American Ice Harvests: A Historical Study in Technology, 1800–1918.* Berkeley, Calif.: University of California Press, 1949.

Current, Richard Nelson. *The Typewriter: And the Men Who Made It.* Champaign, Ill.: University of Illinois Press, 1954.

Cusumano, Michael A., Y. Mylonadis, and R. Rosenbloom. "Strategic Maneuvering and Mass-Market Dynamics: The Triumph of VHS over Beta." *Business History Review,* vol. 66 (Spring 1992), 51–94.

Dagfous Abdelkader, M., and George R. White. "Information and Innovation," *Research Policy* (forthcoming).

David, Paul A. "Clio and the Economics of QWERTY." *American Economic Review,* vol. 75 (May 1985), 332–337.

———. "Understanding the Economics of QWERTY: The Necessity of History." In *Economic History and the Modern Economist,* W.N. Parker, ed. New York: Basil Blackwell, 1986.

———. "Heroes, Herds and Hysteresis in Technological History." *Industrial and Corporate Change,* vol. 1, no. 1 (1992).

Davis, Pearce. *The Development of the American Glass Industry.* Cambridge, Mass.: Harvard University Press, 1948.

De Bresson, Chris. *Understanding Technological Change.* Montreal: Black Rose Books, 1987.

Denoual, Daniel-Guy. *The Diffusion of Innovations: An Institutional Approach.* DBA diss., Harvard Business School, 1980.

Dertouzos, Michael, Richard Lester, and Robert Solow. *Made in America: Regaining the Productive Edge.* Cambridge, Mass.: MIT Press, 1989.

Dorfman, Nancy. *Innovation and Market Structure: Lessons from the Computer and Semiconductor Industries.* Cambridge, Mass.: Ballinger, 1987.

Dosi, Giovanni. "Technological Paradigms and Technological Trajectories: A Suggested Interpretation of the Determininants and directions of Technical Change." *Research Policy,* vol. 11 (1982), 147–162.

Dosi, Giovanni, Christopher Freeman, Richard Nelson, Gerald Silverberg, and Luc Soete. *Technical Change and Economic Theory.* London: Pinter, 1988.

Engler, George Nichols. *The Typewriter Industry: The Impact of a Significant Technological Innovation.* Ph.D. diss., University of California at Los Angeles, 1970.

Enos, John A. "Invention and Innovation in the Petroleum Refinery Industry." In *The Rate and Direction of Inventive Activity: Economic and Social Factors,* a conference report of the National Bureau of Economic Research. Princeton, N.J.: Princeton University Press, 1962.

———. *Petroleum Process and Profits: A History of Process Innovation.* Cambridge, Mass.: MIT Press, 1962.

Fabris, R. *Product Innovation in the Automobile Industry.* Ph.D. diss., University of Michigan, 1966.

Forester, Tom. *High-Tech Society.* Cambridge, Mass.: MIT Press, 1987.

Foster, Richard N. *Innovation: The Attacker's Advantage.* New York: Summit Books, 1986.

Freeman, Christopher. *The Economics of Industrial Innovation,* 2d ed. Cambridge, Mass.: MIT Press, 1982.

———. *Innovation and Long Cycles in Economic Development.* New York: St. Martins Press, 1986.

Freeman, Christopher, Margaret Sharp, and William Walker. *Technology and the Future of Europe.* London: Pinter, 1991.

Freiberger, Paul, and Michael Swaine. *Fire in the Valley: The Making of the Personal Computer.* Berkeley, Calif.: Osborne/McGraw-Hill, 1984.

Friedel, Robert, and Paul Israel. *Edison's Electric Light: Biography of an Invention.* New Brunswick, N.J.: Rutgers University Press, 1986.

Frishmuth, J.S., and T.J. Allen. "A Model for the Description of Technical Problem Solving." *Engineering Management,* May 1969, 79–86.

Gernsheim, Helmut. *A Concise History of Photography.* New York: Grosset & Dunlop, 1965.

Gilfillan, S.C. *The Sociology of Innovation.* Cambridge, Mass.: MIT Press, 1935. Reprinted 1963.

Girifalco, Louis A. *Dynamics of Technological Change.* New York: Van Nostrand Reinhold, 1991.

Gomory, Ralph. "From the 'Ladder of Science' to the Product Development Cycle." *Harvard Business Review,* November–December 1989, 99–105.

Gomory, Ralph, and Roland W. Schmitt, "Science and Product." *Science,* vol. 240 (May 27, 1988), 1131–1132 and 1203–1204.

Guile, Bruce R., and Harvey Brooks, eds. *Technology and Global Industries.* Washington, D.C.: National Academy Press, 1987.

Gullichsen, Johan E. "Innovations Through Exploration of Fibre-Water Interactions." *Innovations For Survival.* Falun, Sweden: The Marcus Wallenberg Foundation, 1986, 44–68.

Hall, Henry. *The Ice Industry of the United States with a Brief Sketch of Its History and Estimates of Production.* U.S. Department of the Interior, Census Division, Tenth Census, 1880, vol. 22. Washington, D.C.: U.S. Government Printing Office, 1888. Reprinted by the Early American Industries Association.

Hamilton, William, and Harbir Singh. "The Evolution of Corporate Capabilities in Emerging Technologies." *Interfaces,* vol. 22, no. 4 (July–August 1992), 13–23.

Henderson, Rebecca M., and Kim B. Clark. "Architectural Innovation: The Reconfiguration of Existing Product Technologies and the Failure of Established Firms." *Administrative Science Quarterly,* vol. 35, no. 1 (1990), 9–30.

Henretta, James A., W. Elliot Brownlee, David Brody, and Susan Ware. *America's History.* Homewood, Ill.: The Dorsey Press, 1987.

Hill, Christopher T., and James M. Utterback. *Technological Innovation for a Dynamic Economy.* New York: Pergamon, 1979.

Hollander, Daniel. *The Sources of Increased Efficiency: A Study of DuPont Rayon Plants.* Cambridge, Mass.: MIT Press, 1965.

Hounshell, David A. *From the American System to Mass Production, 1800–1932: The Development of Manufacturing Technology in the United States.* Baltimore: Johns Hopkins University Press, 1984.

Leeming, J. *Rayon: The First Man-Made Fiber.* New York: Wiley, 1950.

Jenkins, Reese V. *Images and Enterprise: Technology and the American Photographic Industry, 1839–1925.* Baltimore & London: The Johns Hopkins University Press, 1975.

———. "Science, Technology, and the Evolution of Photography, 1790–1925." In *Pioneers of Photography,* Eugene Ostroff, ed. Springfield, Va.: Society of Imaging Science and Technology, 1987.

Jones, Joseph C., Jr. *America's Ice Men: An Illustrative History of the United States Natural Ice Industry, 1665–1925.* Humble, Tex.: Jobeco Books, 1984.

Josephson, Matthew. *Edison: A Biography.* New York: McGraw-Hill, 1959.

Kai, Hidetaka. *Competitive Strategy Under Standardization in the Personal*

Computer Industry and Its Influence on New Entrants. Masters thesis, MIT Sloan School of Management, May 1992.

Kash, Don E. *Perpetual Innovation: The New World of Competition.* New York: Basic Books, 1989.

Kenyon, G.H. *The Glass Industry of the Weald.* Leicester, England: Leicester University Press, 1967.

Kirkpatrick, David. "Breaking Up IBM." *Fortune,* July 27, 1992, 47.

Klein, Burton. *Dynamic Economics.* Cambridge, Mass.: Harvard University Press, 1977.

Kleinschrod, Walter A. *Critical Issues in Office Automation.* New York: McGraw-Hill, 1986.

Kodama, Fumio. *Analysing Japanese High Technologies.* London: Pinter, 1991.

Lehnerd, Alvin P. "Revitalizing the Manufacture and Design of Mature Global Products." *Technology and Global Industries,* Bruce R. Guile and Harvey Brooks, eds. Washington, D.C.: National Academy Press, 1987.

Liebowitz, S.J., and Stephen E. Margolis. "The Fables of the Keys." *The Journal of Law & Economics,* vol. 33, no. 1 (April 1990), 1–25.

Loebbecke, James K., and Miklos Vasarhely. *Microcomputers.* Homewood, Ill.: Irwin, 1986.

Lohr, Steven. "Well, Somebody's Got to Reinvent the I.B.M. Mainframe." *New York Times,* September 12, 1993, 8.

Maidique, M.A., and B.J. Zirger. "The New Product Learning Cycle." *Research Policy,* December 1985.

Majumdar, B. *Innovations, Product Developments, and Technology Transfer: An Empirical Study of Dynamic Competitive Advantage, The Case of Electronic Calculators.* Ph.D. diss., Case Western Reserve University, Cleveland, Ohio, 1977.

Mares, George Carl. *The History of the Typewriter.* London: Guilbert Pitman, 1909.

McCormack, John, and James Utterback. "Technological Discontinuities: The Emergence of Fiber Optics." In Philip Birnbaum, ed., *Competitive Strategies in the Telecommunications Industry,* Greenwich, Conn.: JAI Press, forthcoming.

McCraw, Thomas K., ed. *The Essential Alfred Chandler: Essays Toward an Historical Theory of Big Business.* Boston: Harvard Business School Press, 1991.

Mensch, Gerhard. *Stalemate in Technology.* Cambridge, Mass.: Ballinger, 1979.

Meyer, Marc H. "New Product Strategy in the Technology-Based Firm: Technology, Market Applications and Performance." Ph.D. diss., MIT Sloan School of Management, June 1986.

Meyer, Marc H., and Edward B. Roberts. "Focusing New Product Strategy for Corporate Growth." *Sloan Management Review,* vol. 29, no. 4 (Summer 1988), 7–16.

Meyer, Marc H., and James M. Utterback. "The Product Family and the Dynamics of Core Capability." *Sloan Management Review,* vol. 34, no. 3 (Spring 1993), 29–47.

Modis, T., and A. Debecker. "Innovation in the Computer Industry." *Technological Forecasting and Social Change,* vol. 33 (1988), 267–278.

Montrey, Henry, and James Utterback. "Current Status and Future of Structural Panels in the Wood Products Industry." *Technological Forecasting and Social Change,* vol. 39, no. 4 (December 1990), 15–35.

Morton, Jack A. *Organizing for Innovation.* New York: McGraw Hill, 1971.

Mueller, D.C., and J.E. Tilton. "R&D Costs As a Barrier to Entry." *Canadian Journal of Economics,* vol. 2 (November 1969), 570–579.

Myers, Sumner, and Donald Marquis. *Successful Industrial Innovations.* Washington, D.C.: The National Science Foundation (NSF 69-17), 1969.

Nelson, Richard R., ed. *The Rate and Direction of Inventive Activity: Economic and Social Factors.* Princeton, N.J.: Princeton University Press, National Bureau of Economic Research, 1962.

Nelson, Richard, and Sidney Winter. *An Evolutionary Theory of Economic Change.* Cambridge, Mass.: Harvard University Press, 1982.

Nye, David E. *Electrifying America: Social Meanings of a New Technology, 1880–1940.* Cambridge, Mass.: MIT Press, 1991.

Passer, H.C. *The Electrical Manufacturers: 1875–1900.* New York: Arno Press, 1972.

Phillips, Almarin. *Technology and Market Structure: A Study of the Aircraft Industry.* Lexington, Mass.: Lexington Books, 1971.

Pilkington, Alastair. "The Float Glass Process." Proceedings, Royal Society of London, 1969. A. 314, 1–25, 6–8.

Pilkington ACI Limited. *Ribbons of Glass.* Sydney, Australia: 1989.

Pine, B. Joseph II. *Mass Customization: The Next Frontier of Business Competition.* Boston: Harvard Business School Press, 1993.

Porter, Michael E. *The Competitive Advantage of Nations.* New York: The Free Press, 1990.

Prahalad, C.K., and Gary Hamel. "The Core Competence of the Corporation." *Harvard Business Review,* May–June 1990, 79–91.

Putnam, A.P. "Wenham Lake and the Ice Trade." In *Wenham Great Pond,* John C. Phillips, ed. Salem, Mass.: Peabody Museum, 1938, p. 36.

Quinn, James Brian. "Pilkington Brothers, Ltd." Case Study B.P. 78-0148, Amos Tuck School of Business Administration, Dartmouth College, 1978.

———. "The Intelligent Enterprise: A New Paradigm." *Academy of Management Executive,* vol. 6, no. 4 (November 1992), 48–63.

Roberts, Edward B. *Entrepreneurs in High Technology.* New York: Oxford University Press, 1991.

———. "Managing Invention and Innovation." *Research and Technology Management,* vol. 31, no. 1 (January–February 1988), 11–29.

Roberts, Edward B., and Marc H. Meyer. "A Study of Market and Technological Diversity in New Products." *IEEE Management Review,* vol. 19, no. 1 (Spring 1991), 4–18.

Rogers, Robert P. *Staff Report on the Development and Structure of the Electric Lamp Industry.* Washington, D.C.: U.S. Government Printing Office, February 1980).

Rosenberg, Nathan. *The American System of Manufactures.* Edited version of the Report of the Parliamentary Committee on the Machinery of the United States of 1855 and the Special Reports of George Wallis and Joseph Whitworth of 1854. Edinburgh: The University Press, 1969.

———. *Technology and American Economic Growth*. New York: Harper & Row, 1972.

———. *Perspectives on Technology*. Cambridge, England: Cambridge University Press, 1976.

Rothwell, Roy, C. Freeman, A. Horsley, V.T.P. Jervis, A.B. Robertson, and J. Townsend. "SAPPHO Updated—Project SAPPHO Phase II." *Research Policy*, vol. 3, no. 4 (1974), 258–291.

Sahal, Devendra. *Patterns of Technological Innovation*. Reading, Mass.: Addison-Wesley, 1981.

———. "Technological Guideposts and Innovation Avenues." *Research Policy*, vol. 14 (1985), 61–82.

Sahlman, William A., and Howard H. Stevenson. "Capital Market Myopia." 288-055. Boston: Harvard Business School, 1987).

Sanderson, Susan Walsh. "Managing Generational Change: Product Families Approach to Design." Proceedings of the Design and Manufacturing Systems Conference, National Science Foundation, Washington, D.C., January 19, 1993.

Sanderson, Susan Walsh, and Vic Uzumeri. "Strategies for New Product Development and Renewal: Design-based Incrementalism." Working paper, Rensselaer Polytechnic Institute, Center for Science and Technology Policy, May 1990.

Schon, Donald A. *Technology and Change: The Impact of Invention and Innovation on American Social and Economic Development*. New York: Dell, 1967.

Schumpeter, Joseph. *Business Cycles: A Theoretical, Historical, and Statistical Analysis of the Capitalist Process*. New York: McGraw Hill, 1939.

———. *Capitalism, Socialism, and Democracy*. New York: Harper & Brothers, 1942.

Scoville, Warren. *Revolution in Glassmaking*. Cambridge, Mass.: Harvard University Press, 1948.

Shuon, Marshall. "Chrysler Builds Traffic with its LH Sedans." *New York Times*, Sunday, October 25, 1992, 14.

Smith, Adam. *An Inquiry into the Nature and Causes of the Wealth of Nations*. New York: Modern Library, 1937. Originally published in 1776.

Smith, Douglas K., and Robert C. Alexander. *Fumbling the Future*. New York: William Morrow, 1988.

Smith, Philip Chadwich Foster. *Crystal Blocks of Yankee Coldness: Development of the Massachusetts Ice Trade from Frederic Tudor to Wenham Lake*. Salem, Mass: Essex Institute Historical Collections, vol. XCVII (1961), 203.

Solow, Robert M. "Growth Theory and After." *American Economic Review*, vol. 78, no. 3 (June 1988), 307–317.

Staples, E.P., N.R. Baker, and D. J. Sweeney. "Market Structure and Technological Innovation: A Step Towards a Unifying Theory." Final Technical Report, NSF Grant RDA 75-17332, November 1977.

Stobaugh, Robert. *Innovation and Competition: The Global Management of Petrochemical Products*. Boston: Harvard Business School Press, 1988.

Taub, Eric. *Taurus: The Making of the Car That Saved Ford*. New York: Dutton, 1991.

Teece, David. "Profiting from Technological Innovation." *Research Policy*, vol. 15, no. 6 (1986), 285–306.

Teece, David J., Gary Pisano, and Amy Shuen. "Dynamic Capabilities and Strategic Management." Unpublished manuscript, University of California at Berkeley, 1990.

Thurow, Lester. *Head to Head: The Coming Economic Battle among Japan, Europe and America.* New York: William Morrow, 1992.

Tilton, John E. *International Diffusion of Technology: The Case of Semiconductors.* Washington, D.C.: The Brookings Institution, 1971.

Toynbee, Arnold J., *A Study of History,* rev. ed. New York: Oxford University Press, 1972.

Tushman, Michael, and Philip Anderson. "Technological Discontinuities and Organizational Environment." *Administrative Science Quarterly,* vol. 31 (1986), 439–456.

Utterback, James M. "The Process of Innovation: A Study of the Origination and Development of Ideas for New Scientific Instruments." *IEEE Transactions on Engineering Management,* vol. EM-18, no. 4 (November 1971), 124–131.

———. "Innovation in Industry and the Diffusion of Technology." *Science,* vol. 183, no. 4125 (1974), 620–626.

Utterback, James M., and William J. Abernathy. "A Dynamic Model of Product and Process Innovation." *Omega,* vol. 3, no. 6 (1975), 639–656.

Utterback, James M., and James W. Brown. "Monitoring for Technological Opportunities." *Business Horizons,* vol. 15 (October 1972), 5–15.

Utterback, James M., and Elmer H. Burack. "Identification of Technological Threats and Opportunities by Firms." *Technological Forecasting and Social Change,* vol. 8 (1975), 7–21.

Utterback, James M., and Linsu Kim. "Invasion of a Stable Business by Radical Innovation." In *The Management of Productivity and Technology in Manufacturing,* Paul Kleindorfer, ed. New York: Plenum Press, 1986, 129–130.

Utterback, James M., and Teresa C. Nolet. "Product and Process Change in Non-Assembled Product Industries." Working paper 78-12, MIT Center for Policy Alternatives, September 18, 1978.

Utterback, James W., and Fernando F. Suárez, "Innovation, Competition, and Industry Structure." *Research Policy,* vol. 22, no. 1 (February 1993), 1–21.

von Hippel, Eric. *The Sources of Innovation.* Oxford, England: Oxford University Press, 1988).

Watson, Gregory. *Strategic Benchmarking.* New York: Wiley, 1993.

Wheelwright, Steven, and Kim B. Clark. *Product Development Performance.* New York: The Free Press, 1990.

Womack, James P., Daniel Jones, and Daniel Roos. *The Machine that Changed the World.* New York: Rawson Associates, 1990.

Yates, JoAnne. *Control Through Communication: The Rise of System in American Management.* Baltimore: Johns Hopkins University Press, 1989.

Zorpette, Glenn, issue ed. "Teraflops Galore." *Special Report: Supercomputers, IEEE Spectrum,* September 1992.

Zuboff, Shoshana. *In the Age of the Smart Machine.* New York: Basic Books, 1989.

Index